W9-AQA-767

U·X·L Encyclopedia
of World Mythology

VOLUME 2: C–F

U·X·L Encyclopedia of World Mythology

VOLUME 2: C–F

U·X·L
A part of Gale, Cengage Learning

GALE
CENGAGE Learning™

Detroit • New York • San Francisco • New Haven, Conn • Waterville, Maine • London

BOCA RATON PUBLIC LIBRARY
BOCA RATON, FLORIDA

U·X·L Encyclopedia of World Mythology

Product manager: Meggin Condino

Project editor: Rebecca Parks

Editorial: Jennifer Stock, Kim Hunt

Rights Acquisition and Management: Kelly A. Quin, Scott Bragg, Aja Perales

Composition: Evi Abou-El-Seoud

Manufacturing: Rita Wimberley

Imaging: Lezlie Light

Product Design: Jennifer Wahi

© 2009 Gale, Cengage Learning

ALL RIGHTS RESERVED. No part of this work covered by the copyright herein may be reproduced, transmitted, stored, or used in any form or by any means graphic, electronic, or mechanical, including but not limited to photocopying, recording, scanning, digitizing, taping, Web distribution, information networks, or information storage and retrieval systems, except as permitted under Section 107 or 108 of the 1976 United States Copyright Act, without the prior written permission of the publisher.

For product information and technology assistance, contact us at Gale Customer Support, 1-800-877-4253.
For permission to use material from this text or product, submit all requests online at cengage.com/permissions.
Further permissions questions can be emailed to permissionrequest@cengage.com.

Cover photographs reproduced by permission of Purestock/Getty Images (picture of Statue of Poseidon); Voon Poh Le/Dreamstime.com (drawing of paper cut dragon); Werner Forman/Art Resource, NY (picture of an incense burner of a sun god); Charles Walker/Topfoto/The Image Works (photo of a papyrus drawing of Anubis weighing the heart); and The Art Archive/Richard Wagner/Museum Bayreuth/Gianni Dagli Orti (photo of a drawing of a valkyrie).

While every effort has been made to ensure the reliability of the information presented in this publication, Gale, a part of Cengage Learning, does not guarantee the accuracy of the data contained herein. Gale accepts no payment for listing; and inclusion in the publication of any organization, agency, institution, publication, service, or individual does not imply endorsement of the editors or publisher. Errors brought to the attention of the publisher and verified to the satisfaction of the publisher will be corrected in future editions.

LIBRARY OF CONGRESS CATALOGING-IN-PUBLICATION DATA

U*X*L encyclopedia of world mythology
    p. cm.
    Includes bibliographical references and index.
    ISBN 978-1-4144-3030-0 (set) -- ISBN 978-1-4144-3036-2 (vol. 1) -- ISBN 978-1-4144-3037-9 (vol. 2) -- ISBN 978-1-4144-3038-6 (vol. 3) -- ISBN 978-1-4144-3039-3 (vol. 4) -- ISBN 978-1-4144-3040-9 (vol. 5)
    1. Mythology—Encyclopedias, Juvenile. I. Title: UXL encyclopedia of world mythology. II. Title: Encyclopedia of world mythology.

BL303.U95 2009
201'.303—dc22   2008012696

Gale
27500 Drake
Farmington Hills, MI 48331-3535

ISBN-13: 978-1-4144-3030-0 (set)   ISBN-10: 1-4144-3030-2 (set)
ISBN-13: 978-1-4144-3036-2 (Vol. 1)   ISBN-10: 1-4144-3036-1 (Vol. 1)
ISBN-13: 978-1-4144-3037-9 (Vol. 2)   ISBN-10: 1-4144-3037-X (Vol. 2)
ISBN-13: 978-1-4144-3038-6 (Vol. 3)   ISBN-10: 1-4144-3038-8 (Vol. 3)
ISBN-13: 978-1-4144-3039-3 (Vol. 4)   ISBN-10: 1-4144-3039-6 (Vol. 4)
ISBN-13: 978-1-4144-3040-9 (Vol. 5)   ISBN-10: 1-4144-3040-X (Vol. 5)

This title is also available as an e-book.
ISBN-13: 978-1-4144-3846-7 ISBN-10: 1-4144-3846-X
Contact your Gale, a part of Cengage Learning sales representative for ordering information.

Printed in the United States of America
1 2 3 4 5 6 7 12 11 10 09 08

Table of Contents

Table of Contents by Culture

Reader's Guide

The *U·X·L Encyclopedia of World Mythology* examines the major characters, stories, and themes of mythologies from cultures around the globe, from African to Zoroastrian. Arranged alphabetically in an A–Z format, each entry provides the reader with an overview of the topic as well as contextual analysis to explain the topic's importance to the culture from which it came. In addition, each entry explains the topic's influence on modern life, and prompts the reader with a discussion question or reading/writing suggestion to inspire further analysis. There are five different types of entries: Character, Deity, Myth, Theme, and Culture. The entry types are designated by icons that are shown in a legend that appears on each page starting a new letter grouping so that you can easily tell which type of entry you are reading.

Types of Entries Found in This Book

Character entries generally focus on a single mythical character, such as a hero. In some cases, character entries deal with groups of similar or related beings—for example, Trolls or Valkyries. Deities (gods) are found in their own unique type of entry.

Deity entries contain information about a god or goddess. An example would be Zeus (pronounced ZOOS), the leader of the ancient Greek gods. Deities are very similar to other mythical characters, except that they often appear in many different myths; each Deity entry provides a summary of the most important myths related to that deity.

Myth entries focus on a specific story as opposed to a certain character. One example is the entry on the Holy Grail, which tells the legend of the vessel's origins as well as the many people who sought to locate it. In some cases, the myth is primarily concerned with a single character; the entry on the Golden Fleece, for example, features Jason as the main character. Like the Holy Grail entry, however, this entry focuses on the legends surrounding the object in question rather than the character involved.

Theme entries examine how one single theme, idea, or motif is addressed in the mythologies of different cultures. An example would be the Reincarnation entry that examines different cultural depictions of this eternal cycle of death and rebirth.

Culture entries contain a survey of the myths and beliefs of a particular culture. Each entry also provides historical and cultural context for understanding how the culture helped to shape, or was shaped by, the beliefs of other cultures.

Types of Rubrics Found in This Book

Each entry type is organized in specific rubrics to allow for ease of comparison across entries. The rubrics that appear in these entries are: *Character/Myth/Theme Overview*; *Core Deities and Characters*; *Major Myths*; *[Subject] in Context*; *Key Themes and Symbols*; *[Subject] in Art, Literature, and Everyday Life*; and *Read, Write, Think, Discuss*. In addition, the character, deity, and myth entries all have key facts sections in the margins that provide basic information about the entry, including the country or culture of origin, a pronunciation guide where necessary, alternate names for the character (when applicable), written or other sources in which the subject appears, and information on the character's family (when applicable).

Character Overview offers detailed information about the character's place within the mythology of its given culture. This may include information about the character's personality, summaries of notable feats, and relationships with other mythological characters. *Myth Overview* includes a summary of the myth being discussed. *Theme Overview* provides a brief description of the theme being discussed, as well as a rundown of the major points common when examining that theme in different mythologies.

Core Deities and Characters includes brief descriptions of the main deities and other characters that figure prominently in the given culture's mythology. This is not a comprehensive list of all the gods or characters mentioned in a particular culture.

Major Myths features a brief summary of all the most important or best-known myths related to the subject of the entry. For example, the entry on Odin (pronounced OH-din), chief god of Norse mythology, includes the tale describing how he gave up one of his eyes in order to be able to see the future.

[Subject] in Context provides additional cultural and historical information that helps you understand the subject by seeing through the eyes of the people who made it part of their culture. The entry on the weaver Arachne (pronounced uh-RAK-nee), for instance, includes information on the importance of weaving as a domestic duty in ancient Greece.

Key Themes and Symbols outlines the most important themes in the tales related to the subject. This section also includes explanations of symbols associated with the subject of the entry, or which appear in myths related to the subject. For example, this section may explain the meaning of certain objects a god is usually shown carrying.

[Subject] in Art, Literature, and Everyday Life includes references to the subject in well-known works of art, literature, film, and other media. This section may also mention other ways in which the subject appears in popular culture. For example, the fact that a leprechaun (pronounced LEP-ruh-kawn) appears as the mascot for Lucky Charms cereal is mentioned in this section of the Leprechauns entry.

Read, Write, Think, Discuss uses the material in the entry as a springboard for further discussion and learning. This section may include suggestions for further reading that are related to the subject of the entry, discussion questions regarding topics touched upon in the entry, writing prompts that explore related issues and themes, or research prompts that encourage you to delve deeper into the topics presented.

Most of the entries end with cross-references that point you to related entries in the encyclopedia. In addition, words that appear in bold within the entry are also related entries, making it easy to find additional information that will enhance your understanding of the topic.

Other Sections in This Book

This encyclopedia also contains other sections that you may find useful when studying world mythology. One of these is a "Timeline of World Mythology," which provides important dates from many cultures that are important to the development of their respective mythologies. A glossary in the front matter supplements the definitions that are included within the entries. Teachers will find the section on "Research and Activity Ideas" helpful in coming up with classroom activities related to the topic of mythology to engage students further in the subject. A section titled "Where to Learn More" provides you with other sources to learn more about the topic of mythology, organized by culture. You will also encounter sidebars in many of the entries; these sections offer interesting information that is related to, but not essential to, your understanding of the subject of the entry.

Comments and Suggestions

We welcome your comments on the *U·X·L Encyclopedia of World Mythology* and suggestions for other topics to consider. Please write to Editors, *U·X·L Encyclopedia of World Mythology,* Gale, 27500 Drake Rd., Farmington Hills, Michigan, 48331-3535.

Introduction

On the surface, myths are stories of gods, heroes, and monsters that can include fanciful tales about the creation and destruction of worlds, or awe-inspiring adventures of brave explorers in exotic or supernatural places. However, myths are not just random imaginings; they are cultivated and shaped by the cultures in which they arise. For this reason, a myth can function as a mirror for the culture that created it, reflecting the values, geographic location, natural resources, technological state, and social organization of the people who believe in it.

Values

The values of a culture are often revealed through that culture's myths and legends. For example, a myth common in Micronesian culture tells of a porpoise girl who married a human and had children; after living many years as a human, she decided to return to the sea. Before she left, she warned her children against eating porpoise, since they might unknowingly eat some of their own family members by doing so. Myths such as these are often used to provide colorful reasons for taboos, or rules against certain behaviors. In this case, the myth explains a taboo among the Micronesian peoples against hunting and eating porpoises.

Geography

Myths often reflect a culture's geographic circumstances. For example, the people of the Norse culture live in a region that has harsh, icy winters. It is no coincidence that, according to their myths, the being whose death led to the creation of the world was a giant made of frost. By contrast, the people of ancient Egypt lived in an dry, sunny land; their most important gods, such as Ra, were closely associated with the sun. Geographic features are also often part of a culture's myths, or used as inspiration for mythological tales. Spider Rock, a tall peak located at Canyon de Chelly National Monument in Arizona, is said by the Hopi people to be the home of the creation goddess Spider Woman. The Atlas mountains in northern Africa took their name from the myth that the Titan Atlas (pronounced AT-luhs) had once stood there holding up the heavens, but had been transformed to stone in order to make his task easier.

Natural Resources

Myths can also reflect the natural resources available to a culture, or the resources most prized by a certain group. In Mesoamerican and American Indian myths, maize (commonly referred to as corn) often appears as a food offered directly from gods or goddesses, or grown from the body of a deity. This reflects not only the importance of maize in the diets of early North and Central American cultures, but also the ready availability of maize, which does not appear as a native plant anywhere else in the world. Similarly, the olive tree, which is native to the coastal areas along the Mediterranean Sea, is one of the most important trees in ancient Greek myth. The city of Athens, it is said, was named for the goddess Athena (pronounced uh-THEE-nuh) after she gave its citizens the very first domesticated olive tree.

Sometimes, myths can reflect the importance of natural resources to an outside culture. For example, the Muisca people of what is now Colombia engaged in a ceremony in which their king covered himself in gold dust and took a raft out to the middle of a local lake; there he threw gold trinkets into the water as offerings to the gods. Gold was not commonly available, and was prized for its ceremonial significance; however, when Spanish explorers arrived in the New World and heard of this practice, they interpreted this to mean that gold must be commonplace in the area. This led to the myth of El Dorado, an entire city made of gold that many Spanish explorers believed to exist and spent decades trying to locate.

Technology

A culture's state of technological development can also be reflected in its myths. The earliest ancient Greek myths of Uranus (pronounced

YOOR-uh-nuhs) state that his son Cronus (pronounced KROH-nuhs) attacked him with a sickle made of obsidian. Obsidian is a stone that can be chipped to create a sharp edge, and was used by cultures older than the ancient Greeks, who relied on metals such as bronze and steel for their weapons. This might suggest that the myth arose from an earlier age; at the very least, it reflects the idea that, from the perspective of the Greeks, the myth took place in the distant past.

Social Order

Myths can also offer a snapshot of a culture's social organization. The Old Testament tale of the Tower of Babel offers an explanation for the many tribes found in the ancient Near East: they had once been united, and sought to build a tower that would reach all the way to heaven. In order to stop this act of self-importance, God caused the people to speak in different languages. Unable to understand each other, they abandoned the ambitious project and scattered into groups across the region.

Besides offering social order, myths can reinforce cultural views on the roles different types of individuals should assume in a society. The myth of Arachne (pronounced uh-RAK-nee) illustrates a fact known from other historical sources: weaving and fabric-making was the domestic duty of wives and daughters, and it was a skill highly prized in the homes of ancient Greece. Tales of characters such as Danaë (pronounced DAN-uh-ee), who was imprisoned in a tower by her father in order to prevent her from having a child, indicate the relative powerlessness of many women in ancient Greek society.

Different Cultures, Different Perspectives

To see how cultures reflect their own unique characteristics through myth, one can examine how a single theme—such as fertility—is treated in a variety of different cultures. Fertility is the ability to produce life, growth, or offspring, and is therefore common in most, if not all, mythologies. For many cultures, fertility is a key element in the creation of the world. The egg, one of the most common symbols of fertility, appears in Chinese mythology as the first object to form from the disorder that previously existed in place of the world. In many cultures, including ancient Greece, the main gods are born from a single mother;

in the case of the Greeks, the mother is Gaia (pronounced GAY-uh), also known as Earth.

For cultures that relied upon agriculture, fertility was an important element of the changing seasons and the growth of crops. In these cases, fertility was seen as a gift from nature that could be revoked by cruel weather or the actions of the gods. Such is the case in the ancient Greek myth of Persephone (pronounced per-SEF-uh-nee); when the goddess is taken to the underworld by Hades (pronounced HAY-deez), her mother—the fertility goddess Demeter (pronounced di-MEE-ter)—became sad, which caused all vegetation to wither and die.

For the ancient Egyptians, fertility represented not just crop growth and human birth, but also rebirth into the afterlife through death. This explains why Hathor (pronounced HATH-or), the mother goddess of fertility who supported all life, was also the maintainer of the dead. It was believed that Hathor provided food for the dead to help them make the long journey to the realm of the afterlife.

For early Semitic cultures, the notion of fertility was not always positive. In the story of Lilith, the little-known first wife of Adam (the first man), the independent-minded woman left her husband and went to live by the Red Sea, where she gave birth to many demons each day. The myth seems to suggest that fertility is a power that can be used for good or evil, and that the key to using this power positively is for wives to dutifully respect the wishes of their husbands. This same theme is found in the earlier Babylonian myth of Tiamat (pronounced TYAH-maht), who gave birth to not only the gods but also to an army of monsters that fought to defend her from her son, the hero Marduk (pronounced MAHR-dook).

These are just a few of the many ways in which different cultures can take a single idea and interpret it through their own tales. Rest assured that the myths discussed in this book are wondrous legends that capture the imagination of the reader. They are also mirrors in which we can see not only ourselves, but the reflections of cultures old and new, far and near—allowing us to celebrate their unique differences, and at the same time recognize those common elements that make these enchanting stories universally beloved and appreciated by readers and students around the world.

Timeline of World Mythology

c. 3400 BCE Early Sumerian writing is first developed.

c. 3100 BCE Egyptian writing, commonly known as hieroglyphics, is first developed.

c. 2852–2205 BCE During this time period, China is supposedly ruled by the Three Sovereigns and Five Emperors, mythical figures that may have been based on actual historical leaders.

c. 2100 BCE Earliest known version of the *Epic of Gilgamesh* is recorded in Sumerian.

c. 1553–1536 BCE Egyptian pharaoh Akhenaten establishes official worship of Aten, a single supreme god, instead of the usual group of gods recognized by ancient Egyptians.

c. 1250 BCE The Trojan War supposedly occurs around this time period. Despite the war's importance to Greek and Roman mythology, modern scholars are not sure whether the war was an actual historical event or just a myth.

c. 1100 BCE The Babylonian creation epic *Enuma Elish* is documented on clay tablets discovered nearly three thousand years later in the ruined library of Ashurbanipal, located in modern-day Iraq.

c. 800 BCE The Greek alphabet is invented, leading to a flowering of Greek literature based on myth.

c. 750 BCE The Greek epics known as the *Iliad* and the *Odyssey* are written by the poet Homer. Based on the events surrounding the

Trojan War, these two stories are the source of many myths and characters in Greek and Roman mythology.

c. 750 BCE The Greek poet Hesiod writes his *Theogony*, which details the origins of the Greek gods.

c. 563–480 BCE According to tradition, Gautama Buddha, the founder of Buddhism, is believed to have lived in ancient India and Nepal during this time.

525–456 BCE The Greek dramatist Aeschylus writes tragedies detailing the lives of mythical characters, including *Seven Against Thebes*, *Agamemnon*, and *The Eumenides*.

c. 500–100 BCE The oldest version of the *Ramayana*, the Hindu epic about the incarnation of the god Vishnu named Rama, is written.

c. 496–406 BCE Ancient Greek playwright Sophocles creates classic plays such as *Antigone* and *Oedipus the King*.

c. 450 BCE The Book of Genesis, containing stories fundamental to early Christianity, Judaism, and Islam, is collected and organized into its modern form.

c. 431 BCE Greek builders complete work on the temple of Athena known as the Parthenon, one of the few ancient Greek structures to survive to modern times.

c. 150–50 BCE The Gundestrup cauldron, a silver bowl depicting various Celtic deities and rituals, is created. The bowl is later recovered from a peat bog in Denmark in 1891.

c. 29–19 BCE Roman poet Virgil creates his mythical epic, the *Aeneid*, detailing the founding of Rome.

c. 4 BCE–33 CE Jesus, believed by Christians to be the son of God, supposedly lives during this time period.

c. 8 CE Roman poet Ovid completes his epic work *Metamorphoses*. It is one of the best existing sources for tales of ancient Greek and Roman mythology.

c. 100 CE The *Mahabharata*, a massive epic recognized as one of the most important pieces of literature in Hinduism, is organized into its modern form from source material dating back as far as the ninth century BCE.

c. 570–632 CE The prophet Muhammad, founder of Islam, supposedly lives during this time.

c. 800–840 CE The oldest surviving remnants of *The Book of One Thousand and One Nights*, a collection of Near Eastern folktales and legends, are written in Syrian.

c. 1000 CE The Ramsund carving, a stone artifact bearing an illustration of the tale of Sigurd, is created in Sweden. The tale is documented in the *Volsunga* saga.

c. 1010 CE The oldest surviving manuscript of the Old English epic *Beowulf* is written. It is recognized as the first significant work of English literature.

c. 1100 Monks at the Clonmacnoise monastery compile the *Book of the Dun Cow*, the earliest written collection of Irish myths and legends still in existence.

c. 1138 Geoffrey of Monmouth's *History of the Kings of Britain* is published, featuring the first well-known tales of the legendary King Arthur.

c. 1180–1210 The *Nibelungenlied*, a German epic based largely on earlier German and Norse legends such as the *Volsunga* saga, is written by an unknown poet.

c. 1220 Icelandic scholar Snorri Sturluson writes the Prose Edda, a comprehensive collection of Norse myths and legends gathered from older sources.

c. 1350 The *White Book of Rhydderch*, containing most of the Welsh myths and legends later gathered in the *Mabinogion*, first appears.

1485 Thomas Malory publishes *Le Morte D'Arthur*, widely considered to be the most authoritative version of the legend of King Arthur.

c. 1489 *A Lytell Geste of Robin Hode*, one of the most comprehensive versions of the life of the legendary British character of Robin Hood, is published.

c. 1550 The *Popol Vuh*, a codex containing Mayan creation myths and legends, is written. The book, written in the Quiché language but using Latin characters, was likely based on an older book written in Mayan hieroglyphics that has since been lost.

1835 Elias Lonnrot publishes the *Kalevala*, an epic made up of Finnish songs and oral myths gathered during years of field research.

1849 Archeologist Henry Layard discovers clay tablets containing the Babylonian creation epic *Enuma Elish* in Iraq. The epic, lost for centuries, is unknown to modern scholars before this discovery.

1880 Journalist Joel Chandler Harris publishes *Uncle Remus, His Songs and Sayings: the Folk-Lore of the Old Plantation*, a collection of myths and folktales gathered from African American slaves working in the South. Many of the tales are derived from older stories from African myth. Although the book is successful and spawns three sequels, Harris is accused by some of taking cultural myths and passing them off as his own works.

Words to Know

benevolent: Helpful or well-meaning.

caste: A social level in India's complex social class system.

cauldron: Kettle.

chaos: Disorder.

chivalry: A moral code popularized in Europe in the Middle Ages that stressed such traits as generosity, bravery, courtesy, and respect toward women.

constellation: Group of stars.

cosmogony: The study of, or a theory about, the origin of the universe.

deity: God or goddess.

demigod: Person with one parent who was human and one parent who was a god.

destiny: Predetermined future.

divination: Predicting the future.

dualistic: Having two sides or a double nature.

epic: A long, grand-scale poem.

fertility: The ability to reproduce; can refer to human ability to produce children or the ability of the earth to sustain plant life.

hierarchy: Ranked order of importance.

hubris: Too much self-confidence.

immortal: Living forever.

imperial: Royal, or related to an empire.

indigenous: Native to a given area.

Judeo-Christian: Related to the religious tradition shared by Judaism and Christianity. The faiths share a holy book, many fundamental principles, and a belief in a single, all-powerful god.

matriarchal: Female-dominated. Often refers to societies in which a family's name and property are passed down through the mother's side of the family.

mediator: A go-between.

monotheism: The belief in a single god as opposed to many gods.

mummification: The drying and preserving of a body to keep it from rotting after death.

nymph: A female nature deity.

omen: A mystical sign of an event to come.

oracle: Person through whom the gods communicated with humans.

pagan: Someone who worships pre-Christian gods.

pantheon: The entire collection of gods recognized by a group of people.

patriarchal: Male-dominated. Often refers to societies in which the family name and wealth are passed through the father.

patron: A protector or supporter.

pharaoh: A king of ancient Egypt.

polytheism: Belief in many gods.

primal: Fundamental; existing since the beginning.

prophet: A person able to see the plans of the gods or foretell future events.

pyre: A large pile of burning wood used in some cultures to cremate a dead body.

resurrected: Brought back to life.

revelation: The communication of divine truth or divine will to human beings.

rune: A character from an ancient and magical alphabet.

seer: A person who can see the future.

shaman: A person who uses magic to heal or look after the members of his tribe.

sorcerer: Wizard.

syncretism: The blending or fusion of different religions or belief systems.

tradition: A time-honored practice, or set of such practices.

underworld: Land of the dead.

utopia: A place of social, economic and political perfection.

Research and Activity Ideas

Teachers wishing to enrich their students' understanding of world mythologies might try some of the following group activities. Each uses art, music, drama, speech, research, or scientific experimentation to put the students in closer contact with the cultures, myths, and figures they are studying.

Greek Mythology: A Pageant of Gods

In this activity, students get to be gods and goddesses for a day during the classroom "Pageant of the Gods," an event modeled after a beauty pageant. Each student selects (with teacher approval) a deity from Greek mythology. Students then research their deity, write a 250-word description of the deity, and create costumes so they can dress as their deity. On the day of the pageant, the teacher collects the students' descriptions and reads them aloud as each student models his or her costume for the class.

Materials required for the students:

Common household materials for costume

Materials required for the teacher:

None

Optional extension: The class throws a post-pageant potluck of Greek food.

Anglo-Saxon Mythology: Old English Translation

Students are often surprised to learn that *Beowulf* is written in English. The original Old English text looks almost unrecognizable to them. In this activity (which students may work on in the classroom, in the library, or at home), the teacher begins by discussing the history of the English language and its evolution over the past one thousand years (since the writing of *Beowulf*). The teacher then models how a linguist would go about translating something written in Old English or Middle English (using an accessible text such as *The Canterbury Tales* as an example), and makes various resources for translation available to the students (see below). The class as a whole works on translating the first two lines of *Beowulf*. The teacher then assigns small groups of students a couple lines each of the opening section of *Beowulf* to translate and gloss. When each group is ready with their translations, the students assemble the modern English version of the opening of *Beowulf* and discuss what they learned about the various Old English words they studied.

Materials required for the students:

None

Materials required for the teacher:

Copies of an Old English version of the first part of *Beowulf* for distribution to students.

There are multiple Old English dictionaries available online, so student groups could work on this activity in the classroom if a sufficient number of computer workstations with Internet access are available. There are also many Old English dictionaries in print form. If none is available in the school library, some can be checked out from the public library.

Egyptian Mythology: Mummify a Chicken

The ancient Egyptians believed preserving a person's body ensured their safe passage into the afterlife. The process of Egyptian mummification was a secret for many centuries until ancient Greek historian Herodotus recorded some information about the process in the fifth century BCE. Archaeologists have recently refined their understanding of Egyptian mummification practices. In this activity, students conduct their own mummification experiment on chickens.

The teacher contextualizes the activity by showing students a video on mummies and asking them to read both Herodotus's account of mummification and more recent articles about mummification that center on the research of Egyptologist Bob Brier.

Once students understand the basics of mummification, groups of five or six students can begin their science experiment, outlined below. The teacher should preface the experiment with safety guidelines for handling raw chicken.

Materials required for students:

Scale

One fresh chicken per group (bone-in chicken breast or leg may substitute)

Disposable plastic gloves (available at drugstores)

Carton of salt per group per week

Spice mixture (any strong powdered spices will do; powdered cloves, cinnamon, and ginger are good choices)

Extra-large (gallon size) air-tight freezer bags

Roll of gauze per group (available at drugstore)

Disposable aluminum trays for holding chickens

Cooking oil

Notebook for each group

Materials required for the teacher:

Video on mummies. A good option is: *Mummies: Secrets of the Pharaohs* (2007), available on DVD.

Reading material on mummies, including Herodotus's account. See: http://discovermagazine.com/2007/oct/mummification-is-back-from-the-dead; http://www.nationalgeographic.com/tv/mummy/; http://www.mummytombs.com/egypt/herodotus.htm

Plenty of paper towels and hand soap.

Procedure

1. All students put on plastic gloves.

2. Weigh each chicken (unnecessary if weight printed on packaging) and record the weight in a notebook. Record details of the chicken's appearance in the notebook.

3. Remove chicken organs and dispose of them. Rinse the chicken thoroughly in a sink.

4. Pat the chicken dry with paper towels. Make sure the chicken is completely dry, or the mummification process might not work.

5. Rub the spices all over the chicken, both inside and outside, then salt the entire chicken and fill the chicken cavity with salt.

6. Seal the chicken in the air-tight bag and place it in the aluminum tray.

7. Remove gloves and wash hands thoroughly with soap and water.

8. Once a week, put on plastic gloves, remove the chicken from the bag, dispose of the bag and accumulated liquid, and weigh the chicken. Record the weight in a notebook and make notes on changes in the chicken's appearance. Respice and resalt the chicken, fill the chicken cavity with salt, and seal it in a new bag. Remove gloves and wash hands. Repeat this step until no more liquid drains from the chicken.

9. When liquid no longer drains from the chicken, the mummy is done! Wipe off all the salt and rub a light coat of cooking oil on the mummy. Wrap it tightly in gauze.

Optional extension: Students can decorate their mummies using hieroglyphics and build shoebox sarcophagi for them.

Near Eastern Mythology: Gilgamesh and the Cedar Forest

The story of Gilgamesh's heroics against the demon Humbaba of the Cedar Forest is one of the most exciting parts of the *Epic of Gilgamesh*. In this activity, students write, stage, and perform a three-act play based on this part of the epic. Necessary tasks will include writing, costume design, set design, and acting. The teacher can divide tasks among students as necessary.

Materials required for the students:

Household items for costumes

Cardboard, paint, tape, and other materials for sets

Copy of the *Epic of Gilgamesh*

Materials required for the teacher:

None

Hindu Mythology: Salute the Sun

The practice of yoga, an ancient mental and physical discipline designed to promote spiritual perfection, is mentioned in most of the Hindu holy texts. Today, the physical aspects of yoga have become a widely popular form of exercise around the world. In this activity, the students and teacher will make yoga poses part of their own daily routine.

The teacher introduces the activity by discussing the history of yoga from ancient to modern times, by showing a video on the history of yoga, and by distributing readings from ancient Hindu texts dealing with the practice of yoga. After a class discussion on the video and texts, the teacher leads students through a basic "sun salutation" series of poses with the aid of an instructional yoga video (students may wish to bring a towel or mat from home, as some parts of the sun salutation involve getting on the floor). Students and the teacher will perform the sun salutation every day, preferably at the beginning of class, either for the duration of the semester or for another set period of time. Students will conclude the activity by writing a summary of their feelings about their yoga "experiment."

Materials required for the students:

Towel or mat to put on floor during sun salutations.

Materials required for teacher:

A DVD on the history of yoga. Recommended: *Yoga Unveiled* (2004), an excellent documentary series on the history of yoga.

An instructional yoga video that includes the "sun salutation" sequence (many available).

Handouts of ancient Indian writings on yoga. See *The Shambhala Encyclopedia of Yoga* (2000) and *The Yoga and the Bhagavad Gita* (2007).

African Mythology: Storytelling

Anansi the Spider was a trickster god of West African origin who was known as a master storyteller. In this activity, students work on their own storytelling skills while learning about the spread of Anansi stories from Africa to the Americas.

The teacher begins this activity by discussing the ways that oral traditions have helped the African American community preserve some part of their West African cultural heritage. The spread of stories about Anansi around Caribbean and American slave communities is an example, with the Uncle Remus stories of Joel Chandler Harris being a good demonstration of how the Anansi tales have evolved. The class then conducts a preliminary discussion about what the elements of a good spoken story might be, then watches or listens to models of storytelling. After listening to the stories, the class discusses common elements in the stories and techniques the storytellers used to keep the audience's attention and build interest.

Students then read a variety of Anansi and Uncle Remus stories on their own. With teacher approval, they select one story and prepare it for oral presentation in class (several students may select the same story). After the presentations, students can discuss their reactions to the various oral presentations, pointing out what was effective and ineffective.

Materials required for the students:

Optional: props for story presentation

Materials required for the teacher:

Background reading on West African oral traditions.

Recordings or videos of skilled storytellers. See *The American Storyteller Series* or the CD recording *Tell Me a Story: Timeless Folktales from Around the World* (which includes an Anansi story).

Optional extension: The teacher may arrange for students with especially strong oral presentations to share their stories at a school assembly or as visiting speakers in another classroom.

Micronesian and Melanesian Mythology: Island Hopping

The many islands that make up Micronesia and Melanesia are largely unfamiliar to most students. In this activity, students learn more about these faraway places.

The teacher introduces this activity by hanging up a large map of the South Pacific, with detail of Micronesian and Melanesian islands. The teacher explains that, during every class session, the class will learn the location of and key facts about a particular island. Each day, one student is given the name of an island. It is that student's homework assignment that night to learn the location of the island, its population, and its key industries. The student must also learn two interesting facts about the island. The next day, the student places a push pin (or other marker) on the map showing the location of his or her island. The student presents the information to the class, writes it down on an index card, and files the index card in the class "island" box. In this way, the students learn about a new Micronesian or Melanesian island every day and build a ready resource of information about the islands.

Materials required for the students:

None

Materials required for the teacher:

Large wall map with sufficient detail of Micronesia and Melanesia

Index cards

Box for island index cards

Push pins, stickers, or other markers for islands

Northern European Mythology: The Scroll of the Nibelungen

The *Nibelungenlied* is an epic poem set in pre-Christian Germany. The tale contains many adventures, fights, and triumphs. In this activity, students prepare a graphic-novel version of the *Nibelungenlied*.

To introduce this activity, the teacher gives students a synopsis of the *Nibelungenlied* and describes the various interpretations of the saga (including Richard Wagner's opera and J. R. R. Tolkien's *Lord of the Rings* triology). The teacher then explains that the class will create a graphic novel of the *Nibelungenlied* on a continuous scroll of paper. The teacher shows models of various graphic novels and discusses the conventions of graphic novel representations.

Students are divided into groups of three or four, and each group receives one chapter or section of the *Nibelungenlied* as its assignment.

After reading their sections, the groups meet to discuss possible graphical representations of the action in their chapters and present their ideas to the teacher for approval. After gaining approval, student groups work, one group at a time, to draw and color their chapters on the scroll. When the scroll is finished, each group makes a short presentation explaining what happens in their chapter and how they chose to represent the action. The final scroll can be displayed around the classroom walls or along a school hallway.

Materials required by the students:

None

Materials required by the teacher:

Easel paper roll (200 feet)

Markers, colored pencils, and crayons

Copies of *Nibelungenlied* chapters for students (or refer students to http://omacl.org/Nibelungenlied/)

Inca Mythology: Make a Siku

A siku is an Andean pan pipe. Pipes such as these were important in Inca culture, and remain a prominent feature in Andean music. In this activity, students will make their own sikus.

The teacher begins this activity by playing some Andean pan pipe music, showing students the Andes on a map, and discussing the ways in which Inca culture remains part of the lives of Native Americans in countries like Peru. The teacher shows a picture of a pan pipe (or, ideally, an actual pan pipe) to the students and explains they will build their own.

Students need ten drinking straws each (they can bring them from home, or the teacher can provide them) and a pair of scissors. To make the pipe:

1. Set aside two of the straws. Cut the remaining straws so that each is one-half inch shorter than the next. The first straw is uncut. The second straw is one-half inch shorter than the first. The third is one inch shorter than the first, and so on.

2. Cut the remaining straws into equal pieces. These pieces will be used as spacers between pipe pieces.

3. Arrange the straws from longest to shortest (left to right) with the tops of the straws lined up.

4. Put spacer pieces between each part of the pipe so they are an equal distance apart.

5. Tape the pipe in position, making sure the tops of the straws stay in alignment.

6. The pipe is finished. Cover in paper and decorate if desired. Blow across the tops of straws to play.

Materials required by the students:

Ten drinking straws

Scissors

Tape

Materials required by the teacher:

Andean pipe music

Pictures of a pan pipe or an actual pan pipe

Picture of the Andes on a map

U·X·L Encyclopedia
of World Mythology

VOLUME 2: C–F

C

Character

Deity

Myth

Theme

Culture

Cain and Abel

Character Overview

According to the monotheistic religions (religions in which the people believe in only one god) of the Middle East, Cain and Abel were the sons of the first people, **Adam and Eve**. As told in the book of Genesis in the Bible, Cain and Abel were the first two sons born to Adam and Eve after their banishment from the Garden of **Eden**. Cain, the elder, became a farmer, while Abel became a shepherd. They offered sacrifices to Yahweh, or God. Cain brought fruit and grain; Abel brought lambs. When Yahweh accepted Abel's offerings but rejected those of Cain, Cain was hurt and angry. In a jealous rage, he killed his brother. As punishment, Yahweh ordered Cain to go forth and become "a fugitive and a vagabond in the earth." Then he placed a sign, known as the mark of Cain, on the murderer's forehead to protect him from further punishment.

Cain and Abel in Context

Tradition holds that Cain's son Enoch founded the first city, and that other descendents of Cain invented music and metalworking. Cain may be a mythological representation of a Near Eastern group called the Kenites, who practiced metalworking and musicianship and who may have worn tattoos. Medieval Christians believed that Cain had a

Nationality/Culture
Judeo-Christian

Pronunciation
CAIN and AY-buhl

Alternate Names
Qabil and Habil (Islamic)

Appears In
The Holy Bible, the Torah, the Qur'an

Lineage
Sons of Adam and Eve

In this seventeenth-century painting, Cain runs away after murdering Abel, while God looks down. SCALA/ART RESOURCE, NY.

yellowish beard, so artists and playwrights used yellow beards to identify murderers and traitors. Because some Christians viewed Cain as a forerunner—earlier version—of the Jews, who they believed were responsible for the death of Jesus, yellow became associated with discrimination against Jewish people. During the eighteenth and nineteenth centuries, racists associated the "mark of Cain" with dark-colored skin and used this as proof that African Americans were descended from the wicked Cain. Abel, an innocent and godly victim, was often compared with Jesus.

Key Themes and Symbols

Conflicts between brothers appear often in world mythology, reflecting the widespread view that conflict between good and evil is an inescapable part of human life. One interpretation of the Cain and Abel story is that it reflects the very ancient tension between the different values and ways of life of wandering herders, represented by Abel, and settled farmers, represented by Cain. Other views suggest that the story is about the death of innocence, or that it illustrates the need for self-control and the high cost of giving in to competition and jealousy.

Cain and Abel in Art, Literature, and Everyday Life

The story of Cain and Abel is one of the most well-known legends in the modern world. The characters of Cain and Abel have been tied to many other works of literature, including the Old English epic poem *Beowulf*, where the monster Grendel is described as one of Cain's descendants. The tale of Cain and Abel has been retold in poems by Lord Byron and Charles Baudelaire, and they have even appeared as characters in several comic book series released by DC Comics. John Steinbeck's novel *East of Eden* (1952), a story set in California in the early twentieth century, is also based on the tale of Cain and Abel.

Read, Write, Think, Discuss

One interpretation of the actions of Cain and Abel is that it shows how dangerous jealousy can be. Based on your own experiences or stories you have read, write your own story that illustrates the dangers of jealousy.

SEE ALSO Adam and Eve; Ahriman; Ahura Mazda; Eden, Garden of

Camelot

Myth Overview

Camelot was the location of King **Arthur**'s court and the site of the famous Round Table of **Arthurian legend**. The wedding of Arthur to his queen, **Guinevere**, took place in the town of Camelot, and the

Nationality/Culture
Romano-British/Celtic

Pronunciation
CA-muh-lot

Alternate Names
None

Appears In
Le Morte d'Arthur

Cadbury Castle, a hillfort in Somerset, England, is one of several places thought to have been the possible location of Camelot from the legends of King Arthur. © HOMER SYKES/CORBIS.

magician **Merlin** built a castle there for the couple to live in. The castle served as headquarters for King Arthur and his knights as well. A special hall held the Round Table, where Arthur and the knights would plan their campaigns. The hall also contained lifelike statues of the twelve kings who had tried to overthrow Arthur. All had been defeated by him and were buried at Camelot. Each statue had a lighted candle. According to Merlin, the candles would stay lit until the **Holy Grail**—the cup from which Jesus drank at the Last Supper—was found and brought to Camelot. It was from Camelot that the knights rode out to perform good deeds and to search for the Holy Grail.

Camelot in Context

Scholars have long debated the location of Camelot, just as they have debated the identity of King Arthur. In early times, it was associated with the town of Camulodunum (now called Colchester), an important site during the days of Roman rule in Britain. Other possible sites include Caerleon in Wales and the English towns of Camelford and Cadbury. In his book *Le Morte D'Arthur*, Sir Thomas Malory identified the city of Winchester as Camelot. England's King Henry VII had his first son baptized in Winchester Cathedral and named Arthur. In all likelihood, however, Camelot represents a mythical place, not a real one.

Key Themes and Symbols

As the center of King Arthur's realm, Camelot represents a society in perfect harmony, also known as a utopia. Modern utopias are generally based on the idea of equality among citizens, which is symbolized by the Round Table at Camelot. The kingdom of Camelot ultimately fails due to the flaws of the humans who control it. In this way, Camelot is similar to other mythical places, such as the Garden of **Eden** and **Atlantis**.

Camelot in Art, Literature, and Everyday Life

Camelot appears in some form in nearly all retellings of the King Arthur legend. The 1960 Broadway musical *Camelot*, as well as the 1967 film adaptation of the musical, emphasizes the importance of the setting as a symbol of King Arthur's reign. The mythical Camelot has even inspired the construction of a real-life theme park in Lancashire, England. The term "Camelot" is frequently used to describe the three years (from 1961 to 1963) during which President John F. Kennedy served as president of the United States. Although the United States was hardly considered a utopia during this time, many people felt that Kennedy—like King Arthur—would lead his country and people toward a brighter future.

Read, Write, Think, Discuss

The knights of the Round Table were renowned for their "chivalry." Using your library, the Internet, and other available resources, research the origins and history of chivalry. Where did the idea come from? Why did it take hold among the nobility of Europe? When did the principles of chivalry fall out of favor? Write a brief paper summarizing your findings.

SEE ALSO Arthur, King; Arthurian Legends; Guinevere; Holy Grail; Merlin

Cassandra

Nationality/Culture
Greek/Roman

Pronunciation
kuh-SAN-druh

Alternate Names
Alexandra

Appears In
Homer's *Iliad*, Hyginus's *Fabulae*

Lineage
Daughter of Priam and Hecuba

Character Overview

In **Greek mythology**, Cassandra was the daughter of Priam and **Hecuba**, the king and queen of Troy. Cassandra was the most beautiful of Priam's daughters, and the god **Apollo** fell in love with her. Apollo promised Cassandra the gift of prophecy—the ability to see the future— if she would agree to give herself to him. Cassandra accepted Apollo's gift but then refused his advances. Apollo was furious, but he could not take back the powers he had given her. Instead, he cursed her, proclaiming that although she would be able to tell the future accurately, no one would believe her. Before announcing her prophecies, Cassandra went into a type of trance that made her family believe she was insane.

In Homer's *Iliad*, Cassandra predicted many of the events of the Trojan War. Priam's son Paris planned a trip to Sparta. Cassandra warned against it, but her warnings were ignored. Paris traveled to Sparta, where he kidnapped **Helen**, starting the war with Greece. Cassandra later predicted Troy's defeat and warned the Trojans not to accept the Greek gift of the Trojan horse. Again she was ignored, and Greek troops hidden inside the wooden horse captured the city. During the battle, a Greek soldier known as Ajax the Lesser raped Cassandra in the temple of **Athena**. Athena later punished Ajax and his men for the deed.

After the Greek victory, Cassandra was given to the Greek leader **Agamemnon** as a prize. She bore Agamemnon two sons and later returned to Greece with him. However, she also predicted that a terrible fate awaited Agamemnon and herself. When they reached Agamemnon's home in Mycenae, they were both murdered by Agamemnon's wife, Clytemnestra, and her lover, Aegisthus.

Cassandra. PUBLIC DOMAIN.

Cassandra in Context

In ancient Greece, the belief that certain individuals could see the future—or were told the future by the gods—was common. Those who could see the future were believed to get this power from the god Apollo and were called oracles. Oracles were often found at temples dedicated to Apollo. The most famous ancient Greek oracle, located at **Delphi**, was at the site of a large temple to Apollo. According to legend and historians, the oracle at Delphi, or the Delphic oracle, was always female.

Key Themes and Symbols

In the legends of the Trojan War, Cassandra symbolizes futility, the inability to be useful. Although Cassandra can see exactly what will happen to her family and their city, she cannot do anything about it because no one believes her. In this way, Cassandra also serves as a symbol of destiny, the idea that the future has already been determined by the gods.

Cassandra in Art, Literature, and Everyday Life

Although Cassandra plays a rather small role in the legends of the Trojan War, her unique character has endured and has appeared in numerous other works of art and literature. In modern literature, Cassandra's point of view is told in Marion Zimmer Bradley's historical novel *The Firebrand* (1987). Cassandra also appears in the futuristic tale "Cassandra" by C. J. Cherryh, which won a Hugo Award for Best Short Story in 1979.

The term "Cassandra" is sometimes used in modern times to refer to someone who makes predictions that are ignored or disbelieved, but later proven accurate.

Read, Write, Think, Discuss

Many modern stories include a character similar to Cassandra, who says things that are ignored or considered nonsense until they come true. One example is the title character in the Disney animated film *Chicken Little* (2005), in which the title character tries to warn others about an alien invasion. Try to think of a single example from a book you have read, or a movie or television show you have seen. Describe the story and the character, and explain how the character is like Cassandra. What were the reasons the character's prediction was ignored?

SEE ALSO Agamemnon; Apollo; Athena; Greek Mythology; Hecuba; Helen of Troy; *Iliad, The*

Cassiopeia
See **Andromeda.**

Castor and Pollux

Character Overview

In Greek and **Roman mythology**, Castor and Pollux (known as Polydeuces to the Greeks) were twin brothers who appeared in several prominent myths. The **twins** were worshipped as gods who helped shipwrecked sailors and who brought favorable winds for those who made sacrifices to them. The Romans considered Castor and Pollux the gods who watched over horses and the Roman horsemen known as equites (pronounced EK-wi-teez).

There are many stories about the twins and numerous versions of those stories. According to the Greek poet Homer, Castor and Pollux were the sons of Tyndareus (pronounced tin-DAIR-ee-uhs) and Leda, the king and queen of Sparta. For this reason, they are sometimes called the Tyndaridae (sons of Tyndareus). Another account identifies the twins as the sons of Leda and **Zeus**, from whom they received the name *Dioscuri* (sons of Zeus). Still another legend says that Castor was the son of Leda and Tyndareus—and therefore a human—while Pollux was the son of Zeus—and therefore a god. This difference became significant later in their lives. All tales about the twins agree in portraying Castor as a skilled horse trainer and Pollux as an expert boxer. Inseparable, the brothers always acted together.

In one of the earliest myths about the twins, Castor and Pollux rescued their sister **Helen** after she had been kidnapped by **Theseus** (pronounced THEE-see-uhs), king of Attica. Helen would later gain fame as the queen whose abduction by Paris, a Trojan prince, launched the Trojan War. The twins also accompanied **Jason** and the **Argonauts** on their voyage in search of the **Golden Fleece**. During that expedition, Pollux demonstrated his boxing skills by killing the king of the Bebryces. When a storm arose during the voyage, the Argonaut **Orpheus** prayed to the gods and played his harp. The storm immediately ceased and stars appeared on the heads of the twins. It is because of this myth that Castor and Pollux came to be recognized as the protectors of sailors.

Another story concerns the death of Castor. According to one account, the twins wanted to marry their cousins Phoebe and Hilaria. The women, however, were already promised to two other cousins, Idas

Nationality/Culture
Roman

Pronunciation
KAS-ter and POL-uhks

Alternate Names
Castor and Polydeuces (Greek), the Dioscuri, the Tyndaridae

Appears In
Homer's *Iliad*, Hyginus's *Fabulae*

Lineage
Sons of Zeus and Leda

St. Elmo's Fire

St. Elmo's fire is a natural phenomenon that occurs during certain stormy weather conditions. It appears as a glow on the top of tall pointed objects, such as the masts of ships, and is often accompanied by a cracking noise. When stars appeared on the heads of Castor and Pollux during the voyage of the Argonauts, the twins became known as the protectors of sailors. From that time, sailors believed that St. Elmo's fire was actually Castor and Pollux coming to protect them during a storm.

and Lynceus. Castor and Pollux carried the women away to Sparta, pursued by their male cousins. In the fight that followed, the twins succeeded in killing both Idas and Lynceus, but Castor was fatally wounded.

In another version of this story, the four men conducted a cattle raid together. Idas and Lynceus then tried to cheat Castor and Pollux out of their share of the cattle. The twins decided to take the cattle themselves, but were caught as they started to sneak away. A fight broke out in which Castor, Idas, and Lynceus were all killed.

This story also has several different endings. In one, Castor's spirit went to **Hades**, the place of the dead, because he was a human. Pollux, who was a god, was so devastated at being separated from his brother that he offered to share his immortality (ability to live forever) with Castor, or to give it up so that he could join his brother in Hades. Taking pity on his son Pollux, Zeus declared that the brothers would take turns dwelling in Hades and with the gods on Mount Olympus. On one day, Castor would be with the gods and Pollux would be in Hades; on the next, the two would change places. In another ending, Castor remained in Hades, but Pollux was allowed to visit him every other day. Most versions of the myth say that Zeus placed the brothers in the heavens as part of the constellation—group of stars—known as Gemini. Today the two brightest stars in the constellation Gemini are named Castor and Pollux.

Castor and Pollux in Context

The Romans developed a strong cult—a group that worships a specific god or gods above all others within a religion—around Castor following a military victory by the Romans over the Latins at Lake Regillus in 499

BCE. When the Roman infantry failed to hold its ground in the battle, the dictator Aulus Postumius decided to send in the cavalry (the horsemen of the military) to help. Castor's association with horsemen prompted the dictator to make a vow to build a temple to Castor in exchange for his

The Temple of Castor and Pollux at Agrigento in Sicily. MEDIO IMAGES/ROYALTY-FREE.

help, and the Romans were victorious. The Romans completed the temple in 484 BCE. Pollux joined his brother in the cult much later, but never had quite the same level of honor. The images of Castor and Pollux appear on many early Roman coins. The Romans celebrated the Theoxenia Festival each year on July 15th in their honor, with the Roman cavalry riding in a ceremonial parade.

Key Themes and Symbols

Castor and Pollux are symbols of brotherhood and the bond that unites two people even after death. Castor and Pollux can also be seen as a symbol of inequality: though they are twins, one is immortal while the other is not. Although Castor is known as the patron of horsemen, both Castor and Pollux were known as the "riders on white steeds," and both were thought to represent the spirits of young warriors riding into battle.

Castor and Pollux in Art, Literature, and Everyday Life

Castor and Pollux were featured in the works of many ancient Greek and Roman writers. Besides appearing in Homer's poems, the twins have a role in the play *Helen* by the Greek playwright Euripides. They also figure in Pindar's *Nemean Odes* and in Ovid's *Metamorphoses*. There is even a reference to the twins in the Bible: in the New Testament book Acts of the Apostles, St. Paul is said to sail from Malta aboard a ship bearing the sign of Castor and Pollux. The English poet Edmund Spenser included the twins in his poem *Prothalamion*. The greatest work by the French composer Jean-Phillipe Rameau, the tragic opera *Castor and Pollux*, was based on the story of the brothers.

Read, Write, Think, Discuss

Using your library, the Internet, or other available resources, research the constellation Gemini, and in particular, the stars known as Castor and Pollux. Where in the sky does this constellation appear? Does it always appear in the same place in the sky, or does its position change throughout the year? See if you can spot Castor and Pollux in the nighttime sky.

SEE ALSO *Aeneid, The*; Argonauts; Helen of Troy

Celtic Mythology

Celtic Mythology in Context

Adventure, heroism, romance, and magic are a few of the elements that make Celtic mythology one of the most entrancing mythologies of Europe. Once a powerful people who dominated much of Europe, the Celts were reduced to a few small groups after the Roman invasions. Their mythology survived, however, thanks largely to the efforts of later Irish and Welsh monks who wrote down the stories.

The Celts were a group of people who began to spread throughout Europe in the 1000s BCE. At the peak of their power, they lived in an area extending from the British Isles in the west to what is now Turkey in the east. They conquered northern Italy and Macedonia, plundering both Rome and **Delphi** in the process. They had a reputation as fierce and courageous warriors, and the Romans respected them.

Celtic expansion reached its limit around 225 BCE, when the Celts suffered the first in a series of defeats by the armies of the Roman empire. Gradually, the Romans pushed back the Celts, and by 84 CE, most of Britain was under Roman rule. At the same time, Germanic peoples conquered the Celts living in central Europe. Just a few areas, notably Ireland and northern Britain, managed to remain free and to continue to pass on the Celtic traditions. Six groups of Celts have survived to modern times: the peoples of Ireland, Scotland, the Isle of Man, Wales, Cornwall, and Brittany.

The ancient Celts were neither a race nor a nation. They were a varied people bound together by language, customs, and religion rather than by any central government. They lived off the land, farming and raising stock. No towns existed apart from impressive hill forts. However, by about 100 BCE, large groups of Celts had begun to gather at certain settlements to trade with one another.

Celtic society had a clearly defined structure. Highest in rank was the king, who ruled a particular tribe, or group of people. Each tribe was divided into three classes: the noble knights and warriors, the Druids (religious leaders), and the farmers and commoners. The Druids, who came from noble families, were respected and influential figures. They served not only as priests but also as judges, teachers, and advisers. In addition, it was widely believed that the Druids had magical powers.

The Tragedy of Deirdre

The heroine of the Ulster Cycle is the beautiful Deirdre. King Conchobhar intends to marry the young woman, but she falls in love with Naoise and flees to Scotland with him. When they return, the king has Naoise killed. Forced to lived with Conchobhar, the grief-stricken Deirdre never smiles and makes clear to the king how much she hates him. The story ends with Deirdre taking her own life by striking her head against a rock. Deirdre's tragic tale served as inspiration for poetry, plays, and stories by later Irish writers, including William Butler Yeats and J. M. Synge.

Core Deities and Characters

The Celts worshipped a variety of deities, or gods, who appeared in their tales. Most were all-powerful local deities linked to places rather than to specialized roles. Each tribe had its own god who protected and provided for the welfare of that tribe. Some of them had similar characteristics. For example, **Dagda**, the god of life and death in Ireland—known as the good god—resembled Esus, the "master" god of Gaul.

Some deities had more clearly defined roles. Among these were **Lug**, or Lugus, a **sun** god associated with the arts, war, and healing, and the horned god **Cernunnos**, who was a god of animals and fertility. The Celts also had a large number of important female deities. These included Morrigan, the "Great Queen," who was actually three war goddesses—Morrigan, Badb (pronounced BAV), and Nemain—who appeared as ravens during battle. Another important deity was Brigit, goddess of learning, healing, and metalworking. Epona, the horse goddess, was associated with fertility, water, and death.

Major Myths

The ancient Celts had a vibrant mythology made up of hundreds of tales. They did not, however, record their myths in writing but passed them on orally. Our knowledge of the gods, **heroes**, and villains of Celtic mythology comes mainly from Roman sources. Yet the Romans sometimes referred to Celtic gods by Roman names, so their accounts were not always reliable. Also, because the Romans and Celts were battlefield enemies, Roman descriptions of Celtic beliefs were often unfavorable.

Major Celtic Deities

Brigit: goddess of learning, healing, and metalworking.

Dagda: god of life and death.

Danu: fertility goddess and mother of the Tuatha Dé Danaan.

Epona: goddess associated with fertility, water, and death.

Lug: god of the sun, war, and healing.

Morrigan: goddess of war and death.

Much of what is now known about Celtic mythology is based on manuscripts that were prepared by monks in the Middle Ages. Irish collections dating from the 700s CE and Welsh collections from the 1300s recount many of the myths and legends of the ancient Celts.

Many myths told of the otherworld. In this mysterious place, there was no work and no death, and the gods and spirits who lived there never got old. The Celts believed that humans could enter this enchanted place through burial mounds called *sídhe*, through caves or lakes, or after completing a perilous journey. After reaching the otherworld, they would live happily for all time.

Early Irish myths blend mythology and history by describing how Ireland was settled by different groups of Celtic deities and humans. Filled with magic and excitement, the tales tell of battles between forces of light and darkness. They describe a time when gods lived not in the heavens but on earth, using their powers to create civilization in Ireland and to bring fertility to the land.

There are four cycles, or groups, of connected stories. The Mythological Cycle focuses on the activities of the Celtic gods, describing how five races of supernatural beings battled to gain control of Ireland. The chief god was Dagda, whose magic cauldron could bring the dead back to life. The Ulster Cycle recounts the deeds of warriors and heroes, especially **Cuchulain** (pronounced koo-KUL-in), the warrior and champion of Ireland. The Historical Cycle tells of the adventures and battles of legendary Irish kings. The Fenian Cycle deals with the heroic **Finn** Mac Cumhail, or Finn Mac Cool, leader of a band of bold warriors known as the

Fianna. This cycle is filled with exciting adventures and tales of hand-to-hand combat.

Welsh mythology is found in the Mabinogion (pronounced MAB-eh-no-ghee-on), a collection of eleven tales. In the Welsh myths, as in those of Ireland, the heroes often are half-human and half-divine and may have magical powers. Many of the stories in the Mabinogion deal with **Arthurian legends**, accounts of the deeds of Britain's heroic King **Arthur** and his knights.

In fact, the popular Arthurian tales of medieval European literature are a complex blend of ancient Celtic myths, later stories, and historical events. The legends are clearly rooted in Celtic mythology, however, and references to Arthur appear in a number of ancient Welsh poems. Scholars also note that there are many similarities between the Arthur stories and the tales of the Irish Finn Mac Cumhail, suggesting a shared Celtic origin.

Another famous romantic story of Celtic origin is that of **Tristan and Isolde**. The tragic tale, probably based on an early Cornish poem, concerns the knight Tristan who falls in love with Isolde (pronounced i-SOLE-duh), a princess who is fated to marry his uncle the king. In the Middle Ages, Gottfried von Strassburg wrote a poem based on the legend that is considered a literary masterpiece.

Key Themes and Symbols

Magic, magicians, and the supernatural played a significant role in Celtic mythology. A common theme was the magic cauldron (kettle). The cauldron of plenty was never empty and supplied great quantities of food. The cauldron of rebirth brought slain warriors to life again. Myrddin, a magician in the Welsh tales, later became **Merlin** in the Arthurian legends.

Other important themes in the myths were voyages to mysterious and dangerous lands and larger-than-life heroes. The heroes experienced all kinds of adventures and often had to perform impossible tasks before marrying their loved one. Love, romance, and mischief also figured prominently. The gods played tricks on humans and on one another. Animals changed shape at will.

Celtic Mythology in Art, Literature, and Everyday Life

Celtic mythology has proven to have enduring popularity in modern art and literature. Many tales of Celtic mythology have been retold by later

The Gundestrup Cauldron, which dates to the first century BCE, features many scenes and characters from Celtic mythology. ERICH LESSING/ART RESOURCE, NY.

authors, especially the tales of King Arthur. Other Celtic tales were collected by writers, such as Herminie T. Kavanagh and Lady Gregory. Popular films featuring Celtic mythology include *Excalibur* (1981) and *Darby O'Gill and the Little People* (1959).

Read, Write, Think, Discuss

The Mountain of Marvels: A Celtic Tale of Magic, Retold from the Mabinogion by Aaron Shepard (2007) offers readers a tale of the horse goddess Rhiannon, the nobleman she loves, and an evil magician. The author has been awarded an Aesop Accolade from the American Folklore Society for his myth-based stories for children and young adults.

SEE ALSO Arthurian Legends; Cuchulain; Dagda; Finn; Lug; Tristan and Isolde

Centaurs

Nationality/Culture
Greek/Roman

Pronunciation
SEN-tawrz

Alternate Names
None

Appears In
Ovid's *Metamorphoses*

Lineage
Descendants of Ixion

Character Overview

In **Greek mythology**, centaurs were creatures that had the head, neck, chest, and arms of a man, and the body and legs of a horse. Most centaurs were brutal, violent creatures known for their drunkenness and lawless behavior. They lived mainly around Mount Pelion in Thessaly, a region of northeastern Greece.

According to one account, centaurs were descended from Centaurus, a son of **Apollo**. A more widely accepted account of their origin, however, is that they were descendants of Ixion, the son of **Ares** and king of the Lapiths, a people who lived in Thessaly.

Ixion fell in love with **Hera**, the wife of **Zeus**. Recklessly, Ixion arranged to meet with Hera, planning to seduce her. Zeus heard of the plan and formed a cloud in the shape of Hera. Ixion embraced the cloud form, and from this union, the race of centaurs was created.

The main myth relating to the centaurs involves their battle with the Lapiths. King Pirithous of the Lapiths, son of Ixion, invited the centaurs to his wedding. The centaurs became drunk and disorderly and pursued the Lapith women. One centaur even tried to run off with the king's bride. A fierce battle erupted. The centaurs used tree trunks and slabs of stone as weapons, but eventually the Lapiths won the fight, killing many centaurs. The centaurs were forced to leave Thessaly.

A number of tales describe conflicts between centaurs and the Greek hero **Heracles**. In one such story, Heracles came to the cave of a centaur named Pholus. Pholus served Heracles food but did not offer him any wine, though an unopened jar of wine stood in the cave. Pholus explained that the wine was a gift and was the property of all the centaurs. Nonetheless, Heracles insisted on having some wine, and Pholus opened the jar. The smell of the wine soon brought the other centaurs to the cave and before long a fight broke out. Heracles drove off the centaurs by shooting poisoned arrows at them. Afterward, Pholus was examining one of these arrows when he accidentally dropped it. It struck his foot, and the poison killed him.

In another well-known story, a centaur named Nessus tried to rape Deianira, the wife of Heracles. Heracles caught him and shot the centaur with a poisoned arrow. As he lay dying, Nessus urged Deianira to save some of the blood from his wound. He told her that if Heracles ever stopped loving her, she could regain his love by applying the blood to a garment that Heracles would wear. Deianira did as Nessus suggested and saved some of his blood. Many years later, when Heracles had been unfaithful to her, Deianira gave him a tunic to wear, a tunic that she had smeared with the blood of Nessus. The blood was poisoned, and Heracles died. In this way, Nessus took his revenge on Heracles.

Not all centaurs were savage brutes. One exception was Chiron, a teacher of medicine, music, hunting, and archery. The son of the god **Cronus**, Chiron taught gods and **heroes**, including **Jason**, **Achilles**, Heracles, and Asclepius. Chiron was accidentally wounded by one of Heracles' poisoned arrows. As the son of a god, he would live forever and suffer from the injury forever. Chiron therefore asked Zeus to let him die. Zeus granted his request and placed him in the heavens as a star in the constellation Sagittarius, also known as the Archer.

Centaurs in Context

It is possible that the idea of half-man, half-horse creatures was born when ancient Greeks or Minoans—who did not routinely ride on the backs of horses—first encountered nomads who spent most of their time on horseback. The Lapiths—often associated with centaurs in Greek myth—were considered to be skilled horsemen, and perhaps even the inventors of horseback riding.

Key Themes and Symbols

Centaurs are often associated with wild, reckless behavior. They generally symbolize chaos, or disorder, and may symbolize human traits that were seen as undesirable, such as lust and drunkenness.

Centaurs were invited as guests to the wedding of the King of Lapith, but when they became unruly, a battle erupted between the centaurs and the men of Lapith. © MARY EVANS PICTURE LIBRARY/THE IMAGE WORKS.

Centaurs in Art, Literature, and Everyday Life

Centaurs usually represented wild behavior in Greek literature and art. They appeared on many vases, and their fight with the Lapiths was depicted in sculptures in various temples. Because of their drunken behavior, centaurs were sometimes shown pulling the chariot of **Dionysus**, the god of wine and revelry. At other times, they were pictured being ridden by **Eros**, the god of love, because of their lustful ways. In Christian art of the Middle Ages, centaurs symbolized man's animal nature.

The Roman poet Ovid described the battle of the centaurs and the Lapiths in the *Metamorphoses*. This work, in turn, inspired the English poet Edmund Spenser to write about the battle in his most famous work, *The Faerie Queene*. Centaurs also appear in more recent literary works, such as the *Chronicles of Narnia* fantasy series by C. S. Lewis.

Read, Write, Think, Discuss

Compare centaurs to the mythical creatures known as **satyrs**. What physical and personality traits do satyrs have? How are they similar to centaurs? How are they different? What role do these creatures have in Greek and Roman myths?

SEE ALSO Heracles

Cerberus

Character Overview

In **Greek mythology**, Cerberus was the terrifying three-headed dog who guarded the entrance to the **underworld**. The offspring of the monsters Typhon and Echidna, Cerberus was also the brother of the serpent creature Hydra and the lion-headed beast Chimaera. He is often pictured with the tail of a snake or dragon, and with snakes sprouting from his back.

According to legend, Cerberus's appearance was so fearsome that any living person who saw him turned to stone. The saliva that fell from his mouth produced a deadly poison. Cerberus prevented spirits of the dead from leaving **Hades**, and living mortals from entering. Three humans, however, managed to overcome him: **Orpheus** charmed him with music; the Sibyl of Cumae drugged him with honeycakes to allow the Roman hero **Aeneas** access to the underworld; and **Heracles** (known as Hercules by the Romans) used his sheer strength to take Cerberus from the land of Hades to the kingdom of Mycenae and back again, the twelfth labor of Heracles.

Nationality/Culture
Greek/Roman

Pronunciation
SUR-ber-uhs

Alternate Names
Kerberos

Appears In
Hesiod's *Theogony*, Ovid's *Metamorphoses*, Homer's *Odyssey*

Lineage
Offspring of Typhon and Echidna

Heracles was one of three mortals who tamed Cerberus, done as part of his Twelve Labors. ALINARI/ART RESOURCE, NY.

Cerberus in Context

In ancient Greece and Rome, dogs were sometimes used to guard sacred places, such as temples. At Cumae, a city in southern Italy believed to be near the entrance of the underworld, a cave that housed a sibyl—a woman who, it was believed, could see the future—was discovered in the early twentieth century. At the site, excavators found a wall fixture with three large chains that appear to have been used for a trio of guard dogs.

Key Themes and Symbols

Cerberus is usually associated with the act of guarding or keeping out. He may also symbolize fearsomeness.

Cerberus in Art, Literature, and Everyday Life

Cerberus is one of the most easily recognizable creatures from Greek mythology, and appears in many examples of ancient art. Cerberus has been included as a character in several literary works, most notably Dante's *Inferno* (c. 1320 CE). In modern times, Cerberus has proven especially popular in movies and video games. He appeared in the 1997 Disney animated film *Hercules*, and in the Harry Potter books and film series (under the name Fluffy).

Read, Write, Think, Discuss

Using your library, the Internet, or other available resources, research the history of dogs as human companions. How long ago were dogs domesticated (tamed) by humans? What functions have dogs served over the centuries? What breeds are believed to be the oldest? Then write a brief essay with your views on the relationship between humans and dogs.

SEE ALSO Greek Mythology; Hades; Heracles; Orpheus

Ceres

See **Demeter.**

Cernunnos

Character Overview

Cernunnos is the horned god of **Celtic mythology**. He is represented as a bearded man with antlers sprouting from his head. He is often considered the god of hunters, as well as the lord of the animals.

Nationality/Culture
Irish/Celtic

Pronunciation
kur-NOO-nohs

Alternate Names
None

Appears In
The *Mabinogion*

Lineage
Unknown

Cernunnos. © ROGER-VIOLLET/
THE IMAGE WORKS.

Although Cernunnos is now associated primarily with the Celts and Ireland, images of Cernunnos have been found throughout Europe. Before the rise of the Roman Empire, Celtic tribes covered a large area of Europe, including parts of France, Italy, and Germany. One of the earliest known depictions of Cernunnos was found in northern Italy and has been dated to the fourth century BCE.

A cave painting discovered in France may suggest that Cernunnos is much older than that. The painting, popularly known as "The Sorcerer," depicts an upright figure with antlers that resembles Cernunnos. It is not known whether the painting is meant to show a horned god, or whether it simply shows a person wearing the skin of a deer. The painting has been estimated to be around fifteen thousand years old—more than twelve thousand years older than other existing images of Cernunnos.

Major Myths

Cernunnos does not have any known connections to other Celtic gods. Because Celtic mythology was transmitted orally, or by sharing stories out loud instead of writing them down, it is possible that many tales about Cernunnos have been lost over the centuries. No tales associated with Cernunnos's actions survive.

Cernunnos in Context

In ancient cultures, before the rise of successful farming practices, hunting was of vital importance to a community. People relied on animal meat as a source of protein and animal skins and bones for a variety of purposes. Early hunters lacked guns and sophisticated bows and arrows. Hunting was an incredibly difficult and dangerous task undertaken by groups of men who might spend many days tracking their prey, eventually overtaking it on foot

Cernunnos's Cousins?

The origin of the Celts is uncertain. Archaeological evidence suggests that they came originally from the area around the Black Sea and spread west. It is possible, though, that some Celts spread east, too. The god Pashupati of northern India bears a striking resemblance to Cernunnos—he is a horned hunter and represents untamed male power.

Some scholars have suggested that Cernunnos may be the source of traditional representations of the horned Christian devil. As Christianity spread into Celtic territory, Cernunnos was still a popular deity. It is possible that early Christian church leaders, unable to force the Celts to abandon Cernunnos, reinterpreted the god in a Christian context. His wildness and darkness became connected not with animals and nature but with evil.

and killing it at short range with a spear. The ability to kill a large animal and provide for the community came to be associated with male power. The kingly Cernunnos can be seen as a depiction of man as the ultimate predator.

Key Themes and Symbols

The main symbol of Cernunnos is his horns or antlers, which represent male fertility. Cernunnos is also usually depicted with torcs, or rings that signify Celtic nobility. He is almost always shown to be among animals, especially stags or deer, which indicate his importance to hunters and nature. Cernunnos is also associated with the oak tree, a symbol of wisdom and stability.

Cernunnos in Art, Literature, and Everyday Life

The two most famous depictions of Cernunnos are from the Gundestrup Cauldron and the "Pillar of the Boatmen" monument. The Gundestrup Cauldron, created in the first or second century BCE, is a large silver bowl that was rediscovered in 1891 in a peat bog in Denmark. One decorative panel of the cauldron shows Cernunnos, along with deer, a snake, and other wild animals. The "Pillar of the Boatmen" was created in the first century CE by sailors as a monument to various Roman and Celtic gods. The monument originally stood in a temple in what is now Paris, on the site where Notre Dame Cathedral was later built.

Although familiar to those who study Celtic mythology, Cernunnos is not very well known in modern times. He was featured in an episode of the television show *Hercules: The Legendary Journeys*, and has appeared as a villain to be fought in video games such as *Folklore* for PlayStation 3. A version of Cernunnos appears in Susan Cooper's fantasy novel *The Dark Is Rising* (1973)—as Herne the Hunter, a mounted leader of the hunt with great antlers who, like Cernunnos, is associated with the oak tree (in this case, the oak tree is in Windsor Forest).

Read, Write, Think, Discuss

Although depictions of Cernunnos have been found across Europe, very little is known about his place in ancient Celtic mythology. Based on what you know about Cernunnos, try writing your own short myth about him. Explain where he comes from, how he became associated with deer and other animals, and what relationship he has to other Celtic gods and goddesses.

SEE ALSO Celtic Mythology

Changing Woman

Nationality/Culture
American Indian/Navajo

Alternate Names
None

Appears In
Navajo oral myths and songs

Lineage
Raised by First Man and First Woman

Character Overview

Changing Woman, or Asdzáá Nádleehé, is the most respected goddess of the Navajo people. She represents all changes of life as well as the seasons, and is both a benevolent and a nurturing figure. All Navajo ceremonies must include at least one song dedicated to Changing Woman. She is related to goddesses found in many other Native American traditions, such as the Pawnee Moon Woman and the Apache White Painted Woman.

Major Myths

According to legend, Changing Woman changes continuously but never dies. She grows into an old woman in winter, but by spring she becomes a young woman again. In this way, she represents the power of life, fertility, and changing seasons. In some stories she has a sister, White Shell Woman

(Yoolgai asdzáá), who symbolizes the rain clouds. Ceremonies dedicated to Changing Woman are performed to celebrate childbirth, coming of age for girls, weddings, and to bless a new home.

Changing Woman bears the children of the Sun, Jóhonaa'éí, after he shines his rays on her. Their children are the twin **heroes**, Monster Slayer (Naayéé' neizghání) and Child of Water (Tó bájísh chíní), who cleared the earth of the monsters that once roamed it. Changing Woman lives by herself in a house floating on the western waters, where the Sun visits her every evening. One day she became lonely and decided to make some companions for herself. From pieces of her own skin, she created men and women who became the ancestors of the Navajo people. Changing Woman also created maize, an important food source for the Navajo.

Changing Woman in Context

Changing Woman plays a major role in the Navajo Kinaaldá ceremony, a ceremony that marks a young girl's change into a woman. During the long ceremony the girl impersonates and becomes Changing Woman, and participates in activities that are important to the role of women in the Navajo tribe. For instance, part of the ceremony requires the girl and the women who help her to prepare a large **corn** cake, which is then baked overnight in a pit. The women are not allowed to sleep during this time, and the next day the girl hands out pieces of the cake to guests at the ceremony. The cake represents Mother Earth—with the cake itself coming from the earth—and the girl as Changing Woman is able to change the earth into food. Throughout the ceremony, the girl is supposed to take on the qualities of Changing Woman, including physical strength, endurance, creativity, and fruitfulness.

Key Themes and Symbols

For the Navajo people, Changing Woman represents change—usually the change of seasons, as well as the growth of females into womanhood. She is also a symbol of the sky. She is identified with the earth, vegetation, fertility, growth, abundance, and ideal womanhood.

Changing Woman in Art, Literature, and Everyday Life

As with many characters from American Indian mythology, Changing Woman was known only to a small number of people. Even within that tribe, much of the attention dedicated to Changing Woman was done through song. Only recently have characters such as Changing Woman begun to appear in art and literature beyond members of the Navajo tribe.

Read, Write, Think, Discuss

Changing Woman and Her Sisters: Stories of Goddesses from Around the World by Katrin Hyman Tchana (2006) offers ten stories of goddesses taken from different cultures. Other than Changing Woman, the book features stories of goddesses such as **Amaterasu** from Shinto mythology and Macha from **Celtic mythology**.

SEE ALSO Native American Mythology

Cherubim

Nationality/Culture
Judeo-Christian and Is-
lamic

Pronunciation
CHER-uh-bim

Alternate Names
None

Appears In
The Bible, the Torah

Lineage
Attendants to God

Character Overview

Cherubim (or *cherub* in the singular form) are winged creatures that appear as attendants to God in the Jewish, Christian, and Islamic traditions. Their main duties are to praise God and to support his throne, though their roles vary from culture to culture.

Cherubim were probably introduced into ancient Hebrew culture by the Canaanites. The Hebrews expanded the role of the cherubim somewhat. For example, in the book of Genesis in the Old Testament, cherubim guard the entrance to the Garden of **Eden** after **Adam and Eve** are driven out of Paradise. Cherubim also protect the **Ark of the Covenant** (which contained the original tablets on which the Ten Commandments were inscribed), and God is described as riding on the back of a cherub. In general, cherubim represent the power and glory of the Hebrew god, Yahweh.

In Christian mythology, the cherubim are the second highest of the nine orders of **angels**, second only to the seraphim. The cherubim excel in wisdom and continually praise God. In Islamic mythology, the cherubim (or *karibiyun*) play much the same role, dwelling in **heaven** and constantly praising Allah, the Islamic god.

Scholars disagree about the origin of the word *cherubim*. It may have come from *karabu*, an ancient Near Eastern word meaning "to pray" or

Two cherubs, as portrayed by famous sixteenth-century artist Raphael. ERICH LESSING/ART RESOURCE, NY.

"to bless," or perhaps from *mu-karribim*, the guardians of the shrine of an ancient moon goddess.

Cherubim in Context

Whatever the origin of the name, the cherub itself can be traced to mythologies of the Babylonians, Assyrians, and other peoples of the ancient Near East. In these cultures, cherubim were usually pictured as creatures with parts of four animals: the head of a bull, the wings of an eagle, the feet of a lion, and the tail of a serpent. The four animals represented the four seasons, the four cardinal directions (north, south, east, and west), and the four ancient elements (earth, air, **fire**, and water). These original cherubim guarded the entrances to temples and palaces.

In modern times, cherubim are thought of as the representation of pure, innocent love—God's love particularly. But biblical depictions of cherubim are not so gentle. They guard the gates of Eden with a flaming sword to keep Adam and Eve from returning.

Key Themes and Symbols

Cherubim are often portrayed as human figures having four wings, and they are usually painted blue, which signifies knowledge. Sometimes they

U•X•L Encyclopedia of World Mythology

feature the faces of other animals. In Jewish folklore of the Middle Ages, the cherubim were described as handsome young men. In Christian art, however, cherubim usually appear as children, most often as chubby, winged babies.

Cherubim in Art, Literature, and Everyday Life

Cherubim appear in many ancient illuminated manuscripts, as well as in many Renaissance paintings and sculptures. However, the images of cherubim are often confused with those of *putti*, which are winged infants that do not represent angels but instead symbolize love and innocence. These appeared often in Renaissance and later works, and have become the typical image of cherubim. In modern times, the word "cherub" is often used to describe an innocent-looking child, especially one with chubby or rosy cheeks. This type of representation was particularly popular in the decorative arts of the nineteenth and early twentieth centuries. Plump, rosy-cheeked cherubs appeared on china, lampshades, pillowcases, upholstery, and other household items.

Read, Write, Think, Discuss

CHERUB is a series of novels written by Robert Muchamore about a group of teenage secret agents working for the British government. Like mythical cherubim, they serve as "guardian angels" for the citizens of the world, taking on terrorists and other evil forces. Their young age and seeming innocence allows them to work undetected by criminal organizations. The first volume of the series, *CHERUB: The Recruit*, was first published in the United Kingdom in 2004.

SEE ALSO Angels; Ark of the Covenant; Semitic Mythology

Chinese Mythology

Chinese Mythology in Context

The people of China have a rich and complicated mythology that dates back nearly four thousand years. Throughout Chinese history, myth and reality have been intertwined. Historical figures have been worshipped as gods, and ancient myths are sometimes treated as historical truths. In addition, three great religious traditions—Confucianism, Taoism, and Buddhism—have played a role in shaping the mythology. The result is a rich tapestry of characters and tales, both real and imagined, and a unique pantheon (collection of recognized gods and goddesses) organized very much like ancient Chinese society.

China can trace its historical roots in an unbroken line for more than four thousand years, and its mythological roots extend even farther back in time. From about 2000 to 1500 BCE, a people known as the Xia dominated the northern regions of China. The Xia worshipped the snake, a creature that appears in some of the oldest Chinese myths. Eventually, the snake changed into the dragon, which became one of the most enduring symbols of Chinese culture and mythology.

New Religious Ideas From about 1500 to 1066 BCE, China was ruled by the Shang dynasty. The people at this time worshipped many deities, including natural forces and elements, such as rain, clouds, rivers, mountains, the **sun**, the moon, and the earth. Their greatest deity, Shang Di, remains an important god in the Chinese pantheon.

When a new dynasty, the Zhou, came to power in China in 1066 BCE, significant changes took place in religion. People still worshipped the old gods, but ancestor worship became increasingly important. Confucianism and Taoism appeared near the end of the Zhou dynasty. These two religious traditions had an enormous influence on the development of the most basic and lasting principles of Chinese culture.

Changing Old Beliefs In 213 BCE, many of the original sources of Chinese mythology were lost when Emperor Shi Huangdi of the Qin dynasty ordered the burning of all books on subjects other than medicine, prophecy (predictions of the future), and farming. This order was reversed in 191 BCE, and much of the literature was reconstructed. But works were rewritten to support ideas popular with the royal court at the time. These changes affected religious beliefs, producing a pantheon of deities that mirrored the political organization of the Chinese empire. Gods and spirits had different ranks and areas of responsibility, just like Chinese officials.

Shortly before 100 CE, Buddhism arrived in China from India and added another important influence to Chinese culture and mythology. Buddhist ideas gradually came to be merged with Taoism and

Confucianism in the minds of many Chinese. The three traditions often were seen as different aspects of the same religion and as having basically the same goals. Buddhists and Taoists honored each other's deities in their temples, and both incorporated principles of Confucianism, such as ancestor worship, in their beliefs.

Core Deities and Characters

The deities and characters that make up the body of Chinese mythology originate in many different regions and from several unique belief systems. For this reason, Chinese mythology is less uniform and consistent in its legends than the mythologies of many other cultures, but offers a wide range of tales and mythological figures to appreciate.

Pan Gu was the first living creature and the creator of the world. Among his acts of creation were the separation of the earth and sky, the placement of the stars and planets in the heavens, and the shaping of the earth's surface. It is often said that his body became the world on which all things live.

For the Han people of ancient China, the supreme god was known as Shang Di. In later times, this same deity came to be known as Tian, also used as a word for **heaven** or sky. There are few details about Shang Di in Chinese mythology other than that he was male and his duties involved rewarding those who were deserving and punishing those who were not. Shang Di was not represented in art.

A similar deity is the **Jade Emperor**, also known as Yu Huang, revered by Taoists as the supreme ruler of heaven. According to legend, when Yu Huang was born as a prince the kingdom where he lived was flooded with light. As he grew, he showed a remarkable respect for all living things and devoted himself to helping the least fortunate members of the kingdom. After his father died, he ruled the region with greatness and eventually became immortal, or able to live forever. According to myth, it took Yu Huang millions of years to achieve the status of Jade Emperor, which was bestowed upon him by a group of deities.

Two groups of characters central to Chinese mythology are the Three Sovereigns and the Five Emperors. All of these figures were believed to rule ancient regions of China, and many are credited with uplifting humans to a state of advanced civilization through their leadership or their teachings. The Three Sovereigns are figures of the most ancient times. Two of the three, Fu Xi and Nuwa, were deities who helped humankind continue in the aftermath of a great flood. Fu Xi and Nuwa were brother and sister and were the only two to survive the flood; they prayed to the Jade Emperor, who gave them permission to become a couple and repopulate the land. In many versions of their tale they also teach humans essential skills, such as hunting, fishing with nets, and cooking food. The third of the Three Sovereigns, Shennong, is said to have taught people the arts of agriculture and medicinal herbs. According to legend, Shennong went to the trouble of tasting hundreds of plants and minerals in an effort to determine which could be helpful to humans and which could be harmful (poisonous).

The Five Emperors are believed to be based on historical leaders who brought great advancements to their people. None were emperors in the traditional, later use of the term; rather, they were tribal leaders who may have also been elected to be in charge of a larger group of tribes. The first of the Five Emperors was the **Yellow Emperor**, also known as Huang-Di. The Yellow Emperor was said to be the first to institute laws among the tribes he ruled, and he also brought the first music and art to his people. He became immortal, and eventually power passed to his grandson, Zhuanxu. Zhuanxu made his own contributions to Chinese culture, expanding his kingdom and unifying religious and marriage practices for all his subjects.

The kingdom was later ruled by his son, Ku, and by Ku's son, Yao. It is believed that Ku ruled for seventy years, while his son Yao ruled for over one hundred years. Yao, according to tradition, invented the Chinese board game Go, which was considered an essential way to learn strategy and planning. The last of the Five Emperors was Shun, son-in-law to Yao and ruler for nearly fifty years. He was originally a simple farmer, but his humility and dedication to religion won him a reputation that spread all the way to Yao's throne; since Yao was dissatisfied with his own son's behavior, he allowed Shun to marry two of his daughters and become the next in line to rule. Yao and Shun are often viewed together as the perfect leaders whose behavior rose above any possible hint of misdeed and whose popularity has been unmatched since.

Other important figures from Chinese history have developed their own unique legends that expand upon their true historical accomplishments. Two of the most important of these figures are the religious and philosophical leaders Confucius and Laozi. Born in 551 BCE to a poor family of aristocratic background, Confucius began a teaching career after working as a minor government official. For Confucius, the goal of education and learning was self-knowledge and self-improvement, which would lead one to right conduct. Although his method of education was aimed at ensuring the smooth operation of a stable and well-ordered state, his teachings became a guide to living wisely as well.

Confucius attracted many followers who spread his ideas after his death in 479 BCE. A number of legends grew up about Confucius, including one in which **dragons** guarded his mother when he was born. According to another story, a **unicorn** appeared at his birth and spit out a piece of jade with a prophecy written on it, saying that the infant would become "an uncrowned emperor." Considering the immense impact of Confucius on Chinese culture, the prophecy came true.

Taoism, also known as Daoism, arose about the same time as Confucianism. This religious tradition had its roots in the nature worship of the earliest Chinese people. The word *tao* means "way," and Taoist belief is based on the idea that there is a natural order or a "way of heaven" that one can come to know by living in harmony with nature. Through an understanding of natural laws, an individual can gain eternal life. The main Taoist work, the Tao Te Ching, was supposedly written by Laozi, a scholar at the Chinese royal court in the 500s BCE. Little is known about Laozi. The main sources of information, written hundreds of years after he lived, are legendary in nature. One of the most popular stories about Laozi concerns a voyage to the west, during which he wrote the Tao Te Ching. Other tales claim that Laozi met Confucius and that he lived more than two hundred years. Although the true story of Laozi will probably never be known, he is widely respected in China. Confucianists consider him a great philosopher, while Taoists regard him as the embodiment of the tao and honor him as a saint or god.

Major Myths

According to Chinese mythology, at the beginning of time the universe consisted only of a giant egg. Within the egg lay a sleeping giant named Pan Gu. One day Pan Gu awoke and stretched, causing the egg to split open. After Pan Gu emerged, the light, pure parts of the egg became the sky, while the heavy parts formed the earth. This separation of the earth and sky marked the beginning of yin and yang, the two opposing forces of the universe.

Laozi's fabled meeting with Confucius. © MARY EVANS PICTURE LIBRARY/THE IMAGE WORKS.

Already gigantic in size, Pan Gu grew ten feet taller each day. This went on for eighteen thousand years, and as Pan Gu became taller, he pushed the earth and sky farther apart and shaped them with his tools until they reached their present position and appearance. Exhausted by his work, Pan Gu finally fell asleep and died.

When Pan Gu died, parts of his body were transformed into different features of the world. According to some stories, his head, arms, feet, and stomach became great mountains that help to anchor the world and mark its boundaries. Other stories say that Pan Gu's breath was transformed into wind and clouds; his voice became thunder; and his eyes became the sun and moon. Pan Gu's blood formed rivers and seas; his veins turned into roads and paths; his sweat became rain and dew; his bones and teeth turned into rock and metal; his flesh changed into soil;

the hair on his head became the stars; and the hair on his body turned into vegetation.

Some myths say that humans developed from fleas and parasites that fell from Pan Gu's body and beard. Other stories, however, tell how Pan Gu created humans by shaping them from clay and leaving them in the sun to dry. When a sudden rain began to fall, Pan Gu hastily wrapped up the clay figures, damaging some in the process, which explains why some humans are crippled or disabled.

Another myth tells of the battle between two gods. Zhu Rong was the god of **fire**, while his son Gong Gong was a god of water. The ambitious young Gong Gong decided to attempt an overthrow of heaven so that he could be the ruler of all things. When Zhu Rong heard this, he battled his son for several days to stop him. The two fell down to earth during the fight, and ultimately Zhu Rong was triumphant over his son. However, Gong Gong was so upset that he smashed one of the mountains that held up the heavens. This is why the sun, the moon, and the stars travel through the sky at an angle.

Another popular myth concerns the daughter of the Jade Emperor, a princess who was responsible for weaving the clouds in the sky. She had a magic robe that allowed her to descend to the land of mortals—Earth—in order to bathe each day. On one occasion, a poor cowherd saw her bathing in a stream and fell in love with her. While she was in the water, he took her robe; this kept her from being able to return to the heavens. Trapped with the cowherd, the princess eventually came to love him, and the couple got married. Later, when the princess was feeling homesick and missing her father, she discovered the magic robe that her husband had hidden from her. She used the robe to travel back to the heavens, and her father—not wanting her to return to Earth—created an enormous river across the sky that the princess could not cross. The river is visible in the night sky as the Milky Way. Seeing how upset his daughter became, however, the Jade Emperor decided to allow the couple to meet on a bridge over the river for one day each year. (In one version of the tale, the bridge is made of magpies—birds who have taken pity on the couple.)

A famous literary work that incorporates many elements of Chinese folklore—including animals as main characters—is the sixteenth-century novel *Journey to the West*. The novel tells the story of a famous Buddhist monk named Xuanzang who travels west on a journey to India, where he is tasked with obtaining some sacred Buddhist scriptures. Along the way he encounters several unique characters who join him on his quest, including Sun Wukong, the Monkey King who had been punished by Buddha centuries before when he attempted to take control of heaven. Xuanzang is able to control Sun Wukong's violent outbursts by uttering some magic words. Another companion—the half-human, half-pig Zhu Bajie—was also punished by the gods for his disrespectful behavior. Xuanzang is also joined by a demon named Sha Wujing, a former general in heaven who was punished for breaking a valuable crystal vessel. The group encounters eighty-one different disasters that they must overcome, mostly orchestrated by Buddha himself as a test for the adventurers. What begins as a search for scriptures turns out to be a quest for salvation; Xuanzang and Sun Wukong both achieve the highest level of enlightenment, while the other characters earn the ability to return to heaven.

Key Themes and Symbols

Several common themes appear throughout much of Chinese mythology. Among the most significant are the creation of the world out of chaos or disorder, the importance of nature, and reverence for ancestors. The importance of nature is stressed in legends, such as that of the Five Sacred Mountains that represent the main points of the compass and the axis of the world. The most sacred mountain, T'ai Shan, has Shang Di, the greatest earthly power, as its deity. Mount Kunlun, home of immortals, became the focus of various cults. Many Chinese myths deal with natural disasters, especially **floods**. Others deal with heavenly bodies, such as the sun and moon. Animals, including dragons, pigs, and monkeys, are also important figures in Chinese mythology.

Reverence for ancestors is another common theme in Chinese mythology. Long life is viewed as a sign of the gods' favor, and for many centuries the Chinese have sought the secret of long life and immortality. In the past, Taoists believed that magic potions could be created that bestowed eternal life on people who drank them and that beings known as *hsien* gained immortality in this way. Age is also closely associated with wisdom and enlightenment in many myths. Both Taoism and Confucianism stress the importance of paying proper respect to elders, especially parents and grandparents, and deceased ancestors are honored with various ceremonies and rituals.

Chinese Mythology in Art, Literature, and Everyday Life

Mythology has been one of the richest sources for Chinese artists and writers to draw upon over the centuries. *Journey to the West* is considered to be one of the most important books in Chinese history, and traditional artwork commonly features legendary figures, such as the Five Emperors or the Eight Immortals. In modern times, even with the increasing presence of Western cultural traditions, Chinese mythology remains an integral part of life and art in China.

Journey to the West has appeared in many forms and remains the best-known tale of Chinese mythology to those outside China. The Japanese television series *Monkey* (1978), which also aired in a translated version for British and Australian audiences, was based on the book, and the 2008 English-language film *The Forbidden Kingdom*, starring Chinese cinema legends Jackie Chan and Jet Li, was inspired by the same legendary characters.

Other mythological characters also appear in different aspects of art and culture. Pan Gu is usually portrayed as a little person clothed in a bearskin or leaves, holding a hammer and chisel or the egg of creation. Fu Xi and Nuwa are sometimes depicted in half-human, half-snake form; the two have appeared in several video games, including the popular *Dynasty Warriors* series. In modern times, Shang Di is one name given to God among Chinese Christians. As interest in Asian culture expands throughout the Western world, characters such as these—and the tales that accompany them—will no doubt continue to grow in awareness and popularity.

Read, Write, Think, Discuss

Bridge of Birds: A Novel of an Ancient China that Never Was (1984), by Barry Hughart, is a fantasy tale built largely on the myth of the princess and the cowherd, though it also weaves many other Chinese myths into its adventure. Master Li Kao and his sidekick, Number Ten Ox, venture across a mythical, seventh-century landscape in an attempt to find the Great Root of Power—the only cure for the ailing children of their small village. The book won the 1985 World Fantasy Award for Best Novel, as well as the 1986 Mythopoeic Fantasy Award, and spawned two sequels: *The Story of the Stone* (1988), and *Eight Skilled Gentlemen* (1990).

SEE ALSO Animals in Mythology; Buddhism and Mythology; Creation Stories; Dragons; Reincarnation; Xian; Yellow Emperor

Christopher, St.

Character Overview

In the Christian religion, St. Christopher is thought to have carried the child Jesus across a difficult stream. For this reason, he is associated with helping travelers and is, in fact, the patron (protector) saint of travelers. He is reported to have lived during the third century CE, though little historical evidence exists to support this. The best-known legend about St. Christopher states that he was a giant named Reprobus (or Offero in some versions) who wanted to serve the world's most powerful king. When he found out that Christ was the greatest king, he converted to Christianity. He then took up a post by a river that had no bridge and carried travelers across on his shoulders. One day he was carrying a small child who became so heavy that Christopher could barely make it across. The child turned out to be Christ himself, and Christopher had just carried the weight of the world's sins. He was then given the name Christopher, which translates as "bearer of Christ."

Another legend about St. Christopher suggests that, in addition to being a giant, he had the head of a dog. According to this legend, he was once a fierce cannibal who changed his ways after converting to Christianity. He was later executed for his Christian beliefs.

St. Christopher in Context

Although Christopher has been recognized as a saint by the Roman Catholic Church, there is no verifiable evidence that he ever existed. According to legend, he was executed by the Roman emperor Decius, who served as the leader of Rome from 249–251 CE. During his short reign, Decius was known for persecuting Christians, whom he saw as a threat to traditional Roman beliefs. This may explain why St. Christopher, portrayed as a loyal follower of Christ, is associated with this time period.

Nationality/Culture
Christian

Pronunciation
saynt KRIS-tuh-fer

Alternate Names
Reprobus, Offero

Appears In
Roman Catholic and Eastern Orthodox myths

Lineage
Unknown

St. Christopher carrying Christ (disguised as a child) across the river. CAMERAPHOTO/ART RESOURCE, NY.

In 1969, the Roman Catholic Church removed St. Christopher's feast day from the universal calendar of saints, citing a lack of evidence for his existence. However, he still remains on the list of saints recognized by the Roman Catholic Church.

Key Themes and Symbols

One of the main themes of the myth of St. Christopher is loyalty. St. Christopher's dedication to Christ is why he begins helping people across the river without a bridge. It is also this loyalty that leads to his ultimate execution. The most notable symbol associated with St. Christopher is the dog; he is said to have had a dog's head, and the dog has long been a symbol of loyalty.

St. Christopher in Art, Literature, and Everyday Life

St. Christopher was a popular figure in medieval Christian art. He was sometimes depicted with the head of a dog, and often shown carrying a young Jesus on his back. A famous example of the latter is the painting *St. Christopher Carrying the Christ Child* (1480–1490) by Hieronymus Bosch.

St. Christopher often appears in modern films, music, and literature as a symbolic protector of travelers. An image of St. Christopher is kept by a character in the classic film *The Spirit of St. Louis* (1957, based on Charles Lindbergh's real-life flight across the Atlantic Ocean). St. Christopher is also considered the patron saint of many cities, including Vilnius, Lithuania, and Havana, Cuba.

Read, Write, Think, Discuss

St. Christopher may or may not have been an actual historical figure, but his description qualifies as "larger than life." Some scholars have suggested that the man was referred to as "dog-faced" because he came from a region thought to be savage or primitive. This illustrates the problems of reading a text literally, instead of understanding the symbolic nature of some phrases or descriptions. Although people often use expressions in casual conversation—such as "I'm starving," for example—it can be difficult to spot such expressions in ancient texts originally written in another language.

Write a brief account of a time when you or someone you know mistakenly interpreted a statement literally. If you cannot think of an example, try to come up with at least ten figures of speech that could be easily misunderstood by readers a thousand years in the future.

Circe

Nationality/Culture
Greek/Roman

Pronunciation
SUR-see

Alternate Names
Kirke

Appears In
Homer's *Odyssey*, Hesiod's *Theogony*

Lineage
Daughter of Helios and Perse

Character Overview

In **Greek mythology**, the witch Circe was the daughter of the **sun** god Helios (pronounced HEE-lee-ohs) and the ocean nymph (female nature spirit) called Perse (pronounced PUR-see). According to legend, Circe lived on the island of Aeaea (pronounced ee-EE-uh), where she built a palace for herself and practiced spells that enabled her to turn men into animals.

The two best-known legends involving Circe concern her encounters with the fisherman Glaucus and with **Odysseus**, a Greek hero of the Trojan War.

Glaucus (pronounced GLAW-kus) was changed into a sea god one day while sorting his catch. He became half man and half fish, with long strands of seaweed for hair. Glaucus fell in love with a beautiful girl named Scylla (pronounced SIL-uh), but she was frightened of his appearance and rejected him. He went to Circe and asked for a spell to make Scylla love him. Circe offered Glaucus her love instead, but he refused to have anyone but Scylla. The jealous Circe then enchanted the water where Scylla was swimming, turning her into a horrible sea monster with six heads. Scylla fled to a cave on top of a dangerous cliff and attacked any sailors that came within her reach.

The most famous tale concerning Circe appears in Homer's **Odyssey**. Odysseus (pronounced oh-DIS-ee-uhs) and his crew sailed by Aeaea as they were returning from the Trojan War. Odysseus sent some men ashore, led by a warrior named Eurylochus (pronounced your-i-LOH-kus). The group came upon Circe's palace, which was surrounded by lions, bears, and wolves, which were tame and did not attack them. In fact, the beasts were men that Circe had changed into animal form. Circe then appeared and invited Odysseus's men inside to dine and drink. Everyone accepted the invitation except Eurylochus, who was suspicious. After eating Circe's enchanted food, the men all turned into pigs. Eurylochus alone returned to the ship to tell Odysseus what had happened.

Odysseus decided to go to Circe himself. Along the way, he met a young man, who was actually the god **Hermes** in disguise. Hermes tried to discourage Odysseus from continuing on to the palace, but Odysseus was determined to get his men back. Hermes then gave Odysseus an herb that would protect him from Circe's spells. When Odysseus reached the palace, Circe invited him in and attempted to enchant him. However, the herb protected him against her spell, and he drew his sword and threatened her. The sorceress fell to her knees and pleaded for her life. Odysseus agreed to spare her if she would return his men to their normal condition and release them safely.

Circe restored the crew to human form and offered to entertain them before they returned to sea. Odysseus and his men found life on the island so pleasurable that they remained there a full year before resuming the journey home. When they finally left, Circe sent them on their way with a favorable wind and advice about how to avoid the many dangers that lay before them.

In an Italian version of this legend, Circe and Odysseus had three children: Telegonus (pronounced tuh-LEG-uh-nus), Agrius (pronounced AG-ree-us), and Latinus (pronounced LA-tin-us). Telegonus traveled to Ithaca to seek his father but then killed him by accident. He brought Odysseus's body back to Aeaea, accompanied by Odysseus's widow, **Penelope** (pronounced puh-NEL-uh-pee), and their son Telemachus (pronounced tuh-LEM-uh-kuhs). Circe made them all immortal (able to live forever) and married Telemachus, and Telegonus married Penelope. Circe also played a role in the legend of the **Argonauts**, ritually purifying **Jason** and **Medea** after they killed Medea's brother.

Circe in Context

Ancient Greek women did not enjoy the same status as men. They were expected to remain at home, tend to the household, and nurture their families. The aggressive actions of the female figures in ancient Greek myths show that the Greeks were well aware, however, that women might have more than meal-planning and child-rearing on their minds. The witch, Circe, possesses qualities that would both entice and frighten men. Circe is beautiful, entertaining, generous, a wonderful hostess, and a capable healer—all things that, to the ancient Greeks, a perfect woman must be. She offers rest and restoration to Odysseus's weary men, and she helps them along in their journey—but not, of course, before turning them into pigs. Thus, Circe's two-sided female nature becomes clear. She is not only nurturing and feminine; she is dangerous, deceptive, and powerful.

Real Magic?

Although there is no evidence that Circe is based on a real historical figure, medical experts have speculated about a possible scientific explanation for her potions and Odysseus's antidote. This assumes the effect of Circe's potion is not taken literally—in other words, victims are not actually transformed into animals.

A potion that causes hallucinations, memory loss, and confusion could be made from a group of naturally occurring substances known as anticholinergics. These substances are found in deadly nightshade and other plants found in the region associated with the Circe myth. Such a potion could result in a victim feeling as if he or she were under a magical spell. (It is important to note that deadly nightshade is one of the most poisonous plants known to humans and should never be consumed or fed to anyone.)

In addition, the plant that Homer describes as protection against Circe's potion—referred to as "moly"—matches descriptions of a plant known today as the snowdrop. The snowdrop contains a natural substance that can reduce the effects of anticholinergics, thus offering protection from such a potion.

She controls wild beasts such as lions and wolves, and has a deep connection with the ancient, dark forces of nature. This dark, mysterious connection with nature is something that was, long before the ancient Greeks, associated with women. Odysseus, a clever man, recognizes and respects Circe's power. It is only with divine help that he outmaneuvers her. The story of Circe seems to be a warning to Greek men that if they did not firmly control women, women would control them.

Circe has much in common with later conceptions of witches in Europe and North America. She knows how to use herbs to create spells and potions, which she whips up in a bubbling cauldron. She even has a stick or staff, much like a witch's wand.

Key Themes and Symbols

Because of the details of her tale in the *Odyssey*, Circe has become associated with men in animal form, usually as swine. She is commonly shown surrounded by animals and holding a cup of her potion. Many scholars view Circe as a symbol of the luxury and unchecked desire that seduces people and causes them to ignore their duty and thus lose their dignity. Since nearly all the victims of her wrath were male, Circe may also represent the power that a woman can have over men.

Circe in Art, Literature, and Everyday Life

Though Circe is hardly a major character in Greek mythology, she has endured in art and popular culture better than some Greek gods. Her story is recognized well enough that she is mentioned in passing in many works, including the Ernest Hemingway novel *The Sun Also Rises* (1926). Nathaniel Hawthorne offered a retelling of Circe's story in his 1853 collection *Tanglewood Tales*. Literary legends as diverse as Edmund Spenser, James Joyce, and Toni Morrison included female characters based on Circe in their most popular works.

Circe has also appeared as a villain in several DC Comics series, including *Wonder Woman*, and has also appeared on the animated television series *Hercules*.

Read, Write, Think, Discuss

Waiting for Odysseus by Clemence McLaren (2004) offers a unique new perspective on the story of Homer's *Odyssey*: each of the four sections of the book is told in the voice of a woman from Odysseus's life. The second section of the book, "Circe's Story: A Witch Takes a Lover," tells of the sorceress and her affair with the adventurous hero. The author includes an epilogue that offers additional information about the themes of the book and the original Greek myths.

SEE ALSO Jason; Nymphs; Odysseus; *Odyssey, The*

Coatlicue

Character Overview

Coatlicue, the earth goddess of **Aztec mythology**, was the mother of the **sun**, the moon, the stars, and all the Aztec gods and goddesses. Her name means "serpent skirt." Coatlicue was the source of all life on earth and took the dead back again into her body.

Nationality/Culture
Aztec

Pronunciation
koh-aht-LEE-kway

Alternate Names
Teteoinan

Appears In
Aztec oral legends

Lineage
Mother of Huitzilopochtli and Quetzalcoatl

Major Myths

According to legend, Coatlicue had several hundred children. Once, she became pregnant after a ball of feathers fell from the sky and she stuffed it into her bosom. One of Coatlicue's daughters, Coyolxauhqui (pronounced koh-yohl-SHAW-kee), was outraged by this and led a group of Coatlicue's other children to destroy their mother. Just as Coatlicue was about to be killed, the god **Huitzilopochtli** (pronounced wee-tsee-loh-POCH-tlee) emerged fully grown from her womb and protected her, slaying many of her rebellious children in the process.

Coatlicue in Context

The Aztecs, like other early American tribes, engaged in human sacrifices to their gods. The victims were usually enemy soldiers or captives of war, and the method of **sacrifice** depended upon which god the Aztecs meant to please. For Huitzilopochtli, a priest would slice open the stomach and chest of the victim and pull the still-beating heart out of the victim's body. For Huehueteotl (pronounced way-way-tay-OH-tul), the god of **fire**, victims would be burned alive. The skulls of sacrificed victims were then displayed on a large rack known as a *tzompantli*. The largest tzompantli, just one of at least six located at the capital city of Tenochtitlán (pronounced teh-nowch-TEE-tlan), is estimated to have contained approximately sixty thousand skulls.

Estimates for the number of sacrifices performed by the Aztecs each year during the height of their empire range from twenty thousand to nearly a quarter of a million. Although Coatlicue was a goddess of death and is depicted wearing body parts, sacrifices made in her honor are not documented.

In many mythologies, a "mother" goddess gives birth to the cosmos and all the deities. The creation of new life was seen as a female power, for the obvious reason that women are able to produce life from their bodies. The particular ferocity and grim depiction of Coatlicue were reflections of the violence that was part of Aztec society.

Key Themes and Symbols

One of the main symbols of Coatlicue is the snake. Her skirt is made of entwined serpents, and her head consists of two snakes facing each other. Snakes are symbols of both death and fertility in many cultures. Her massive breasts show her as a nourishing mother, while her clawlike

A statue of Coatlicue, the Aztec goddess of the earth.
THE LIBRARY OF CONGRESS.

fingers and toes show her as a devouring monster and a digger of graves. She wears a necklace made of the hands and hearts of her children, with a single skull in the center. This symbolizes both the giving and taking of life.

Coatlicue in Art, Literature, and Everyday Life

As with many Aztec gods and goddesses, Coatlicue appears in relatively few existing works of art. A statue in Mexico's National Museum of Anthropology and History represents the idea of Coatlicue as creator and destroyer, and is undoubtedly the most well-known representation of the goddess. Several illustrated Aztec calendars and tribal histories were also created at around the time Spanish colonists settled in the region in the early sixteenth century.

Read, Write, Think, Discuss

Spanish conquistadors viewed Aztec rituals of human sacrifice as barbaric and used this as one of their main justifications for overthrowing the Aztec empire. In modern times, the principle of freedom of religion allows people the right to worship as they wish, but does not make allowances for human or animal sacrifices. Some Aztec rituals required self-sacrifice, which involved piercing one's own skin and offering the blood to the gods.

Do you think freedom of religion should protect certain rituals such as blood or animal sacrifices? Why or why not? Do you think animal sacrifice is fundamentally different from hunting, which is largely legal and regulated by the government? Why or why not?

SEE ALSO Aztec Mythology; Serpents and Snakes

Corn

Theme Overview

First grown in Mexico thousands of years ago, corn soon became the most important food crop in Central and North America. Throughout the region, Maya, Aztecs, and other Native Americans worshiped corn gods and developed a variety of myths about the origin, planting, growing, and harvesting of corn (also known as maize).

Major Myths

Corn Gods and Goddesses The majority of corn deities (gods) are female and associated with fertility. They include the Cherokee goddess Selu; Yellow Woman and the Corn Mother goddess Iyatiku of the

Keresan people of the American Southwest; and Chicomecoatl (pronounced chee-co-meh-KWAH-tl), the goddess of maize who was worshipped by the Aztecs of Mexico. The Maya believed that humans had been fashioned out of corn, and they based their calendar on the planting of the cornfield.

Male corn gods do appear in some legends. The Aztecs had a male counterpart to Chicomecoatl, called Centeotl (pronounced sen-teh-OH-tl), to whom they offered their blood each year, as well as some minor corn gods known as the Centzon Totochtin, or "the 400 rabbits." The Seminole figure Fas-ta-chee, a dwarf whose hair and body were made of corn, was another male corn god. He carried a bag of corn and taught the Seminoles how to grow, grind, and store corn for food. The Hurons of northeastern North America worshipped Ioskeha (pronounced i-oh-WISS-keh-ha), who made corn, gave **fire** to the Hurons, and brought good weather.

The Zuni people of the southwestern United States have a myth about eight corn maidens. The young women are invisible, but their beautiful dancing movements can be seen when they dance with the growing corn as it waves in the wind. One day the young god Paiyatemu fell in love with the maidens, and they fled from him. While they were gone, a terrible famine spread across the land. Paiyatemu begged the maidens to turn back, and they returned to the Zuni and resumed their dance. As a result, the corn started to grow again.

Origin Myths A large number of American Indian myths deal with the origin of corn and how it came to be grown by humans. Many of the tales center on a "Corn Mother" or other female figure who introduces corn to the people.

In one myth, told by the Creeks and other tribes of the southeastern United States, the Corn Woman is an old woman living with a family that does not know who she is. Every day she feeds the family corn dishes, but the members of the family cannot figure out where she gets the food.

One day, wanting to discover where the old woman gets the corn, the sons spy on her. Depending on the version of the story, the corn is either scabs or sores that she rubs off her body, washings from her feet, nail clippings, or even her feces. In all versions, the origin of the corn is disgusting, and once the family members know its origin, they refuse to eat it.

This painting by George Catlin shows the Hidatsa people of the North American plains celebrating the corn harvest with the Green Corn Dance. The ceremony, held in the middle of the summer, marks the beginning of the New Year. SMITHSONIAN AMERICAN ART MUSEUM, WASHINGTON, D.C./ART RESOURCE, NY.

The Corn Woman solves the problem in one of several ways. In one version, she tells the sons to clear a large piece of ground, kill her, and drag her body around the clearing seven times. However, the sons clear only seven small spaces, cut off her head, and drag it around the seven spots. Wherever her blood fell, corn grew. According to the story, this is why corn grows only in some places and not all over the world.

In another account, the Corn Woman tells the boys to build a corn crib and lock her inside it for four days. At the end of that time, they open the crib and find it filled with corn. The Corn Woman then shows them how to use the corn.

Other stories of the origin of corn involve goddesses who choose men to teach the uses of corn and to spread the knowledge to their people. The Seneca Indians of the Northeast tell of a beautiful woman who lived on a cliff and sang to the village below. Her song told an old

---

King Corn

The 2007 documentary *King Corn* examines the way corn is grown, fertilized, harvested, and marketed by American farms. The filmmakers, Aaron Wolf and Curt Ellis, follow the many paths corn takes as it becomes everything from car fuel to livestock feed to soda sweetener. The film shows the surprising ways in which corn, considered a blessing from the gods by the Native Americans, has become a low-quality, non-nutritious ingredient present in almost every packaged food we eat.

---

man to climb to the top and be her husband. At first, he refused because the climb was so steep, but the villagers persuaded him to go.

When the old man reached the top, the woman asked him to make love to her. She also taught him how to care for a young plant that would grow on the spot where they made love. The old man fainted as he embraced the woman, and when he awoke, the woman was gone. Five days later, he returned to the spot to find a corn plant. He husked the corn and gave some grains to each member of the tribe. The Seneca then shared their knowledge with other tribes, spreading corn around the world.

Mayan stories give the ant—or some other small creature—credit for the discovery of corn. The ant hid the corn away in a hole in a mountain, but eventually the other animals found out about the corn and arranged for a bolt of lightning to split open the mountain so that they could have some corn too. The fox, coyote, parrot, and crow gave corn to the gods, who used it to create the first people. Although the gods' earlier attempts to create human beings out of mud or wood had failed, the corn people were perfect. However, the gods decided that their new creations were able to see too clearly, so they clouded the people's sight to prevent them from competing with their makers.

The Lakota Plains Indians say that a white she-buffalo brought their first corn. A beautiful woman appeared on the plain one day. When hunters approached her, she told them to prepare to welcome her. They built a lodge for the woman and waited for her to reappear. When she came, she gave four drops of her milk and told them to plant them, explaining that they would grow into corn. The woman then changed into a buffalo and disappeared.

According to the Penobscot Indians, the Corn Mother was also the first mother of the people. Their creation myth says that after people began to fill the earth, they became so good at hunting that they killed most of the animals. The first mother of all the people cried because she had nothing to feed her children. When her husband asked what he could do, she told him to kill her and have her sons drag her body by its silky hair until her flesh was scraped from her bones. After burying her bones, they should return in seven months, when there would be food for the people. When the sons returned, they found corn plants with tassels like silken hair. Their mother's flesh had become the tender fruit of the corn.

Another Corn Mother goddess is Iyatiku, who appears in legends of the Keresan people, a Pueblo group of the American Southwest. In the Keresan story, Iyatiku leads human beings on a journey from underground up to the earth's surface. To provide food for them, she plants bits of her heart in fields to the north, west, south, and east. Later the pieces of Iyatiku's heart grow into fields of corn.

Corn in Context

Though it is now grown and consumed worldwide, corn originated in Mexico around nine thousand years ago. It was most likely developed from a wild maize native to the area; local farmers created hybrid versions that maximized its benefit as a food. By around 1500 BCE, corn was one of the main foods for many of the tribes found in Central America. However, it was unknown to the rest of the world until Spanish explorers arrived in the late fifteenth and early sixteenth centuries. Today, corn is grown in places such as China, Italy, and India, and is the number one grain crop (measured by weight) in the world. The United States produces more corn by itself than the rest of the top ten corn-producing countries combined.

In the mythologies of the American Southwest, corn is often said to arise from the flesh of a woman. This reflects the woman's role as both the giver of life through childbirth, and the gatherer of food in tribes that developed stable agricultural methods. While men would provide meat from hunting, much of a tribe's dietary needs were met by the women who harvested crops and prepared the food. The growing of corn from a dead body also reflects an understanding that organic matter, such as a dead body, provides nutrients for soil that aid in plant growth.

Corn in Art, Literature, and Everyday Life

Corn played an important part in the art of many ancient American cultures. The Moches of Peru, for example, immortalized corn by representing it in their works of pottery.

Today, for most people, corn is a common food item that is consumed in some form—corn flakes, corn syrup, corn oil—practically every day. Livestock are fed corn. Corn has also recently become a source of fuel; corn can be used to produce ethanol, which can be used to power automobiles. Even as more people depend upon corn for their daily needs, its status as a mythical food given by the gods has faded.

However, some groups still recognize the mythical importance of corn. American Indians of the Southeast still hold a Green Corn Dance to celebrate the New Year. This important ceremony, thanking the spirits for the harvest, takes place in July or August. None of the new corn can be eaten before the ceremony, which involves rituals of purification and forgiveness and a variety of dances. Finally, the new corn can be offered to a ceremonial fire, and a great feast follows.

Read, Write, Think, Discuss

Find ten multi-ingredient snacks or food items in your kitchen. Read the ingredient list on each package. How many of the items contain at least one corn-based ingredient? Keep an eye out for things like "high fructose corn syrup" and "modified corn starch." Based on your findings, do you think corn is as important to modern society as it was to ancient Americans? Why or why not?

SEE ALSO Aztec Mythology; Mayan Mythology; Native American Mythology

Creation Stories

Theme Overview

People have long wondered how the world came into being. They have answered the question with stories that describe the origin of the universe or the world and usually of human life as well. Creation myths, known as cosmogonies, express people's understanding of the world and their place in it.

Major Myths

Some methods of creation appear again and again in cosmogonies from different parts of the world. One of the most common images is a description of the beginning of the world as a birth, a kind of creation familiar to everyone. The birth may result from the mating of a pair of gods as parents. The Maori of New Zealand, for example, say that the union of **Rangi and Papa** (Father Sky and Mother Earth) produced all things.

The hatching of an egg is another familiar kind of birth. Some creation myths tell of a cosmic egg containing the seeds or possibilities of everything. The hatching of the egg lets the possibilities take form. The Hindu texts known as the Upanishads describe the creation of the world as the breaking of a cosmic egg.

Another type of cosmogony says that the actions, thoughts, or desires of a supreme being or creator god brought the world into existence. The book of Genesis in the Bible tells how God created the world and everything in it. Other accounts of creation by a supreme being can be found in many regions, from the island of Hokkaido in northern Japan to the islands of Tierra del Fuego in southern South America.

Sometimes the created order simply emerges from chaos—a state of disorder. In **Norse mythology**, the scene of creation is an emptiness of wind and mist that forms into clouds and hardens into the frost giant **Ymir** (pronounced EE-mir), from whose body the world is made. Many Native American myths tell how animals and people appeared on earth by climbing out of a chaotic or primitive underground world.

The primal chaos is often a flood or a vast expanse of water. The people of ancient Egypt—who relied on the yearly **floods** of the Nile River to support their agriculture—said that before creation there existed only Nun, a watery abyss (bottomless depth). In some flood myths, creation takes place as the waters recede or as land rises. In others, an earth diver, a bird or an animal, plunges to the bottom of the water and brings up mud that becomes the earth. Such myths, which are common among American Indians, seldom explain where the mud or the earth-

The Omaha Big Bang

Many modern scientists think that the universe began billions of years ago with an explosion of matter and energy called the Big Bang. The Omaha people of the Great Plains have their own "big bang" account of creation. At first all living things were spirits floating through space, looking for a place to exist in bodily form. The sun was too hot. The moon was too cold. The earth was covered with water. Then a huge boulder rose out of the water and exploded with a roar and a burst of flame that dried the water. Land appeared. The spirits of plants settled on earth. Animal spirits followed. Finally the spirits of people took bodily form on earth.

diving creature came from. Many cosmogonies describe the shaping or ordering of the world rather than its creation from nothingness. They often begin with some substance, being, or active force already in existence.

In some mythologies, the creation of people occurs through emergence from the earth. American Indian groups such as the Hopi, Zuni, and Navajo say that the first people traveled though a series of lower worlds to reach their permanent home. In some stories, a flood forces the occupants of the lower worlds to climb upward until they arrive on the surface.

Themes in Creation Myths In explaining how creation led to the world as it now exists, cosmogonies explore several basic themes. Most creation myths illustrate one or more of these themes.

Separation The theme of separation deals with the forming of distinct things out of what was once a formless unity. Separation may be a physical act. In Polynesian myth, for example, the children of Mother Earth and Father Sky force their parents apart so that the world can exist between them. Cosmogonies may describe creation as taking place in stages that mark the process of differentiation. The Old Testament states that God took six days to create light and darkness, the heavens, the earth and plants, the **sun** and moon, the sea creatures and animals, and the first people.

Imperfection A second theme is imperfection. According to many cosmogonies, the creator planned to make a perfect world, but something went wrong. As a result, flaws such as evil, illness, and death entered the creation. The Dogon of West Africa say that the world is imperfect because one of a pair of **twins** broke out early from the cosmic egg. The Hawaiians relate that the earth goddess Papa cursed humans with death after she discovered an incestuous affair between her husband and daughter.

Dualism Dualism, or tension between opposing forces, is an underlying theme of many creation stories, especially those that revolve around conflict. Greek myths about the war between the **Titans** and the gods are just one example of conflict between cosmic parents and their offspring. Sometimes the conflict involves twins or brothers. Some American Indians of the northeast woodlands explain that the world is the way it is because two gods played a role in its creation. **Gluskap**, good and wise, created plants, animals, and people. His evil, selfish brother Malsum made poisonous snakes and plants.

Sacrifice The theme of **sacrifice** reflects the idea that life is born out of death. Someone must die, or at least shed blood, before the world and life can begin. The *Enuma Elish* tells how the god **Marduk** killed the goddess **Tiamat** and cut her body into two parts that became the heavens and the earth. Sometimes the first people are made from a god's blood, perhaps mixed with dust or clay. Creation may also involve the slaying of a primal beast or monster.

Cycles of creation and destruction A few cosmogonies describe cycles in which the world is created and destroyed a number of times. Hindu scriptures say that **Brahma** has remade the world many times. Four ages, or *yugas*, make a *kalpa*, or eon. When a *kalpa* ends, creation dissolves into chaos.

The Aztecs of Mexico believed that the present world was the fifth that the gods had created. It was fated to end in universal destruction by earthquakes. The four previous worlds had been destroyed by a great flood, the falling of the sky, a fire storm, and a wind storm. The Maya believed that the gods made three unsuccessful attempts to create human beings before achieving a satisfactory result. Their first creations—animals, people made of mud, and wooden people—disappointed them in various ways, and they abandoned or destroyed them. Finally, the gods made people of maize (corn) who were perfect—so perfect that their creators clouded their vision to prevent them from seeing too far.

Every region of the world has produced numerous creation stories, and some cultures and religions have more than one. A sampling of myths from various sources shows both the endless variety of cosmogonies and the similarities in their structures and themes.

African Creation Myths Some African creation myths feature a huge snake, often identified with the rainbow, whose coils make up the universe. In West and Central Africa the idea of creation from a cosmic egg is common.

Twins or paired, dualistic powers appear in many African creation stories. The Fon of West Africa tell of the first mother, Nana Buluku, who gave birth to the twins Mawu (moon) and Lisa (sun), the parents of all the other gods, who were also born in sets of twins. Some African cosmogonies, however, are less concerned with the creation of the physical universe and the gods than with the appearance of the first man and first woman and the ordering of human society.

The notion of a supreme creator god appears throughout Africa. The Bushongo people of the Congo region called the creator Bumba. He was the sole inhabitant of a watery universe until he vomited out the sun, which dried the water. Then he vomited out the first animals and people.

Creation Myths of the Americas The Incas of South America claimed that darkness covered the earth until the god Con Tiqui **Viracocha** rose out of a lake, bringing with him the first people. He made more people out of rocks, then sent them out to populate the whole world. When these inhabitants rebelled against Con Tiqui Viracocha, he punished them by stopping the rainfall. A god named Pachachamac overthrew Con Tiqui Viracocha and created a new race of people, the ancestors of humans.

Creation myths of American Indians generally explain how the world took its present form, including the origins of human culture. Some tales feature a creator god or pair of gods, such as the Sun Father and Moonlight-giving Mother of the Zuni people. Many groups, including the Cheyenne, have stories of an earth diver.

Indians of the Southwest may have developed myths of emergence because their agricultural way of life led them to think of growth as a movement upward from below the earth's surface. The Hopi of Arizona say that creation brought four worlds into existence. Life began in the bottom level or cave, which eventually grew dirty and crowded. A pair of twin brothers carried plants from **heaven**, and the people climbed up the cane plant into the second cave. When that place became too crowded, they climbed up again into the third cave. Finally, the brother gods led the people out into this world, the fourth level of creation.

Creation Myths of the Near East The ancient Egyptians believed that before the world existed there was only Nun, the watery nothingness. Then a mound of land rose, giving the first deity (god) a place to live. In some accounts, the first deity took the form of a bird. Others said that a lotus flower containing a god rose from the water. Several Egyptian creator gods were worshipped by different people: **Amun** and Atum, the sun gods; Khnum, who made men and women from clay and breathed life into them; and Ptah, who created the other gods by saying their names.

Among the Semitic creation myths of western Asia is the story of how God formed the world, the Garden of **Eden**, and **Adam and Eve**, the first parents. It is the cosmogony of the Christian, Jewish, and Islamic faiths.

In the dualistic Persian, or Iranian, cosmogony, the good and wise lord **Ahura Mazda** began creation by sending beams of light into an abyss where **Ahriman**, lord of evil and sin, lived. Ahura Mazda cast Ahriman into **hell** for three thousand years. This gave Ahura Mazda time to create spirits of virtue, **angels**, and the creatures of earth, including Gayomart, the first man. When Ahriman's time in hell ended, he created flies, germs, pests, and other evils. One of his wicked followers brought disease and death to Gayomart, but a plant that grew from Gayomart's remains bore fruit that became the human race.

Asian Creation Myths Japanese tradition, preserved in a volume of mythological history called the *Kojiki*, states that before creation there was an oily sea. Gods came into being in the High Plains of Heaven. After seven generations of deities, came the first human ancestors, whose task was to make solid land. They stirred the sea with a jeweled spear. Drops that fell from the spear formed the islands of Japan.

A Chinese creation myth tells how Pan Gu hatched from a cosmic egg. One part of the eggshell formed the heavens; the other part became the earth. For eighteen thousand years, Pan Gu stood between them, keeping them apart by growing ever taller. Finally he became weary, lay down, and died. From his eyes came the sun and moon, from his hair the stars, from his breath the wind, and from his body the earth.

In the Judeo-Christian tradition, God created a different part of the world each day by simply speaking it into existence. This manuscript illumination shows God creating the earth (upper left), the sun and moon (upper right), the animals (lower left), and the birds (lower right). © MUSEE MARMOTTAN, PARIS, FRANCE/GIRAUDON/THE BRIDGEMAN ART LIBRARY.

Indian mythology, linked to both the Hindu and the Buddhist religions, contains many creation stories. Hindus often speak of Brahma as the creator god who brought the universe into being through his thoughts. Sometimes creation involves the sacrifice of a primal being such as Purusha, from whose body all the gods were made. Other myths describe the breaking of a cosmic egg or the union of heaven and earth as cosmic parents.

Creation Myths of Australia and the Pacific In the mythology of Australia's native peoples, or Aborigines, the period of creation was called **Dreamtime**, or the Dreaming. During this time, ancestral beings created the landscape, made the first people, and taught them how to survive. Some Aboriginal myths tell of a great flood that destroyed the previous landscape and the former society. According to many accounts, a great serpent caused the flood when he became angry with the ancestral people.

The vast Pacific Ocean contains the Polynesian, Melanesian, and Micronesian island groups, which produced a variety of cosmogonies. Not surprisingly, many of these myths involve water.

According to some Polynesians, a creator god named Tangaloa sent a bird messenger over an endless primal sea. At last Tangaloa threw a rock into the sea so the tired bird would have a place to land. Then the god created all the islands in the same way. The bird made the first people by giving arms, legs, hearts, and souls to maggots. Other Polynesian stories describe creation as the union of two opposing qualities: Po (darkness) and Ao (light). Polynesian and Micronesian cosmogonies often include the act of separating the earth from the sky. Melanesian creation myths generally involve ancestral **heroes** who wander from place to place, forming the landscape and creating the rules of society.

European Creation Myths Norse creation myths tell how the giant Ymir took shape in the huge icy emptiness called Ginnungagap. Ymir's great cow licked the ice, creating the first gods, including **Odin**. The gods killed Ymir and divided his body into a series of worlds on three levels: Asgard, the realm of gods; Midgard, the realm of people, **giants**, dwarfs, and elves; and Niflheim, the realm of the dead. The gods created the first man and woman from an ash tree and an elm tree.

Greek cosmogonies, echoed by the Romans, begin with birth and end with struggle. **Gaia**, the earth mother, emerged from chaos and gave birth to **Uranus**, the sky. The union of Uranus and Gaia produced plants, animals, and children, the Titans. The Titans overthrew Uranus, only to be overthrown later by their own children, the gods. Another Greek creation myth, possibly borrowed from the ancient Near East, combines many images and themes. It tells how a primal goddess emerged from the waters of chaos. Her union with a serpent produced a cosmic egg that split to become the heaven and the earth.

Creation Stories in Context

Throughout history, humans have pondered the question, "Where did this world I live in come from?" The world's mythologies and religions offer an immense variety of answers to this question. Yet scholars have discovered that the cosmogonies of different cultures fall into broad categories and contain many shared themes, as discussed above. Most creation myths reflect human understanding of how creation of new material takes place on Earth—through birth or through changes in states of matter.

The creation stories of different cultures generally reflect the importance of different elements within each culture. For example, according to **Japanese mythology**, the world began with an ancient ocean; the gods created the islands of Japan to occupy it. This reflects the importance of the ocean in an island culture. By contrast, the American Plains Indians speak of humans arising from clay, indicating the importance of the earth in their culture and daily life. For Aboriginal Australians, the Rainbow Serpent creates the all-important waterholes that dot the Australian landscape and provide the people with their only reliable source of fresh water. In each example, those things that are considered most important to the people of a culture play a key part in the culture's creation myths.

Creation Stories in Art, Literature, and Everyday Life

Because of their very nature, creation myths in various cultures have remained fairly stable over the centuries. Once a creation myth becomes a part of a belief system, it will likely remain a part of that belief system. This means that new creation myths tend to arise only with new belief systems or mythologies. In modern times, such new belief systems are usually considered cults.

Some creation stories, such as those of Africa and Polynesia, existed for years in spoken form, but were not written down until recently. Other cultures preserved their cosmogonies in written texts, and some of these have survived from ancient times. The Babylonian epic *Enuma Elish*, written thousands of years ago, tells how people in Mesopotamia explained the beginning of the world. A Mayan text called the ***Popol Vuh*** describes the creation of the ancestors of the Maya.

Depictions of the ancient creation myths by modern artists can be found in many cultures. However, because some of these myths provide settings or details that are hard to visualize, creation myths do not appear in art as often as other, more visually familiar myths. One example of a modern artist depicting a creation myth is Bill Reid's sculpture *The Raven and the First Men*, which can be found in the University of British Columbia Museum of Anthropology.

The Christian version of the beginning of the world was the inspiration for both Joseph Haydn's symphony *Creation* (1798) and Scottish composer William Wallace's piece *Creation Symphony*.

Read, Write, Think, Discuss

Virginia Hamilton's *In the Beginning: Creation Stories from Around the World* (1988) offers an excellent sampling of creation myths from a variety of cultures. The author includes explanatory notes for each myth to help provide context for the reader, and each myth features at least one watercolor illustration by artist Barry Moser. Hamilton has won numerous awards for her books, including the Newbery Medal and the National Book Award.

SEE ALSO African Mythology; Australian Mythology; Aztec Mythology; Buddhism and Mythology; Celtic Mythology; Chinese Mythology; Dreamtime; Egyptian Mythology; *Enuma Elish*; Finnish Mythology; Floods; Gluskap; Greek Mythology; Hinduism and Mythology; Inca Mythology; Japanese Mythology; Mayan Mythology; Melanesian Mythology; Micronesian Mythology; Native American Mythology; Norse Mythology; Persian Mythology; Polynesian Mythology; Roman Mythology; Semitic Mythology

Cronos

See **Cronus.**

Cronus

Character Overview

Cronus was the youngest of the **Titans**, the Greek deities (gods) who ruled the world before the arrival of **Zeus** and the other Olympian gods

Nationality/Culture
Greek

Pronunciation
KROH-nuhs

Alternate Names
Saturn (Roman), Kronos

Appears In
Hesiod's *Theogony*, Ovid's *Metamorphoses*, Hyginus's *Fabulae*

Lineage
Son of Uranus and Gaia

and goddesses. Cronus seized power from his father, the sky god **Uranus** (pronounced YOOR-uh-nuhs), and was later overthrown by his own children. The Romans adopted Cronus as a member of their pantheon—or group of recognized gods—renaming him Saturn and worshipping him as a god of agriculture.

Major Myths

According to legend, Uranus had imprisoned several of his children in the body of his wife, the earth goddess **Gaia**. To punish him, Gaia asked her son Cronus to cut off Uranus's sex organs during the night. After carrying out his mother's wishes, Cronus replaced his father as ruler. He imprisoned races of **giants** and **Cyclopes** (pronounced sigh-KLOH-peez), who he considered dangerous. He married his sister, Rhea, another Titan, and they began to have children. Learning that one of his offspring was fated to overcome him just as he had overcome his father, Cronus swallowed each baby as it was born. Rhea, however, managed to save their youngest child, Zeus (pronounced ZOOS), by feeding Cronus a stone wrapped in infant clothing. She then arranged for the baby to be raised in secret in a cave on the highest mountain of the island of Crete.

When Zeus was grown, he forced Cronus to vomit up the swallowed children: the deities Hestia (pronounced HESS-tee-uh), **Demeter** (pronounced di-MEE-ter), **Hera** (pronounced HAIR-uh), **Hades** (pronounced HAY-deez), and **Poseidon** (pronounced poh-SYE-dun). Zeus also freed the giants and the Cyclopes who had been imprisoned by his father. Together they went to war against Cronus and the Titans and, after a violent struggle, emerged victorious. Zeus then banished the Titans to Tartarus (pronounced TAR-tur-uhs), a place deep in the **underworld**. In another version of the myth, Cronus's rise to power ushered in a peaceful golden age, which ended when the Titans were defeated. Following the battle, Cronus was sent to rule a distant paradise known as the Islands of the Blessed.

Cronus in Context

Even though Cronus was the father of Zeus and other Olympian gods, he did not play a major role in ancient Greek worship or daily life; he did receive worship in parts of Greece, particularly as part of a harvest festival called the "Kronia." During the festival, masters and slaves ate together,

Rhea prevented her husband Cronus from eating their son Zeus by giving him a stone to eat instead. ERICH LESSING/ ART RESOURCE, NY.

thereby "overthrowing" social rules that separated the classes, and allowing social equality—just for a day. The Romans, who worshipped Cronus as "Saturn," held a similar festival called the "Saturnalia" in which slaves had temporary freedom to do as they please. The festival coincided with the Christian Christmas season, and involved the exchange of presents, a practice adopted by the Christians when Christianity became the official religion of the Roman Empire. Although the Romans were much more active in their worship of Cronus than the Greeks were, the Romans recognized Saturn as a Greek import; when the Roman priests presented sacrifices to him, they left their heads uncovered, as was customary in Greek worship and contrary to Roman practice.

Key Themes and Symbols

The Greeks viewed Cronus as a symbol of great power and fate. Although he overthrows his father and becomes the leader of the gods, he later falls victim to his son. Although he tries to control his fate by swallowing his children, his plan fails and his destiny—a predetermined path in life—remains the same.

As a god of harvests, Cronus is sometimes shown holding a pruning hook. The similarity between the name "Cronus" and the Greek word for time *chronos* inspired his transformation into the Western figure of "Father Time," the elderly man with a scythe who is ushered out at the end of each year by a child who represents the New Year.

Cronus in Art, Literature, and Everyday Life

Saturn was the source of the modern word "Saturday," and his name was given to the sixth planet from the Sun in our solar system. Perhaps because of the Romans' admiration of Cronus as Saturn, the god is better known and more commonly depicted as Saturn from the Renaissance through the modern age. One of the most famous images of Saturn is Francisco Goya's grisly painting *Saturn Devouring One of His Children*, completed around 1823 as a mural on a wall in his home and never meant for public display. Another famous image of Cronus/Saturn eating one of his children was created by Peter paul Rubens in 1636. Cronus is also the evil force at work pitting the gods against each other in the award-winning young readers book *The Lightning Thief* (2005) by Rick Riordan.

Read, Write, Think, Discuss

The Cronus Chronicles, written by Anne Ursu and illustrated by Eric Fortune, is a series about two modern-day kids who become caught up in a supernatural world of Greek myths. In the first volume of the series, *The Shadow Thieves* (2007), the kids—Charlotte Mielswetzki and her cousin Zee—must stop Philonecron, the grandson of Poseidon, from stealing the shadows of children in order to build an army and take over the underworld.

SEE ALSO Cyclopes; Gaia; Giants; Greek Mythology; Oedipus; Uranus; Zeus

Cuchulain

Nationality/Culture
Irish/Celtic

Pronunciation
koo-KUL-in

Alternate Names
Sétanta

Appears In
The Ulster Cycle

Lineage
Son of Lug and Dechtire

Character Overview

Cuchulain, one of the greatest **heroes** of Irish mythology and legend, was a warrior in the service of Conchobhar (pronounced KON-kvar), king of Ulster. Best known for his single-handed defense of Ulster, Cuchulain is said to have lived in the first century BCE, and tales about him and other heroes began to be written down in the 700s CE. Cuchulain's adventures were recorded in a series of tales known as the Ulster Cycle.

Like many Irish heroes, Cuchulain had a short, adventurous, and tragic life. He was the son of Dechtire (pronounced DEK-tir-uh), sister of King Conchobhar. She and some of her handmaidens were kidnapped on her wedding night by **Lug**, the **sun** god, who appeared to her as a fly. Dechtire swallowed the fly and later gave birth to a son whose original name was Sétanta.

From the beginning, the child possessed extraordinary powers. He could swim like a fish at birth. He had seven fingers on each hand, seven toes on each foot, and seven pupils in each eye. At the age of seven, he fought off 150 boy warriors to gain entrance to his uncle's court. When he was twelve, Sétanta accidentally killed the watchdog of the smith Cullan and offered to guard Cullan's property until another dog could be trained. It was at that time that he changed his name to Cuchulain, which means "hound of Cullan." He grew up to be a handsome, well-spoken man who was very popular with women.

Training with Scatha Cuchulain fell in love with a woman named Emer and asked her to marry him. Emer's father insisted that Cuchulain must first prove his valor by undergoing a series of trials and sent him to the war goddess Scatha to be trained in warfare. On his journey to Scatha, Cuchulain had to pass through the plain of Ill Luck, where sharp grasses cut travelers' feet, and through the Perilous Glen, where dangerous animals roamed. Then Cuchulain had to cross the Bridge of the Cliff, which raised itself vertically when someone tried to cross it. Cuchulain jumped to the center and slid to the opposite side.

To repay Scatha for his training, Cuchulain fought her enemy Aife (pronounced EE-va), the strongest woman in the world. After defeating Aife, he made peace with her, and she bore him a son, Connla. While

The Irish hero Cuchulain asked to be tied to a pole so he could continue to fight even while dying. © MARY EVANS PICTURE LIBRARY/THE IMAGE WORKS.

returning home to claim his bride, Cuchulain rescued a princess and visited the **underworld**, or land of the dead.

The Cattle Raid of Cooley Back home, Cuchulain achieved his greatest victory. When Queen Medb (pronounced MAVE) of Connacht (pronounced KON-et) sent a great army to steal the Brown Bull of Cooley, in Ulster, Cuchulain stopped them single-handedly. He alone, of all the Ulster warriors, was unaffected by a curse that had weakened the strength of the fighting force. Unfortunately, during one of the battles, he was forced to fight and kill his good friend Ferdiad. On numerous other occasions, Cuchulain defended Ulster against the rest of Ireland and won numerous contests of bravery and trustworthiness.

But misfortune followed him. Cuchulain killed his own son, Connla, learning his identity too late. In addition, Cuchulain died as a result of trickery. After offending Morrigan, the goddess of death and battles, he was summoned to fight at a time when he was ill. On the way to battle, he saw a vision of a woman washing the body and weapons of a dead warrior, and he recognized the warrior as himself. Knowing then that his own death was unavoidable, he fought bravely. When he was too weak to stand, Cuchulain tied himself to a pillar so that he could die fighting on his feet. He was twenty-seven years old.

Cuchulain the Warrior Cuchulain had several magical weapons: his sword, his visor, and his barbed spear, Gae Bulga, which inflicted wounds from which nobody ever recovered. When Cuchulain went into battle, he would go into a frenzy known as a "warp spasm." His cry alone would kill a hundred warriors, frightening them to death. His physical appearance—namely, that of a handsome man—changed completely. Cuchulain's hair stood on end, one of his eyes bulged out while the other disappeared in his head, his legs and feet turned to face backward, his muscles swelled, and a column of blood spurted up from his head. His body became so hot that it could melt snow.

When swept away in a war frenzy, Cuchulain could not distinguish between friends and enemies. On one occasion, he was so full of the lust for battle that he needed to be stopped. A group of Ulster women marched out naked carrying vats of cold water to bring him to his senses. When Cuchulain stopped his chariot in embarrassment, he was grabbed by warriors who threw him into three vats of cold water to calm him down. The first vat burst apart, the second boiled over, but the third merely got hot.

Cuchulain in Context

Cuchulain is often seen as a cultural hero, but exactly whose culture he represents has been a subject for debate. He has been adopted by Irish

National Heroes

Certain traits are common to almost all national heroes.

Figure	Nationality	Major Deeds	Description
Aeneas	Roman	Defended Troy, founded Rome	Brave, devoted to duty, ruled capably for a long time
King Arthur	British	Established law and order in Britain, founded Camelot	Brave, just, ruled capably for a long time
Beowulf	Norse	Killed the monster Grendel, Grendel's mother, and a dragon; ruled Geatland	Brave, selfless, ruled capably for a long time
Cuchulain	Irish	Defended the city of Ulster	Brave, handsome, smooth-talking, popular with women, extremely strong, dead at a young age (27)
Robin Hood	British	Robbed the rich to give to the poor	Brave, selfless, concerned about common people

ILLUSTRATION BY ANAXOS, INC./CENGAGE LEARNING, GALE.

nationalists as an important symbol supporting Ireland's independence from England. Cuchulain has also been used as a symbol by those supporting Ireland's union with England, since many of these supporters are based in the region of Ulster—home to the Cuchulain legend.

The Celts, like the Norse, valued their warriors and respected those with great skill in battle. Cuchulain, like the Norse hero **Beowulf**, is nearly unbeatable. The Celts also valued beautiful speech and charm, and Irish culture in modern times is still associated with lyricism, poetry, song, and a special persuasiveness. Cuchulain was a fearsome warrior, but also a charming, handsome, smooth-talking man: the cultural ideal.

Key Themes and Symbols

Much like **Achilles** from ancient Greek myth, Cuchulain symbolizes both legendary strength and rage that can, at times, hardly be controlled. He is a symbol of the perfect warrior and ideal protector of his people, defending Ulster even when he could no longer stand on his own.

One of the main themes of the legend of Cuchulain is that great fame and glory are often paid for with an early death. This theme is also seen in the tale of Achilles, though Cuchulain's destiny is unknown to him.

Cuchulain in Art, Literature, and Everyday Life

Cuchulain is one of the most popular figures in Irish legend, and has remained an important part of Irish literature. Modern Irish author William Butler Yeats wrote several works about Cuchulain and his adventures, including plays and poetry. A famous bronze statue of Cuchulain created by Oliver Sheppard can be found in the Dublin Post Office. In addition, the highest honor awarded to adult Scouts in the Irish equivalent of the Boy Scouts is named after Cuchulain.

Read, Write, Think, Discuss

Cuchulain has been used as a symbol for several different groups of people, some with opposing viewpoints (such as the Irish nationalists and the Unionists). Do you think mythological figures such as Cuchulain "belong" to a specific culture, or do you think they should be free to be adopted by anyone who wishes? Should a terrorist organization be free to use a culture hero like Cuchulain as a symbol for their cause? Why or why not?

SEE ALSO Celtic Mythology; Lug

Cupid

See **Eros.**

Cybele

Character Overview

Cybele was the fertility goddess of Phrygia, an ancient country of Asia Minor. In Greek and **Roman mythology**, Cybele personified Mother Earth and was worshipped as the Great Mother of the Gods. The Greeks associated her with some of their existing goddesses, such as Rhea and **Demeter** (pronounced di-MEE-ter), and sometimes referred to her as Meter. She was also associated with forests, mountains, and nature. Although usually shown wearing a crown in the form of a city wall or carrying a drum, the goddess may also appear on a throne or in a chariot, accompanied by lions and sometimes bees.

Major Myths

According to myth, Cybele discovered that her youthful lover—and in some versions, her son—Attis was unfaithful. In a jealous rage, she made him go mad and mutilate himself under a pine tree, where he bled to death. Regretting what she had done, Cybele mourned her loss. **Zeus** (pronounced ZOOS) promised her that the pine tree would remain sacred forever.

In his *Aeneid*, Virgil relates a uniquely Roman myth about Cybele. Before the Trojan War, Cybele allowed her trees to be used by the Trojans to make warships. The goddess then asked Jupiter to make the ships so they could not be destroyed; Jupiter agreed to turn the ships into sea **nymphs** (female nature deities) after they had served their purpose, so that they would never be destroyed. After **Aeneas** (pronounced i-NEE-uhs) led his soldiers to Italy using the ships, his foes attempted to burn the ships. Since the ships had already served their purpose—to transport Aeneas and his army to Italy—the ships disappeared and became sea nymphs.

Cybele in Context

From Asia Minor, Cybele's popularity spread to Greece, where she was associated with Demeter, the Greek goddess of fruitfulness. She was regarded as the mother of all the gods. Around 200 BCE, the worship of

Nationality/Culture
Phrygian/Greek/Roman

Pronunciation
SIB-uh-lee

Alternate Names
Meter

Appears In
Virgil's *Aeneid*, Pausanias's *Description of Greece*

Lineage
Mother of the gods

A fountain showing the goddess Cybele in her chariot. © PLAZA DE CIBELES, MADRID, SPAIN/KEN WELSH/THE BRIDGEMAN ART LIBRARY.

Cybele reached Rome, and she became well known throughout the Roman world.

During the Roman empire, followers of Cybele held an annual spring festival dedicated to the goddess. The ceremonies involved cutting down a pine tree that represented the dead Attis. After wrapping the tree in bandages, the followers took it to Cybele's shrine. There they honored the tree and decorated it with violets, which they considered to have sprung from Attis's blood. As part of this religious ceremony, priests cut their arms so that their blood fell on Cybele's altar and the sacred pine tree. They also danced to the music of cymbals, drums, and flutes. During these wild ceremonies, some followers even mutilated themselves by castration, as Attis had. The idea of death and rebirth, prominent in her relationship with Attis, also reflects the changing of the seasons.

Key Themes and Symbols

Cybele is widely regarded as a symbol of fertility and motherhood. Like many fertility gods and goddesses, she is also associated with agriculture and forests. She is sometimes depicted with tame lions, which may symbolize great power that can be easily controlled.

Cybele in Art, Literature, and Everyday Life

Though the Greeks imported Cybele from Phrygian mythology, she was a popular subject in both Greek and Roman art. Rome in particular was home to several temples honoring Cybele, including a shrine at the Circus Maximus. However, one of the most famous sculptures of Cybele can be found as part of a fountain built in Madrid, Spain, in the late eighteenth century. The fountain is located at a town square known as Plaza de Cibeles.

As with many ancient mythological figures, Cybele has appeared with somewhat altered characteristics as a character in the Marvel Comics universe. In the comic world, Cybele is one of the Eternals, a race of superhumans conceived by Jack Kirby that first appeared in print in 1976.

Read, Write, Think, Discuss

Some ancient Roman followers of Cybele became so overwhelmed while celebrating that they would mutilate themselves in her honor. Some religious traditions, even in modern times, call for ritual mutilation or alteration of some part of the subject's body. Using your library, the Internet, or other resources, can you find similar modern examples of mutilation as part of a religious tradition? How does such an act compare to non-religious but culturally accepted acts of body alteration, such as ear piercing?

SEE ALSO Demeter; Zeus

Cyclopes

Character Overview

In **Greek mythology**, the Cyclopes were a group of **giants** who possessed only one eye set in the middle of their forehead. They were

Nationality/Culture
Greek/Roman

Pronunciation
sigh-KLOH-peez

Alternate Names
Kyklopes

Appears In
Hesiod's *Theogony*, Homer's *Odyssey*

Lineage
Sons of Uranus and Gaia

said to be skilled workers, and the Greeks credited them with building the walls of several ancient cities. The Romans believed that the Cyclopes worked at Mount Etna with **Hephaestus** (pronounced hi-FES-tuhs), the god of **fire** and metalworking.

The Greek poet Hesiod wrote about three of the Cyclopes: Brontes (pronounced BRON-teez; thunder), Steropes (pronounced stuh-ROH-peez; lightning), and Arges (pronounced AR-jeez; brightness). The sons of **Uranus** (sky) and **Gaia** (earth), these Cyclopes were banished by their father to Tartarus after they were born. They eventually gave **Zeus** the gifts of thunder and lightning with which he defeated the **Titans** and became ruler of the universe. Later authors related that Zeus killed **Apollo**'s son Asclepius, causing Apollo to kill the Cyclopes in revenge.

In the *Odyssey*, Homer described how **Odysseus** (pronounced oh-DIS-ee-uhs) was captured by the cruel and barbaric Cyclops named Polyphemus (pronounced pol-uh-FEE-muhs), the son of **Poseidon**. Polyphemus ate six of Odysseus's crew members. However, Odysseus and the rest of his crew managed to escape by blinding the single eye of Polyphemus with a long, sharpened pole.

Cyclopes in Context

The notion of Cyclopes may have originated from the practice of ancient metalworkers wearing an eye patch for protection from sparks while working. This explains the Cyclopes' close association with metalworking and the god Hephaestus.

Another theory, first suggested by paleontologist Othenio Abel in the early twentieth century, is that dwarf elephant skulls found in the region may have led to myths of Cyclopes. The skulls of these elephants—which lived in the area until about eight thousand years ago—feature a deep nasal cavity directly in the center of the skull. This cavity could easily have been mistaken for a giant eye socket, especially by people who had never seen living elephants.

Key Themes and Symbols

The Cyclopes are usually associated with fire and lightning. They are also associated with metalworking and are commonly thought to work alongside Hephaestus. Later Cyclopes such as Polyphemus, unlike the original Cyclopes, symbolized savagery and lawlessness.

The giant cyclops Polyphemus. GUILIO ROMANO/THE BRIDGEMAN ART LIBRARY/ GETTY IMAGES.

The story of Odysseus and Polyphemus is usually used to highlight the craftiness of Odysseus, a quality the Greeks valued. Odysseus proves that cunning can be more valuable than physical force. The lesson was not lost on ancient Greek military commanders. When an overwhelming

Persian invasion force threatened Greece, the Greek commander Themistocles (pronounced thuh-MISS-tuh-kleez) was able to decisively rout the Persian navy at the key battle of Salamis in 480 BCE largely through sheer nerve and clever trickery. Odysseus would have been proud.

Cyclopes in Art, Literature, and Everyday Life

The Cyclops is an enduring image in art and literature. Cyclopes have appeared in films such as *Krull* (1983) and *The 7th Voyage of Sinbad* (1958). On the animated television show *Futurama*, one of the main characters—Leela—has only one eye in the center of her head, though she is unrelated to the Cyclopes of Greek myth. Also unrelated to Greek myth is the Marvel superhero Cyclops, a member of the X-Men who can shoot powerful optic blasts from his shielded eyes. The character Polyphemus appears in Rick Riordan's novel *Sea of Monsters* (2006), in which he must once again tangle with a clever hero, this time the young demigod Percy Jackson.

The Cyclops has also lent its name to a genus of small freshwater crustaceans. Like their mythical namesakes, each of the crustaceans has a single large eye.

Read, Write, Think, Discuss

Many myths around the world feature monsters that are similar to humans, but possess a characteristic or deformity that separates them from normal people. In modern times, many medical disorders have been discovered that cause similar physical traits; for example, cyclopia is a rare condition that results in the eye sockets of an embryo failing to separate into two cavities.

Do you think rare medical conditions in ancient times could have been the source for some monster myths? Explain your reasoning.

SEE ALSO Hephaestus; Odysseus

D

Character

Deity

Myth

Theme

Culture

Nationality/Culture
Greek/Roman

Pronunciation
DED-uh-lus

Alternate Names
Daidalos

Appears In
Ovid's *Metamorphoses*,
Virgil's *Aeneid*

Lineage
Father of Icarus

Daedalus

Character Overview

The name Daedalus means "ingenious" or "clever." Daedalus lived in Athens, where he was known for his skills as an inventor, artist, and sculptor. Indeed, it was said that the statues Daedalus made were so realistic that they had to be chained to keep them from running away.

Daedalus's nephew Talus (also called Perdix) came to serve as an apprentice to his uncle. The boy soon showed remarkable talent, inventing the saw by copying either the jawbone of a snake or the spine of a fish. Before long, Daedalus grew jealous of Talus, believing that the boy might become as great a craftsman as he was. This idea was more than Daedalus could bear. He killed Talus by pushing him off a cliff into the sea. In some versions, **Athena** (pronounced uh-THEE-nuh)—or her Roman equivalent Minerva (pronounced mi-NUR-vuh)—saved Talus by transforming him into a partridge. Because of his crime, Daedalus was forced to leave Athens. He went to Crete, an island in the Mediterranean Sea, and began working for King Minos, the Cretan ruler.

Minos had asked the sea god **Poseidon** (pronounced poh-SYE-dun) for a sacrificial bull, and a beautiful white bull had emerged from the sea. The bull was so magnificent that Minos decided to keep it rather than **sacrifice** it to Poseidon. The angry sea god punished the king by causing his wife, Pasiphaë (pronounced pa-SIF-ah-ee), to fall helplessly in love with the bull. At the request of the queen, Daedalus built a lifelike model of a cow in which she could conceal herself and spend time with her beloved bull. As a result of these visits, Pasiphaë gave birth to the **Minotaur**, a monstrous creature with the body of a man and the head of a bull.

The Labyrinth King Minos wanted to hide the Minotaur. He ordered Daedalus to construct a prison from which the monster could never escape. Daedalus designed the Labyrinth, a mazelike network of winding passages that had only one entrance. Its layout was so complex that no one who entered it could ever find a way out. King Minos kept the Minotaur imprisoned in the Labyrinth.

The Minotaur was given humans to eat. Some were provided by the city of Athens. After suffering defeat in battle with Crete, Athens had to send King Minos a yearly tribute of seven boys and seven girls. These unfortunate Athenians were sent into the Labyrinth one by one as food for the Minotaur.

One year the Greek hero **Theseus** (pronounced THEE-see-uhs) came to Crete as one of the youths. He was determined to put an end to the human sacrifice. **Ariadne** (pronounced ar-ee-AD-nee), the king's daughter, fell in love with Theseus and asked Daedalus to help her find a way of saving him. When Theseus went into the Labyrinth to slay the Minotaur, Ariadne gave him a ball of string that she had obtained from Daedalus. Theseus tied the string to the entrance of the Labyrinth and unwound it as he made his way toward the Minotaur. He killed the beast and then used the string to find his way out of the Labyrinth.

When King Minos discovered what had happened, he was furious. To punish Daedalus for his role in the escape, the king imprisoned him and his young son Icarus in the Labyrinth.

The Winged Escape Daedalus put his talents to work. Day after day, he collected the feathers of birds. He also gathered wax from a beehive. When he had enough feathers and wax, Daedalus set to work making two pairs of enormous wings, one pair for himself and the other for Icarus.

Daedalus carefully instructed his son on how to use the wings to fly. He warned Icarus not to fly too high or too low. If he flew too high, the **sun**'s heat could melt the wax that held the wings together. If he flew too low, he risked being swept up by the sea.

Daedalus watches helplessly as his son Icarus falls from the sky. Icarus had flown too close to the sun, which caused his wings to melt. SCALA/ART RESOURCE, NY.

With that, father and son took off from Crete. The wings worked well, and Daedalus and Icarus began to fly across the sea. However, Icarus did not pay attention to his father's warning. He flew higher and higher until the sun's heat melted the wax in his wings. Icarus fell into the ocean and drowned. Daedalus managed to fly safely to Sicily.

Daedalus in Context

Archaeologists uncovered an area of ruins on the island of Crete in the late nineteenth century. The ruins came to be known as Knossos, and are believed by some to be the remains of the palace of King Minos. The main building was less a palace than an enormous administrative center with approximately thirteen hundred rooms. It has been suggested that the intricate and confusing layout of the building may have led to the myth of the Labyrinth.

Daedalus embodies the cleverness and ingenuity valued by the ancient Greeks. Many ancient Greeks such as Pliny the Elder credited him with inventing carpentry and basic carpenter's tools. The ancient Greeks revered their thinkers and inventors. The famous inventor and mathematician Archimedes (pronounced ar-ki-MEE-deez), for example, designed a variety of ingenious inventions to defend Syracuse against the invading Romans in 213 BCE—including a reported "death ray" that used a system of mirrors to set **fire** to Roman ships in the harbor. Apparently, the Romans valued Greek genius, too. The Romans finally won Syracuse after a two-year siege, and Archimedes was killed. The Roman commander Marcellus was greatly distressed and ordered that Archimedes be buried with honors.

Key Themes and Symbols

The fate of Icarus has endured as an example of human folly or bravado. Icarus would not accept reasonable limits. He went too far, flying beyond the bounds that had been set. As a result, he met with disaster.

Daedalus in Art, Literature, and Everyday Life

The story of Daedalus and Icarus has inspired many writers and artists. The Roman poet Ovid told the myth in his work *Metamorphoses*, and Irish novelist James Joyce named his literary hero Stephen Dedalus (he appears both in the 1916 novel *Portrait of the Artist as a Young Man* and in the 1922 novel *Ulysses*). The Flemish artist Pieter Brueghel the Elder painted a landscape showing Icarus's fall.

In modern times, the myth of Daedalus is better known to most people as the story of Icarus, the son who flew too close to the sun.

Read, Write, Think, Discuss

In the myth of Daedalus, the clever craftsman warns his son Icarus not to fly too high or too low as they escape Crete on his homemade wings. Icarus fails to listen, which leads to his demise.

It might sometimes be difficult to follow parents' advice, but sometimes—as in the case of Icarus—it proves to be very important. Write an essay recounting an instance where you followed your parents' advice and it paid off—or you did not follow your parents' advice and later regretted it.

SEE ALSO Ariadne; Minotaur; Theseus

Dagda

Character Overview

In **Celtic mythology**, Dagda (often referred to as "the" Dagda) was an Irish god who was head of a group of Irish gods called the Tuatha Dé Danaan (pronounced TOO-uh-huh day DAH-nuhn). He was considered the father of the gods and the lord of fertility, plenty, and knowledge. The word Dagda means "the good god."

Major Myths

According to legend, Dagda had several possessions associated with power and position. One was a huge cauldron, or pot, that was never empty and from which no one went away hungry. The ladle was so big that two people could lie in it. Dagda also owned an orchard of fruit trees where the fruit was always ripe, and two pigs, one of which was always cooked and ready to eat. In addition, he had a club with two ends—one for killing living people and the other for bringing the dead back to life. Dagda used his magic harp to order the seasons to change. In spite of his great power, Dagda was pictured as a fat man, plainly dressed and pulling his club on wheels. His favorite food was porridge. As the god of knowledge, he was the protector of the druids, the priests of the Celtic religious order.

When the Tuatha Dé Danaan were forced to go underground, Dagda divided the land among the gods. His son Aonghus (pronounced AHN-gus), the god of love, was absent during the division, and Dagda did not give his son a section because he wanted to keep Aonghus's palace for himself. When Aonghus returned, he tricked his father to get

Nationality/Culture
Irish/Celtic

Pronunciation
DAHG-duh

Alternate Names
Eochaid Ollathair

Appears In
The *Yellow Book of Lecan*, *The Book of Invasions*

Lineage
Son of Elatha or Ethlinn

his palace back, leaving Dagda without land or power. Dagda was later fatally wounded in battle by a woman named Cethlenn.

Dagda in Context

The Tuatha Dé Danaan were a group of gods founded by the goddess Danu who once ruled Ireland. They fought off many other invaders and older Irish gods to retain control, sometimes granting certain regions to other races as a way of settling a battle. The Tuatha Dé Danaan were eventually driven underground by a race known as the Milesians. However, the gods of the Tuatha Dé Danaan continued to appear in Celtic myths centuries later and appear to have taken on immortal status.

Key Themes and Symbols

In Celtic mythology, Dagda fulfills the role of provider. He can feed an army with his magic cauldron, his fruit trees, and his pigs. He also ensures that the seasons follow as they should by playing his harp. Harps figure prominently in Celtic and Irish mythology as powerful instruments, indicating the importance of music in Celtic culture.

Dagda in Art, Literature, and Everyday Life

The Dagda is one of the gods pictured on the Gundestrup Cauldron, perhaps the most famous Celtic artifact. The large silver bowl is decorated with panels dedicated to different Celtic gods. The Dagda may also be the subject known as the Cerne Abbas (pronounced KERN AB-bus) giant, an enormous image of a nude man with a club that was dug into a hillside near Dorset, England, centuries ago.

Read, Write, Think, Discuss

The Dagda is a god who can provide food in abundance from his magic cauldron. For people in many parts of the world, however, hunger is an all-too-real daily struggle. Would you expect to find myths similar to the Dagda and his cauldron in places experiencing widespread famine? Why or why not?

SEE ALSO Celtic Mythology

Damocles, Sword of

Myth Overview

Damocles was a member of the court of Dionysius (pronounced dye-uh-NIGH-see-us) the Younger, ruler of the Sicilian city of Syracuse during the 300s BCE.

According to a legend passed on by the Roman writer Cicero, Damocles told Dionysius how much he envied his kingly wealth, power, and happiness. In response, Dionysius invited Damocles to come to a magnificent banquet.

Damocles was seated before a marvelous feast, enjoying the benefits of a ruler, when he happened to glance up in horror. Above his head hung a sharp sword, suspended by nothing more than a single thread. Damocles was no longer able to enjoy the food, wine, or entertainment before him. In this way, Dionysius showed Damocles that a ruler's life may appear grand, but it is filled with uncertainty and danger.

The Sword of Damocles in Context

Although Damocles appears to be a work of legend, Dionysius the Younger was an actual ruler in fourth-century Sicily. He originally ruled under the guidance of his uncle Dion and his uncle's teacher, the philosopher Plato, but Dionysius grew tired of what he viewed as their attempts to control him. He drove his uncle out of Syracuse, but after years of his unpopular rule, his uncle amassed an army and returned to take over the city. Dionysius fled, and years after his uncle died, returned to reclaim leadership of Syracuse. Still unpopular, he was driven out once again, and lived the last years of his life in Corinth, Greece.

The real-life events of Dionysius the Younger help to illustrate the message of the legend of Damocles: though he ruled Syracuse twice, it is not likely he enjoyed much peace or satisfaction as its leader. Few kings in ancient cultures did. Positions of power were often gained, maintained, or lost by force.

Key Themes and Symbols

One of the key themes of the tale of Damocles is that one should not be envious of another person's position. Although they may appear to have

Nationality/Culture
Greek/Roman

Pronunciation
DAM-uh-kleez

Alternate Names
None

Appears In
Cicero's *Tusculan Disputations*

a perfect life, they may also bear burdens that cannot be seen. The "sword of Damocles" symbolizes a threat that can come to pass at any moment; for Dionysius, the sword represented the threat of murder or betrayal by his own followers.

The Sword of Damocles in Art, Literature, and Everyday Life

The legend of Damocles has endured as a popular tale for centuries. The climax of the tale is famously depicted in Richard Westall's 1812 painting *Sword of Damocles*. In modern usage, the phrase "sword of Damocles" is commonly used to refer to a potentially tragic threat or situation that seems inches away.

Read, Write, Think, Discuss

Because of their unprecedented destructive power, nuclear weapons have been described as a sword of Damocles hanging over modern civilization. Others have argued that nuclear weapons are necessary to keep some nations from attacking peaceful countries without provocation. Do you think nuclear weapons are a necessary enforcement tool or a potentially tragic threat? Can they be both? Explain your opinion.

Nationality/Culture
Greek

Pronunciation
DAN-uh-ee

Alternate Names
None

Appears In
Ovid's *Metamorphoses*, Hyginus's *Fabulae*

Lineage
Daughter of Acrisius and Eurydice

Danaë

Character Overview

In **Greek mythology**, Danaë was the daughter of Acrisius (pronounced uh-KREE-see-us), the king of Argos. An oracle, or person through which the gods communicated with humans, told Acrisius that Danaë's son would someday kill him. To prevent the prediction from coming true, Acrisius had his daughter imprisoned in a bronze tower so she could not marry. There the god **Zeus**, smitten by her beauty, went to her in a shower of gold, and she became pregnant with a son, the hero **Perseus** (pronounced PUR-see-uhs). When Acrisius learned of the baby's birth, he ordered Danaë and her son locked inside a chest and set adrift at sea.

The chest reached the island of Seriphos, where it was discovered by a fisherman named Dictys (pronounced DIK-tis), whose brother Polydectes (pronounced pol-ee-DEK-teez) was king. Dictys helped Danaë raise her son on the island. When Perseus was grown, Polydectes fell in love with Danaë, but she did not love him in return. Believing that he could pressure Danaë into marrying him if her son were absent, Polydectes sent Perseus on a quest for the head of the gorgon **Medusa**, whose gaze could turn men into stone. Some sources say that Danaë went into hiding during Perseus's absence, while others state that Polydectes locked her away. In any event, Danaë resisted Polydectes' advances.

When Perseus returned, he saved Danaë by turning Polydectes to stone with the head of Medusa. Dictys became king, and Danaë and Perseus returned to Argos. According to some writers, she went on to found the city of Ardea in Italy. The original prophecy was fulfilled when Perseus accidentally killed Acrisius with a stray discus—a heavy disc thrown for sport—during some athletic games.

Danaë in Context

According to myth, Danaë becomes pregnant after Zeus visits her in the form of a shower of gold. However, she is just one of many women in Greek mythology reported to have had an unusual encounter with Zeus. The god transformed himself into a swan to seduce Leda (LEE-duh), the Queen of Sparta. He appeared to Antiope (an-TYE-uh-pee) in the form of a satyr, half human and half goat, in order to seduce her. Alcmena (alk-MEE-nuh), a lady of Thebes, was deceived by Zeus when he took the form of her husband and seduced her. The nymph Callisto was loved by Zeus after he appeared to her in the form of her master, the goddess **Artemis**. These many stories of Zeus's exploits with women indicate that virility, or male fertility, was respected by the ancient Greeks. Fathering many children would be considered a sign of manliness. Danaë's story points to the Greek belief in the power of fate. Despite the pains he takes to protect himself, Acrisius cannot thwart destiny.

Key Themes and Symbols

Danaë is portrayed as a victim of fate. She is imprisoned by her father because he fears death at the hands of her future child. She becomes pregnant after a mysterious visit by Zeus over which she has no control. She is protected by her son from a dangerous king against whom she

Red figure bell crater showing Danaë's encounter with Zeus as a shower of gold. RÉUNION DES MUSÉES NATIONAUX/ART RESOURCE, NY.

cannot defend herself. In this way, Danaë symbolizes innocence and helplessness.

Danaë in Art, Literature, and Everyday Life

Though Danaë is not as well known as other characters of Greek mythology, several artists, including Titian, Rembrandt, and Gustav Klimt, have captured the story of Danaë in their paintings: Titian's *Danaë* (1554), Rembrandt's *Danaë* (1636), and Klimt's *Danaë* (1907). She is nearly always pictured at the moment Zeus visits her in the form of a shower of gold.

Read, Write, Think, Discuss

In the myth of Danaë, she becomes impregnated by Zeus in the form of a shower of gold—a mysterious and unavoidable form of sexual reproduction.

How do you think myths such as that of Danaë reflect ancient understanding about human reproduction? Compare the myth of Danaë to modern belief in the story of the Virgin Mary. How are the stories similar?

For centuries, the biological processes involved in reproduction were not considered appropriate subjects for people to study. By contrast, modern supporters of sex education aim to inform students about sex so that it is not viewed as mysterious or beyond their understanding. Do you think that offering facts about the reproductive process is an effective way of dealing with issues like teen pregnancy and the prevention of sexually transmitted diseases? Or do you think examining such topics in detail might encourage sexual behavior?

SEE ALSO Greek Mythology; Medusa; Perseus

Delphi

Myth Overview

Delphi, a town on the slopes of Mount Parnassus in Greece, was the site of the main temple of **Apollo** (pronounced uh-POL-oh) and of the Delphic oracle, the most famous oracle (someone who makes predictions about the future) of ancient times. Before making important decisions, Greeks and other peoples traveled to this sacred place to consult the oracle and learn the gods' wishes.

According to **Greek mythology**, **Zeus** (pronounced ZOOS) wanted to locate the exact center of the world. To do this, he released two eagles from opposite ends of the earth. The eagles met at Delphi. Zeus marked the spot with a large, egg-shaped stone called the omphalos (pronounced AHM-fuh-lus), meaning "navel."

Originally, Delphi was the site of an oracle of the earth goddess **Gaia** (pronounced GAY-uh). The site was guarded by a monstrous serpent (or dragon, in some accounts) called Pytho (pronounced PYE-thoh). Apollo killed Pytho and forced Gaia to leave Delphi. Thereafter, the temple at Delphi belonged to Apollo's oracle.

No one knows for certain how the process of consulting the Delphic oracle worked. However, over the years, a traditional account has been

Nationality/Culture
Greek

Pronunciation
DEL-fye

Alternate Names
None

Appears In
The Homeric Hymns, Pausanias's *Description of Greece*

widely accepted. According to this description, a visitor who wanted to submit a question to the oracle would first make an appropriate offering and **sacrifice** a goat. Then a priestess known as the Pythia (pronounced PI-thee-uh) would take the visitor's question into the inner part of Apollo's temple, which contained the omphalos and a golden statue of Apollo. Seated on a three-legged stool, the priestess would fall into a trance.

After some time, the priestess would start to writhe around and foam at the mouth. In a frenzy, she would begin to voice strange words and sounds. Priests and interpreters would listen carefully and record her words in verse or in prose. The message was then passed on to the visitor who had posed the question. Some modern scholars believe that the priestess did not become delirious but rather sat quietly as she delivered her divine message.

Many rulers consulted the oracle at Delphi about political matters, such as whether to wage a war or establish a colony. However, the oracle's answers were often vague or ambiguous, leaving interpretation to the listener. Sometimes such uncertainty had ironic results. For example, King Croesus (pronounced KREE-sus) of Lydia asked the oracle if he should attack Cyrus the Great of Persia. The oracle responded that such an attack would destroy a great empire. Croesus attacked, expecting victory. However, his own forces were overwhelmed, and it was the Lydian empire of Croesus that was destroyed.

Anyone could approach the oracle, whether king, public official, or private citizen. At first, a person could consult the oracle only once a year, but this restriction was later changed to once a month.

Delphi in Context

The ancient Greeks believed in fate and destiny—the idea that one's path in life was already determined by the gods and could not be changed. They had complete faith in the oracle's words, even though the meaning of the message was often unclear. As the oracle's fame spread, people came from all over the Mediterranean region seeking advice. Numerous well-known figures of history and mythology visited Delphi, including the philosopher Socrates and the doomed King **Oedipus**.

Visitors would ask not only about private matters but also about affairs of state. As a result, the oracle at Delphi had great influence on

The Oracle of Delphi. STOCK MONTAGE/HULTON AR-CHIVE/GETTY IMAGES.

political, economic, and religious events. Moreover, Delphi itself became rich from the gifts sent by many believers.

The worship of Apollo at Delphi probably dates back to the 700s BCE, although the fame of the oracle did not reach its peak until the 500s BCE. In about 590 BCE, war broke out between Delphi and the nearby town of Crisa because Crisa had been demanding that visitors to the

Delphic oracle pay taxes. The war destroyed Crisa and opened free access to Delphi. To celebrate the victory, Delphi introduced the Pythian Games, an athletic festival that took place every four years.

In early Roman times, Delphi was often plundered. For example, the Roman dictator Sulla took many of Delphi's treasures, and the emperor Nero is said to have carried off some 500 bronze statues. With Rome's conquest of Greece and the spread of Christianity, Delphi's importance declined. The oracle was finally silenced in 390 CE to discourage the spread of non-Christian beliefs.

The modern village of Kastri stood on the site of ancient Delphi until 1890. Then the Greek government moved the village to a nearby location, making the site of the ancient town available for excavation. Archaeologists have been working on the site since that time and have made many important discoveries relating to the temple of Apollo.

Key Themes and Symbols

For the people of ancient Greece, the oracle at Delphi came to symbolize wisdom and the voice of the gods. People journeyed from throughout the Greek empire to seek the wisdom of the oracle. Its importance as a central location was also symbolized by the omphalos located there, which was said to mark the center of the world.

Delphi in Art, Literature, and Everyday Life

The oracle at Delphi appeared in numerous ancient works, including a description of the battle of Thermopylae between the Spartans and the invading Persians in 480 BCE by Herodotus.

Read, Write, Think, Discuss

To most people in the modern world, the idea of consulting an oracle for guidance may seem foolish. However, people routinely read horoscopes and consult fortune-tellers and psychics, even if only for entertainment. Do you think there is any value in astrological or psychic predictions? Are there tools or pathways people can use to get a glimpse of the future?

SEE ALSO Apollo; Gaia; Serpents and Snakes

Demeter

Character Overview

Demeter, the Greek goddess of vegetation and fruitfulness, was known to the Romans as Ceres (pronounced SEER-eez). She was the daughter of **Cronus** (pronounced KROH-nuhs) and Rhea (pronounced REE-uh), and the sister of **Zeus** (pronounced ZOOS). Although Demeter was not one of the twelve gods of Olympus, her origins can be traced back to very ancient times, perhaps to the Egyptian goddess **Isis**. Her name means "mother goddess" or "barley mother." Demeter had a daughter by Zeus called **Persephone** (pronounced per-SEF-uh-nee). The figures of Demeter and Persephone are closely related, and certain aspects of Persephone—for example, as a goddess of the **underworld**—are also associated with Demeter in different versions of the same myth.

Major Myths

In one tale, **Hades** (pronounced HAY-deez), the ruler of the underworld, fell in love with Persephone and kidnapped her to make her his queen. Demeter spent nine days and nights searching for her daughter, bearing a torch. When she failed to find Persephone, she took on the form of an old woman and sat down by a well in the town of Eleusis (pronounced i-LOO-sis). The king's daughters soon came along to draw water from the well and saw the old woman, who appeared to be crying. Taking pity on her, they asked her to return home with them to rest under their roof and take refreshment. At the palace, the queen and her servants showed so much hospitality that Demeter agreed to stay and care for the king's son Demophon (pronounced DEM-uh-fon).

Demeter secretly planned to reward the king and queen by making their son immortal, or able to live forever. During the day, she fed the boy with ambrosia, the food of the gods. At night, she laid him in the ashes of the **fire** to burn off his mortality. However, one night one of the queen's maids saw Demeter lay the boy in the fire and told the queen. The queen surprised Demeter and cried out for her to stop. Demeter then revealed her true identity and proclaimed that the child would not be immortal but would grow up to do great things. According to legend, Triptolemus (pronounced trip-tuh-LEE-mus), probably another name

Nationality/Culture
Greek

Pronunciation
di-MEE-ter

Alternate Names
Ceres (Roman)

Appears In
Hesiod's *Theogony*, Ovid's *Metamorphoses*

Lineage
Daughter of Cronus and Rhea

Statue of the Greek goddess Demeter. SCALA/ART RE-SOURCE, NY.

for Demophon, later traveled around the earth introducing agriculture to all the peoples of the world. Demeter commanded the king to build a temple to her and taught him secret rituals that the people should perform in her honor.

Still grieving for Persephone, Demeter neglected the earth. As a result, all the crops withered and died, and famine spread over the world.

Zeus was alarmed because he feared that all the humans would die, leaving no one to perform sacrifices to the gods. But Demeter would not restore life to the earth unless Persephone was returned to her. Zeus persuaded Hades to release Persephone, but during her stay in the underworld, she had eaten some pomegranate seeds. Because of this, Persephone was forever tied to Hades and required to spend part of the year with him in the underworld and only part on earth with her mother. This story was used to explain the cycle of the seasons. When Demeter was without her daughter, the earth was barren. When Persephone rejoined her mother, plants could grow.

Demeter in Context

Agriculture was without a doubt the foundation of the ancient Greek economy. Three out of every four ancient Greeks were involved in growing, preparing, or distributing food as their occupation. For this reason, Demeter—who had full control over the seasons and the crops— was an extremely important goddess to worship. The main crops grown were cereals such as barley and wheat. Olive trees, which provided rich and flavorful olive oil, were also important to Greek agriculture.

The rites held in Demeter's honor became the Eleusinian Mysteries, some of the most important ceremonies in ancient Greece. Scholars still do not know everything that took place during the secret rites. However, it is thought that the mysteries involved fasting, a procession from Athens to Eleusis, sacred dances, and a reenactment of the story of Persephone. Those who participated were promised a special future in the underworld after death.

Key Themes and Symbols

In Greek and Roman myths, Demeter represents fertility, agriculture, and motherhood. She also represents the seasons of the year. Symbols associated with Demeter include wheat stalks, barley, poppies, and the horn of plenty. She may be depicted holding a torch (as when searching for Persephone) or carrying grain, and is sometimes shown riding a chariot pulled by winged serpents.

Demeter in Art, Literature, and Everyday Life

Demeter appears in many ancient works, especially hymns. However, she was not embraced by medieval or Renaissance artists the way many

Death, Rebirth, and Fertility

Many world myths describe nature's cycles in terms of the death of a god or goddess and that figure's subsequent rebirth or return to earth. Often, the deity's death is associated with winter on Earth, and his/her return is associated with spring or summer.

Figure	Nationality	Myth Summary
Adonis and Aphrodite	Greek	The handsome Adonis captures the heart of both Aphrodite, goddess of love, and Persephone, queen of the underworld. Zeus orders him to divide his time between them. Half the time he spends with Aphrodite—spring and summer—and half with Persephone—fall and winter.
Ishtar and Tammuz	Near Eastern	Mother goddess Ishtar, trapped in the underworld, must offer her beloved young husband Tammuz in her place so she can return to the living. Ishtar is able to rescue her husband for part of each year—spring and summer.
Demeter and Persephone	Greek	Hades, god of the underworld, falls in love with Persephone, the daughter of Demeter, goddess of fertility and fruitfulness. He kidnaps her, and Demeter is so upset she neglects the crops and plants. Zeus persuades Hades to let Persephone spend part of each year with her mother. The time with her mother becomes spring and summer, and the time with Hades becomes winter and fall.

ILLUSTRATION BY ANAXOS, INC./CENGAGE LEARNING, GALE.

other Greek and Roman gods and goddesses were. Demeter's Roman name, Ceres, lives on in the word "cereal," used to refer to all types of grain. The Spanish word for beer, *cerveza*, also comes from the name of the Roman goddess, because beer is made from grain. Ceres is also the name given to a dwarf planet that lies in the asteroid belt between Mars and Jupiter in our solar system.

Read, Write, Think, Discuss

The Gods in Winter by Patricia Miles is a modernized retelling of the myth of Persephone, Demeter, and Hades. In the novel, the Bramble family moves to the English countryside and hires an unusual housekeeper named Mrs. Korngold. When strange events begin happening—and it seems like winter will never end—the Bramble children decide to investigate. Originally published in 1978, the book was reprinted in 2005 with an afterword by Tamora Pierce.

SEE ALSO Cybele; Hades; Isis; Persephone; Underworld

Devi

Character Overview

Devi is the major goddess in the Hindu pantheon, or collection of gods. Known both as Devi (which in Sanskrit means "goddess") and Mahadevi ("great goddess"), she takes many different forms and is worshipped both as a kind goddess and as a fierce one. In all of her forms, she is the wife of the **Shiva** (pronounced SHEE-vuh), the god of destruction.

Major Myths

In the form of Durga, Devi is a warrior goddess charged with protecting the gods and the world from powerful demons. The gods used their combined strength to create Durga when they were unable to overpower a terrible buffalo demon named Mahisha (pronounced muh-HEE-shuh). They gave Durga ten arms—so she could hold many weapons—and a tiger to carry her into battle. Durga and Mahisha fought a long, terrible, and bloody battle in which the two opponents changed shape many times. Durga finally managed to kill the demon by piercing his heart with a trident and cutting off his head.

Nationality/Culture
Hindu

Pronunciation
DEY-vee

Alternate Names
Mahadevi, Kali, Durga, Parvati

Appears In
The Vedas

Lineage
Wife of Shiva

Devi also takes gentler forms. As Sati (pronounced suh-TEE), a loyal wife to Shiva, she burned herself alive to defend his honor and prove her love. When Shiva refused to let go of Sati's burning body, the god **Vishnu** (pronounced VISH-noo) had to cut her body out of his arms. Her remains were then cut into fifty pieces and scattered to different places that became shrines. As Parvati (pronounced PAR-vuh-tee), Devi is a gentle and loving wife who went through great **sacrifice** to win Shiva's love. Parvati has a softening influence on the harsh god and is often portrayed as an idealized beauty or pictured with Shiva in domestic scenes.

Another, and quite different, form of Devi is the fierce Kali (pronounced KAH-lee). Like Durga, Kali defends the world from demons, but she can go into a rage and lose control. When she blindly begins to kill innocent people, the gods have to intervene. On one occasion, Shiva threw himself among the bodies she was trampling to bring her out of her madness. Images of Kali show her with black skin, three eyes, fangs, and four arms. She wears a necklace of skulls and carries weapons and a severed head. She is usually portrayed with her tongue hanging out in recognition of her victory over the demon Raktavira (pronounced rahk-tah-VEER-uh). To make sure that Raktavira was truly dead, Kali had to suck the blood out of his body because any drop that fell to the ground would produce a duplicate of him.

There are numerous other forms of Devi. As Uma (pronounced OO-ma), she appears as the golden goddess, personifying light and beauty. As Hariti (pronounced huh-REE-tee), she is the goddess of childbirth. As Gauri (pronounced GAH-ree), she represents the harvest or fertility, and as Manasa (pronounced mah-NAH-sah), she is the goddess of snakes. When she takes the role of mother of the world, Devi is known as Jaganmata (pronounced jahg-ahn-MAH-tah).

Devi in Context

It is not uncommon in Hinduism for one god or goddess to have many different forms. For example, the god Shiva is known as Rudra (pronounced ROOD-ruh) in his fierce and wild form, and Bhairava (bah-ee-RAH-vah) in one of his more destructive forms. Sankara (pronounced SAHN-kah-rah) and Sambhu (pronounced sahm-BOO) are two of the god's more helpful or beneficent representations.

In the case of Devi, the one single goddess can serve a great number of functions to those who worship her, depending upon the form of Devi

Worshippers immerse a statue of the goddess Devi, in the form of Durga, in a river on the final day of a festival in her honor to secure her blessings. MANPREET ROMANA/AFP/GETTY IMAGES.

they praise. This makes her one of the most important figures in the Hindu religion.

Devi and her many forms probably date back to the mother goddess worshipped in India in prehistoric times. Ancient civilizations around the world, including India, worshipped mother goddesses because in human fertility they saw a parallel to the fertility of the earth around them—the growth of plants and abundance of wild and domesticated animals they relied on for survival. While these mother goddesses eventually became secondary to male gods in much of the world, Devi has retained a place of great stature in India.

Key Themes and Symbols

Because Devi can be found in so many different forms, she may symbolize many different things. For example, Sati and Parvati symbolize love and loyalty. The goddess Saraswati (pronounced sah-rah-SWAH-tee) symbolizes knowledge, art, and science. Durga and Kali both can represent strength and vengeance. In addition, Kali often symbolizes uncontrollable violence and rage. Most often, however, Devi symbolizes motherhood, fertility, and beauty.

The image of the goddess as Kali is perhaps the depiction best known to those outside the Hindu culture, and her fierce wild image can be bewildering to Western eyes, to whom she resembles a black, fanged, bloodthirsty beast. But in the Hindu faith, she represents the unformed, terrifying, true chaotic beginning of all things—the origin, the mother, but also death and destruction. Her blackness symbolizes the void, the beginning of everything, including space and time. Her nakedness represents her freedom from illusions. Her breasts represent her motherhood of all.

Devi in Art, Literature, and Everyday Life

Devi appears throughout ancient Hindu literature in her many forms. Some of these forms were once considered separate goddesses, such as Kali. Each of these different forms is depicted differently in Hindu art. For example, Kali is often depicted as having four arms, blue skin, and wearing a necklace of human heads. Saraswati is shown with yellow skin and wearing white.

Kali is also often pictured standing or trampling on Shiva, her husband, which also presents some confusion. Scholars debate the symbolic meaning of these images. Is she trampling her own husband because she wants to destroy the world? Is she just asserting her dominance? There is no single, accepted interpretation.

Read, Write, Think, Discuss

In Hindu mythology, the goddess Devi has many different forms, only some of which are mentioned here. Using your library, the Internet, or other resources, find at least two other forms of the goddess Devi that have not already been mentioned. Write a description of each form, and explain why you think that form is important to Hindu mythology.

SEE ALSO Hinduism and Mythology; Shiva; Vishnu

The God Marduk Sets Out to Attack the Evil Goddess Tiamat

In the Babylonian creation myth *Enuma Elish*, the god Marduk killed the evil goddess Tiamat and divided her corpse into two parts, which became heaven and earth. *See Enuma Elish*.

© Charles Walker/Topfoto/The Image Works.

The Norse Goddess Freyja Wearing the Necklace of the Brisings

The Norse goddess of love Freyja acquired her favorite possession, the Necklace of the Brisings, by agreeing to spend the night with each of the necklace's creators. *See* Freyja.

© Mary Evans Picture Library/The Image Works.

The Sword of Damocles

Damocles learned how uncertain things are for rulers, despite the apparent ease of their lives, when he attended a magnificent banquet held by the ruler of Syracuse and saw a sword suspended by a thread above his head. The sword represented how quickly life can change for the worse for those in power. *See* Damocles, Sword of.

Réunion des Musées Nationaux/Art Resource, NY.

वाल्मीकी लं॰६४

श्रीलम्भागली आं॰ अनिकायंनेयुद्ध

The Demon King Ravana Battles with the Army of Rama

Hindu mythology describes a group of demons known as *Rakshasas* who served the demon king Ravana. *See* Devils and Demons.

© Private Collection/The Bridgeman Art Library.

Aztec Creation Myth

Aztec mythology tells of four creator gods, each associated with a direction and a color: Tezcatlipoca, the north and black; Quetzalcoatl, the west and white; Huitzilopochtli, the south and blue; and Xipe Totec, the east and red. This drawing shows Hueheuteotl, the god of fire, surrounded by the four directions. *See* Creation Stories.

Werner Forman/Art Resource, NY.

The Garden of Eden

According to the book of
Genesis in the Bible, the
Garden of Eden was an
earthly paradise created by
God as a home for the first
people, Adam and Eve.
They lived there until their
disobedience introduced sin
and death into the world.
See Eden, Garden of.

Bildarchiv Preussischer Kulturbesitz/Art
Resource, NY.

Circe Preparing a Potion

The sorceress Circe used her spells to
turn men into animals, according to
Greek mythology. *See* Circe.

The Bridgeman Art Library/Getty Images.

People Left Behind by Noah's Ark
According to the book of Genesis in
the Bible, God caused a flood to cover
the earth because the people were so
sinful. God chose to save Noah and
his family, along with pairs of all the
animals, in an ark because Noah was
righteous. *See* Floods.

© Private Collection/Index/The Bridgeman Art Library.

Statue of a Dragon on a Malaysian Temple

In some Asian cultures, dragons are seen as a positive symbol of power and happiness. *See* Dragons.

John W. Banagan/Iconica/Getty Images.

Devils and Demons

Theme Overview

In myths, legends, and various religions, devils and demons are evil or harmful supernatural beings. Devils are generally regarded as the adversaries (enemies) of the gods, while the image of demons ranges from mischief makers to powerful destructive forces. In many religions, devils and demons stand on the opposite side of the cosmic balance from gods and **angels**. Although devils and demons have been pictured in many different ways, they are usually associated with darkness, danger, violence, and death.

Some people, including many Christian writers, have used the terms *devil* and *demon* almost interchangeably. Although devils and demons sometimes seem to be closely related or even identical, they also appear in myth and religion as two quite different creatures.

In most mythologies and religions, a devil is a leader or ruler among evil spirits, a being who acts in direct opposition to the gods. The general view is that devils are trying to destroy humans, to tempt them into sinning, or to turn them against their gods. Monotheistic religions, which recognize only a single supreme God, also often speak of one devil.

Devils and gods may be opposites, but they are also usually linked in some way. Many religious and mythological explanations say that devils are related to the gods or that they are gods of evil.

A demon (sometimes spelled *daemon*) is generally thought to be a harmful or evil spirit or supernatural being, sometimes a god or the offspring of a god. Demons may be the messengers, attendants, or servants of the Devil. They are often monstrous in appearance, combining the features of different animals or of animals and humans.

Demons were not always regarded as evil. The ancient Greeks spoke of a person's *daimon* as his or her personal spirit, guardian angel, or soul. In many cultures, demons were merely inhuman supernatural powers that could be evil or good at various times, depending on whether their actions harmed or helped people. Human witches, wizards, and sorcerers were thought to gain some of their abilities by summoning and controlling demons through magical practices.

Major Myths

Devilish and demonic forces have taken many shapes and forms around the world. Frightening and dramatic stories and images of them have always had considerable appeal.

Egyptian Mythology The devil could be seen in the evil god **Set** in ancient **Egyptian mythology**. Once a helpful god who ruled the kingdom of the blessed dead, Set's place in the Egyptian pantheon—or collection of recognized gods—changed after he murdered his brother. Followers of the supreme god **Horus** conquered Set's followers, and the priests of Horus made Set the enemy of the other gods and the source of evil.

The Egyptians believed in the existence of demons. One such demon was Nehebkau (pronounced neh-HEB-kah), who appeared at times as a powerful earth spirit, a source of strength for the other gods. At other times, though, he was a menacing monster, a serpent with human arms and legs who threatened the souls of the dead. Like many demons, Nehebkau had more than one role.

Persian Mythology In the mythology of Persia, now known as Iran, two opposing powers struggled for control of the universe. **Ahura Mazda** (pronounced ah-HOO-ruh MAHZ-duh) was the god of goodness and order, while his twin brother, **Ahriman** (pronounced AH-ri-muhn), was the god of evil and chaos (disorder). The Zoroastrian religion that developed in Persia pictured the world in terms of tension between opposites: God (Ahura Mazda) and the Devil (Ahriman), light and darkness, health and illness, life and death. Ahriman ruled demons called *daevas* that represented death, violence, and other negative forces.

Judaism and Christianity Hebrew or Jewish tradition, later adopted by Christians, calls the Devil **Satan**, which means "adversary." Satan took on qualities of Ahriman, becoming the prince of evil, lies, and darkness. Jewish tradition also includes a female demon known as **Lilith**. Said to be the first wife of Adam, Lilith was cast out when she refused to obey her husband and was replaced by Eve.

In Christian belief, the Devil came to be seen as a fallen angel who chose to become evil rather than worship God. Satan rules the demons in **hell**, the place of punishment and despair. In the Middle Ages, some Christians believed that a separate devil—or a separate aspect of the

Devil—existed for each of the seven deadly sins. In their view, Lucifer (pronounced LOOS-i-fur) represented pride, Mammon (pronounced MAM-uhn) greed, Asmodeus (pronounced az-MOH-dee-us) lust, Satan anger, Beelzebub (pronounced bee-ELL-zuh-bub) gluttony, **Leviathan** (pronounced luh-VYE-uh-thuhn) envy, and Belphegor (pronounced BEL-feh-gore) sloth.

The common image of the Devil in Western culture is drawn from many sources. The Devil's pointed ears, wings, and sharp protruding teeth resemble those of Charu (pronounced CHAH-roo), the **underworld** demon of the Etruscans of ancient Italy. The Devil's tail, horns, and hooves are like those of **satyrs** (half-man, half-goat creatures) and other animal gods of ancient Greece, and **Cernunnos**, the ancient Celtic lord of the hunt. The trident he is often shown brandishing is similar to those carried by the Greek gods **Poseidon** (pronounced poh-SYE-dun), god of the sea, and **Hades** (pronounced HAY-deez), lord of the underworld. The Hindu god **Shiva** (pronounced SHEE-vuh), who represents the powers of destruction, also carries a trident. The Devil sometimes appears in other forms, such as a winged snake or dragon.

Islam In the Muslim religion of Islam, which shares many elements of Jewish and Christian tradition, the Devil is called Iblis (pronounced IB-liss) or Shaitan (pronounced SHAY-tan). Like Satan, he is a fallen angel. He commands an army of ugly demons called shaitans, who tempt humans to sin. The shaitans belong to a class of supernatural beings called djinni (pronounced JEE-nee) or jinni (genies). Some djinni are helpful or neutral toward the human world, but those who do not believe in God are evil.

Hinduism and Buddhism In the earliest form of Hinduism in India, the gods were sometimes called Asuras (pronounced ah-SOO-rahs). But as the religion developed the Asuras came to be seen as demons who battled the gods. Another group of demons, the Rakshasas (pronounced RAHK-shah-sahs), served the demon king Ravana. Some were beautiful, but others were monstrous or hideously deformed. One demon, Hayagriva (pronounced hah-yah-GREE-vah) (meaning "horse-necked"), was a huge and powerful enemy of the gods whose troublemaking constantly threatened to overturn the cosmic order.

The Buddhist religion incorporated many elements of Hinduism, including the demon Hayagriva. It turned the Hindu demon Namuchi

A Deal with the Devil

Christians of the Middle Ages and afterward believed that humans occasionally made bargains with the Devil, selling their souls to him in exchange for riches, power, or other benefits they would enjoy before they died. Witches were said to have made such bargains, an act that condemned them to death in the eyes of the church. An obscure German schoolmaster-turned-magician named Faust, who lived in the 1500s, gave rise to one of the most famous stories about a deal with the Devil. The legend of Dr. Faustus has been the subject of many plays, books, and operas. Two of the most famous were the 1564 play *Doctor Faustus* by British playwright Christopher Marlowe, and the 1808 play *Faust*, by German Johann von Goethe. The story was adapted as a successful Broadway musical, *Damn Yankees*, in 1955, in which a middle-aged man sells his soul to the devil to become a successful baseball player.

(pronounced nah-MOO-chee) into Mara, the Evil One who tempts people with desires and deceives them with illusions. Mara tried to tempt the Buddha. He failed—but he still tries to keep others from reaching enlightenment.

Chinese and Japanese Mythology Although traditional Chinese and Japanese religions did not recognize a single powerful devil, they had demons. In Chinese legends, the souls of the dead become either *shen*, good spirits who join the gods, or *gui*, malevolent ghosts or demons who wander the earth, usually because their descendants do not offer them the proper funeral ceremonies.

Japanese mythology includes stories about demons called Oni, generally portrayed with square, horned heads, sharp teeth and claws, and sometimes three eyes. Oni may have the size and strength of **giants**. Although these demons are cruel and mischievous, some tales tell of Oni who change their ways and become Buddhist monks.

African Mythology The Bushpeople of southern Africa say that Gauna, the ruler of the underworld, is the enemy of Cagn, the god who created the world. Gauna visits the earth to cause trouble in human society and

Robert Johnson at the Crossroads

Legendary blues guitarist and song writer Robert Johnson (1911–1938) wrote several songs that mention the devil. The circumstances of his life and death are a bit hazy, and over time the myth developed (probably based on jealous gossip by his musical rivals) that Johnson got his talent from the devil, whom he met at a crossroads in Mississippi. A crossroads has particular unholy significance in several cultures. In parts of Europe, the bodies of those who could not be buried in consecrated (holy) ground (suicides and executed criminals, for example) were often buried at a crossroads. In the folklore of the southeast United States, the devil could be met at a crossroads at midnight. The crossroads symbolizes a choice between two very different paths.

to seize people to take to the realm of the dead. He also sends the souls of the dead to haunt their living family members.

Devils and Demons in Context

The spread of religions has had an interesting effect on demons in world mythology. When one religion replaces another, the gods of the former religion may become demons in the new faith. For example, as Islam spread through West Africa, Central Asia, and Indonesia, some local deities (gods) did not disappear but were transformed into demons within a universe governed by the god of Islam. Similarly, as Christianity spread through Europe and the eastern Mediterranean area, local gods and goddesses were adapted. The ancient Celtic god of the hunt, Cernunnos (pronounced ker-NOO-nohs), for example, who had the body of a man and a great stag's head, may even have been the basis of the traditional Christian image of a devil as a man with horns.

Devils and Demons in Art, Literature, and Everyday Life

Devils and demons were frequently depicted as grotesque figures in ancient and medieval art. More recently, some of the most recognizable traits of devils and demons—such as red skin, pointed tails, and horns—have been incorporated into pop-art imagery. Devils and other demonic imagery are commonly associated with certain types of music, such as heavy metal. Devils and demons are also common in horror films and comic books, such as the Vertigo Comics series *Hellblazer.* The Dark Horse Comics character Hellboy spawned a movie, *Hellboy,* in 2004. The devil appears frequently in films as a character; both Peter Cook and Tim Curry have played the devil in movies—Cook in the 1967 comedy *Bedazzled,* and Curry in the movie *Legend* (1985).

In the realm of technology, the *daimons* of ancient Greece have given rise to *daemons* of computer programming. Like the helpful household spirits of ancient Greece, daemons are processes that run in the background of a computer operating system and perform mundane tasks for the user, such as responding to network requests. The idea of daemons as souls, not evil creatures, plays a prominent part in Phillip Pullman's *His Dark Materials* trilogy (published between 1995 and 2000), in which some characters have animal-formed daemons that live with them and cannot be separated from them without dire consequences.

The Demonata #1: Lord Loss by Darren Shan (2006) is the first book in the *Demonata* series of horror novels for young adults. It is about a boy whose family is killed by a demon and who narrowly escapes death himself. After he goes to live with his uncle Dervish, he discovers dark secrets about his family and the supernatural world that exists around him.

Read, Write, Think, Discuss

The United States was first referred to as "the Great Satan" in 1979 by the Ayatollah Ruhollah Khomeini, the leader of the Islamic government of Iran. Since then, the term has been used by many groups and leaders throughout the Middle East to describe the United States. Why do you think so many people believe the United States deserves this label?

SEE ALSO African Mythology; Ahriman; Angels; Buddhism and Mythology; Chinese Mythology; Genies; Hell; Hinduism and Mythology; Japanese Mythology; Lilith; Persian Mythology; Satan; Set; Witches and Wizards

Diana

See **Artemis.**

Dido

Character Overview

In **Greek mythology**, Dido was the founder and queen of Carthage, a city on the northern coast of Africa. She was the daughter of Belus (or Mutto), a king of Tyre in Phoenicia (pronounced fuh-NEE-shuh), and the sister of Pygmalion (pronounced pig-MAY-lee-uhn). Dido is best known for her love affair with the Trojan hero **Aeneas** (pronounced i-NEE-uhs).

King Belus had wanted his son and daughter to share royal power equally after his death, but Pygmalion seized the throne and murdered Dido's husband. Dido and her followers fled from Tyre, landing on the shores of North Africa. There a local ruler named Iarbas (pronounced ee-AR-bus) agreed to sell Dido as much land as the hide of a bull could cover. Dido cut a bull's hide into thin strips and used it to outline a large area of land. On that site, Dido built Carthage and became its queen.

Carthage became a prosperous city. Iarbas pursued Dido, hoping to marry her, but Dido refused. After her husband's death, she had sworn never to marry again. Iarbas continued his advances, and even threatened Carthage with war unless Dido agreed to be his wife. Seeing no other alternative, Dido killed herself by throwing herself into the flames of a funeral pyre, a large pile of burning wood used in some cultures to cremate a dead body. In another version of the story, she mounted the pyre and stabbed herself, surrounded by her people.

The Roman poet Virgil used part of the story of Dido in his epic poem the **_Aeneid_**. In Virgil's account, the Trojan leader Aeneas was shipwrecked on the shore near Carthage at the time when Dido was building the new city. After welcoming Aeneas and his men, the queen fell deeply in love with him. In time, the two lived together as wife and husband, and Aeneas began to act as though he were king of Carthage. Then the god Jupiter (the Roman version of the Greek god Zeus) sent a messenger to tell Aeneas that he could not remain in Carthage. Rather, his destiny—or future path in life as determined by the gods—was to found a new city for the Trojans in Italy that would eventually become Rome.

Nationality/Culture
Greek/Roman

Pronunciation
DYE-doh

Alternate Names
Elissa

Appears In
Virgil's _Aeneid_, Ovid's _Heroides_

Lineage
Daughter of King Belus of Tyre

Aeneas tells Dido of his misfortunes at Troy. RÉUNION DES MUSÉES NATIONAUX/ART RESOURCE, NY.

Dido was devastated when she heard that Aeneas planned to leave. She had believed that the two of them would eventually marry. Aeneas insisted that he had no choice but to obey the gods, and shortly afterward, he and his men set sail for Italy. When Dido saw the ships sail out to sea, she ordered a funeral pyre to be built. She climbed onto it, cursed Aeneas, and using a sword he had given her, stabbed herself to death.

Dido in Context

For Romans, the story of Dido and Aeneas is a convenient way of explaining the rift between the people of Carthage and the people of Rome. Before Dido killed herself, she cursed not only Aeneas but all Trojans and their descendants (the Romans). This hatred between the two regions was seen as the cause of the Punic Wars, fought between the Romans and the Carthaginians. Unlike the Trojan War, the mythical battle mentioned in Homer's **Iliad** and Virgil's *Aeneid*, the Punic Wars were historical events well documented by people living at the time.

The Punic Wars took place during the second and third centuries BCE. As the Roman Empire expanded throughout the region of the Mediterranean Sea, small but prosperous kingdoms such as Carthage were subject to attack by Roman forces. The Carthaginians held off many Roman assaults; during the Second Punic War, the master military commander Hannibal even marched his forces—including a group of elephants—across the Alps into Italy, earning several victories against the Romans. In the end, however, a Roman attack on Carthage resulted in the city's complete surrender and subsequent destruction in 146 BCE.

Key Themes and Symbols

Although the story of Dido and Aeneas may seem to represent tragic love, Romans viewed Dido as a symbol of the bad feelings between Carthage and Rome. She was not seen as a sympathetic character, but as a vengeful enemy or a woman scorned. In the myth, Aeneas—who is viewed as the hero and founder of the Roman Empire—chooses his destiny to found Rome over his love for Dido. The themes of abandonment and the importance of duty over love are central to the myth.

Dido in Art, Literature, and Everyday Life

Famed English playwright Christopher Marlowe wrote a play about the legend titled *Dido, Queen of Carthage*, which was first published in 1594. In 1689, the English composer Henry Purcell wrote an opera, *Dido and Aeneas*, that was based on the story and characters from the myth. Dido also appears as a character in Dante's *Inferno*, as one of the damned souls in the second circle of **hell**.

The popular singer/songwriter Dido Armstrong, better known simply as Dido, was named after the mythical queen of Carthage.

Read, Write, Think, Discuss

Dido commits suicide after Aeneas leaves her behind to continue on his journey to found Rome. In modern societies, suicide is seen as a serious problem, especially among teenagers. In the United States, suicide is the third most common cause of death for people between the ages of fifteen and twenty-four. Why do you think teen suicide occurs at such an alarming rate? Do failed relationships, such as the one between Dido and Aeneas, often play a role in teen suicide? Using your library, the Internet, or other available resources, find a list of risk factors for teen suicide and compare these to the reasons you listed.

SEE ALSO Aeneas; *Aeneid, The*; *Iliad, The*; Pygmalion and Galatea

Dionysus

Nationality/Culture
Greek

Pronunciation
dye-uh-NYE-suhs

Alternate Names
Bacchus (Roman)

Appears In
Homer's *Iliad*, Ovid's *Metamorphoses*, Euripides' *Bacchae*

Lineage
Son of Zeus and Semele

Character Overview

Dionysus, the Greek god of fertility, wine, and ecstasy, was popular throughout much of the ancient world. In Rome he was known as Bacchus (pronounced BAHK-us). A complex deity, Dionysus played two very different roles in **Greek mythology**. As the god of fertility, he was closely linked with crops, the harvest, and the changing of the seasons. As the god of wine and ecstasy, he was associated with drunkenness, madness, and wild sexuality. His nature included a productive, life-giving side and an animal-like, destructive side.

Major Myths

The most common myth about the origins of Dionysus says that he was the son of **Zeus** (pronounced ZOOS) and of Semele (pronounced SEM-uh-lee), daughter of the founder of Thebes. Zeus's jealous wife, **Hera**, wanted to know the identity of the child's father. She disguised herself as Semele's old nurse and went to see Semele. When Semele told her that Zeus was the father, Hera challenged her to prove her claim by having Zeus appear in all his glory. Semele did so. However, because Zeus was the god of lightning, his power was too much for a human to bear. Semele was turned into ashes.

Before Semele died, Zeus pulled Dionysus out of her womb. Then cutting open his thigh, Zeus placed the unborn child inside. A few months later he opened up his thigh, and Dionysus was born. The infant was left with Semele's sister Ino, who disguised him as a girl to protect him from Hera. As punishment for helping Dionysus, Hera drove Ino and her husband insane.

Some legends say that Hera also drove Dionysus insane. Afterward, Dionysus wandered the world accompanied by his teacher, Silenus (pronounced sye-LEE-nus), bands of **satyrs** (pronounced SAY-turz, half-human, half-goat creatures), and his women followers, who were known as maenads (pronounced MEE-nads). When Dionysus traveled to Egypt, he introduced the cultivation of grapes and the art of winemaking. When he went to Libya, he established an oracle—a place where mortals could communicate with the gods—in the desert. He also journeyed to India, conquering all who opposed him and bringing laws, cities, and wine to the country. On his way back to Greece, he met his grand-mother, the earth goddess **Cybele** (pronounced SIB-uh-lee). She cured him of his madness and taught him the mysteries of life and resurrection (rebirth).

In another story about his birth, Dionysus was the son of Zeus and **Demeter**, the goddess of crops and vegetation. Hera was jealous of the child and convinced the **Titans** to destroy him. Although Dionysus was disguised as a baby goat, the Titans found him, caught him, and tore him to pieces. They ate all of his body except his heart, which was rescued by **Athena**. She gave the heart to Zeus, who gave it to Semele to eat. Semele later gave birth to Dionysus again. The story represents the earth (Demeter) and sky (Zeus) giving birth to the crops (Dionysus), which die each winter and are reborn again in the spring.

Drunkenness and madness are elements that appear in many of the stories about Dionysus. In one tale, Dionysus disguised himself as a young boy and got drunk on an island near Greece. Some pirates found him and promised to take him to Naxos, which Dionysus said was his home. However, the pirates decided to sell the boy into slavery. Only one of them, Acoetes, objected to the plan. When the pirates steered their ship away from Naxos, the wind died. Suddenly, a tangle of grapevines covered the ship. The oars turned into snakes, clusters of grapes grew on Dionysus's head, and wild animals appeared and played at his feet. Driven to madness, the pirates jumped overboard. Only Acoetes was spared. He sailed the ship to Naxos, where Dionysus made him a priest of his followers. It was on Naxos that Dionysus also met the princess **Ariadne** (pronounced ar-ee-AD-nee), who became his wife.

Dionysus. MICHELANGELO
MERISI DA CARAVAGGIO/THE
BRIDGEMAN ART LIBRARY/
GETTY IMAGES.

The Worship of Dionysus Dionysus's influence over fertility extended beyond crops to animals and humans as well. This power made him the symbol of creative forces, the lifeblood of nature. Women flocked to his cult because of its association with the female responsibilities of childbearing and harvesting. According to tradition, these women would abandon their families and travel to the countryside to participate in Dionysia festivals, known in Rome as Bacchanalia. They wore animal skins and carried wands called *thyrsi*, made of fennel stalks bound together with grapevines and ivy. The thyrsi were symbols of fertility and reproduction and also of intoxication.

During the Dionysia festivals the maenads would enter a trance, dancing to the beat of drums and waving thyrsi. Sometimes they would go into a frenzy during which they gained supernatural powers. It was said that the maenads could tear apart animals—and even humans—with their bare hands.

In one myth, the worship of Dionysus has tragic consequences. Dionysus visited Thebes disguised as a young man and caused the women there to fall under his power. He led them to a mountain outside the city, where they took part in his rituals. Pentheus, the king of Thebes, was furious and imprisoned Dionysus. Miraculously, the chains fell off and the jail cell opened by itself. Dionysus then told Pentheus of the wild celebrations he would see if he disguised himself as a woman and went to the mountain. The king, dressed as a woman, hid in a tree to watch the Dionysia. However, the women saw him and, in their madness, mistook him for a mountain lion. They killed him, tearing him limb from limb.

King Midas One of the best-known tales about Dionysus concerns King **Midas** and the golden touch. Dionysus's teacher, Silenus, had a habit of getting drunk and forgetting where he was. One day after drinking, Silenus became lost while traveling in Midas's kingdom. He fell in a whirlpool and would have drowned if Midas had not saved him. As a reward, Dionysus granted Midas anything he wished. Midas asked that everything he touched turn to gold. After the wish was granted, however, Midas discovered that all his food turned to gold and he was unable to eat. Then, when he hugged his daughter, she turned to gold too. Dionysus removed Midas's golden touch after the king had learned the price of his greed.

Dionysus in Context

Dionysus did not start out as a Greek god. His following had its roots in Thrace (north of Greece), in Phrygia (in modern Turkey), or possibly on the island of Crete. Many Greek city-states at first rejected the cult of Dionysus because of its foreign origins and its wild, drunken rituals. When the cult first arrived in Rome, worshippers held their celebrations in secret. However, in both Greece and Rome, the cult of Dionysus overcame resistance and gained many followers.

Though many cultures view drinking and drunkenness as undesirable at best and a sin at worst, for the ancient Greeks and Romans it was, within certain contexts, considered an appropriate way to honor and connect with the gods. The Greek philosopher Plato's Symposium, in

Dionysus and Apollo

In his discussion of the ancient Greeks, the German philosopher Friedrich Nietzsche used the terms *Dionysian* and *Apollonian* to describe the two sides of human nature. Dionysian urges—sensual and irrational impulses—are named for Dionysus. The term *Apollonian* refers to the rational side of human behavior associated with the god Apollo. Interestingly, these two gods, with their very different natures, actually shared a shrine at Delphi. Dionysus was said to have the gift of prophecy, and the priests at Delphi honored him almost as much as they honored Apollo.

fact, records a drinking party attended by his teacher Socrates and several other notable Athenians during the festival of Dionysus. It seems clear from the text that the men present have been drinking heavily, and that the ability to do so was considered a positive trait.

While agriculture as a whole was important to ancient Romans, winemaking in particular was considered an especially critical part of Roman agriculture. Dionysus, often depicted with grapes and wine, enjoyed more popularity among ancient Romans than many other gods of agriculture because of this connection.

Key Themes and Symbols

There are three important themes that run through the myth of Dionysus. One theme is the hostility that Dionysus and his cult face both from Hera and from the inhabitants of the places he visits. He is often viewed as the outsider or foreigner, which is a reflection of his origins outside Greece and Rome. The second is the association of Dionysus with madness. This may also symbolize the loss of control caused by drunkenness. The third is the idea of death and rebirth, an essential part of Dionysus's identity as god of the harvest and of fertility. Because crops die in winter and return in spring, Dionysus—like many other agricultural gods—was seen as a symbol of death and resurrection.

Dionysus in Art, Literature, and Everyday Life

Because of his popularity and the colorful stories about him and his followers, Dionysus has been a favorite subject of writers and artists. He appears in early Greek poetry such as Homer's *Iliad*, where he is pictured as a young god. He is later mentioned in works of the Greek playwright Euripides and the Roman poet Ovid. Many poems and stories by English and American writers such as John Milton, John Keats, and Ralph Waldo Emerson include descriptions of Dionysus or his rituals. Famous sculptors such as Michelangelo have carved images of him, and artists throughout history have used him as the subject for paintings. He is sometimes portrayed as old and bearded and sometimes as youthful. Often he is shown surrounded by powerful animals, such as bulls and goats.

Dionysus appears as a character in Rick Riordan's award-winning book *The Lightning Thief* (2005). The story of an attempted re-creation of a Dionysian ritual that goes horribly wrong forms the basis of Donna Tartt's 1992 novel *The Secret History*.

Read, Write, Think, Discuss

Alcoholic beverages, especially wine, have long played an important part in Greek culture. In modern times, Greece does not have a legal drinking age for consuming alcohol in private, and for many years, was well-known for having no age restrictions on the purchase of alcohol (though this is no longer the case). However, the rate of alcoholism in Greece is generally acknowledged to be lower than in many other countries. Do you think legalized drinking for teenagers in the United States would result in increased rates of alcoholism among teens? Why or why not? Are there basic differences between Greek and American culture that would lead to different results?

SEE ALSO Apollo; Ariadne; Athena; Demeter; Hera; *Iliad, The*; Midas; Satyrs; Zeus

Djang'kawu

Character Overview

In **Australian mythology**, the Djang'kawu were three sacred beings—a brother and two sisters—who created all life on earth. The Aborigines of

Nationality/Culture
Australian/Aboriginal

Pronunciation
jang-kuh-WOO

Alternate Names
Djanggawul

Appears In
Australian Aboriginal oral mythology

Lineage
Unknown

Arnhem Land in northern Australia tell the story of the three siblings in a series of five hundred songs.

Major Myths

Arriving from **heaven** in a canoe with their companion Bralbral, the Djang'kawu set off to walk across the land carrying digging sticks called *rangga*. When the Djang'kawu sisters touched the ground with these sticks, they created the water, trees, animals, and all other features of the earth. The sisters were always pregnant, and their children populated the earth.

Originally, the sisters controlled the magic objects that created life. However, one day while they were sleeping, their brother stole these objects. In the beginning, the sisters had both male and female sex organs, but their brother cut off the male parts so that the sisters appeared like other women.

Djang'kawu in Context

The Australian landscape is largely harsh and unforgiving. It is in fact the driest and flattest of all the continents, and consists mostly of desert. The only reliable source of water is an underground basin accessible through various springs, or small pockets where water rises up to the surface, that dot the land. Because of the importance of these springs, it makes sense that the Aboriginal people of Australia would include them in their creation myth as being made by the Djang'kawu.

Key Themes and Symbols

The story of the Djang'kawu is a story about fertility and the creation of the living world. The sisters symbolize motherhood, as well as water, which is seen as the source of all life. The myth of the Djang'kawu is also about how, according to myth, men control the power to perform sacred rituals. This is explained by the brother taking his sisters' rangga sticks so that he can control the magic.

Djang'kawu in Art, Literature, and Everyday Life

The Aboriginal people of Australia have passed on their myths largely through oral tales and songs. Though their culture has recently started to become assimilated into Australian culture as a whole, the myths of the

Aborigines have yet to become widespread in the public consciousness. For this reason, examples of the Djang'kawu in art and literature are mostly limited to tribal songs and art.

Read, Write, Think, Discuss

In Australia, there has been an effort over the years to assimilate or absorb Aboriginal cultures into the mainstream. A similar effort was made with many American Indian tribes in the United States during the early twentieth century. Supporters of assimilation argue that it helps members of small, alienated communities become a successful part of the national culture, which helps create economic and emotional prosperity while bringing diversity into the mainstream. Opponents of assimilation argue that it only serves to destroy the remaining traces of Aboriginal culture and force Aboriginal people to change their ways to match everyone else.

Do you think assimilation is good or bad for native cultures such as the Aborigines? Support your opinion with reasons and examples. You can research the topic for additional information that may help you establish your position.

SEE ALSO Australian Mythology; Creation Stories

Dragons

Character Overview

In myths and legends, dragons are reptilian creatures with horns, huge claws, and long tails. Though they can be found in cultures across the globe, they tend to share these same basic physical features. Some dragons are capable of breathing **fire**, and many have wings. Dragons are usually described as living in a cave or underground lair.

The oldest myths involving dragons come from the ancient Sumerian, Akkadian, and Egyptian mythologies. The dragons in these stories are generally evil forces that disrupt the correct order of the natural world. A god typically defeats the dragon in order to protect the world. The dragon Apophis (pronounced uh-POH-fis) in **Egyptian mythology** was the

Nationality/Culture
Various

Alternate Names
Lindworm (Scandinavian), Wyvern (Saxon)

Appears In
Various myths around the world

enemy of **Ra**, the **sun** god, and is slain by the god **Set**. Babylonian creation myths describe the dragonlike monster **Tiamat** (pronounced TYAH-maht), who was associated with chaos or disorder, and who died at the hands of the god **Marduk**. Dragons also play a role in the Bible, where they are frequently identified with **Satan**; the book of Revelations in the Bible describes the defeat of a dragon at the end of the world. Later Christian legends continued the theme of the dragon as a satanic figure; in one famous legend, **St. George**, the protector saint of England, saved the daughter of a king from a dragon, symbolizing the triumph of the church over the devil. The dragon played a similar symbolic role in Christian art, representing sin that must be overcome by saints and martyrs.

In various Greek and Roman myths, dragons were thought to understand the secrets of the earth. They had both protective and fearsome qualities. For example, **Apollo** fought the dragon Pytho (pronounced PYE-thoh), which guarded the oracle at **Delphi**—a place where mortals could communicate with the gods. Dragons guarded other valuable objects in Greek myths, notably the **Golden Fleece** and the golden apples of the Hesperides; in both stories, the dragons are defeated by **heroes** seeking to obtain the treasure. Dragons served as guardians of valuable things in other cultures, as well. In **Norse mythology**, the best-known dragon is Fafnir, a dwarf who transformed himself into a dragon to guard riches on which a curse had been placed. The young hero **Sigurd** slays Fafnir. In the Anglo-Saxon story of **Beowulf**, the hero slays a dragon that guards an ancient treasure.

Chinese mythology is not without its dragon-slayers; the mythical emperors Yu and Chuan-hin kill dragons in order to establish order in the world. But this view of dragons as things that must be destroyed or controlled is balanced by positive aspects of dragons. For instance, Chinese mythology draws a strong connection between dragons and water. Dragons are thought to symbolize the rhythmic forces of life, and so are held in high regard. In East Asian mythology and tradition, dragons symbolize power, happiness, and fertility and are believed to bring good fortune and wealth. Statues and carvings of dragons are common, and garments are often decorated with the dragon image.

Dragons in Context

In some mythologies, the story of a god's victory over a dragon can be interpreted as a fertility myth because the god is often a storm god, and the dragon is threatening a natural resource. The dragon represents a chaotic force that must be destroyed in order to preserve order in the world. It has been speculated that dinosaur remains, found throughout the world, could have sparked the imagination of ancient peoples, leading them to invent dragons as the fearsome creatures that left such large bones.

The dragon's fierce and ancient power caused many cultures to adopt it as a military and political symbol. Roman soldiers of the first century CE inscribed dragons on the flags that they carried into battle. The ancient Celts also used the dragon symbol on their battle gear, and to this day, a red dragon appears on the flag of Wales.

Key Themes and Symbols

In ancient times, dragons often represented evil, destruction, and death. In some cases, as in Norse myth, dragons represent greed. They are usually portrayed as frightening and destructive monsters. Gods and heroes must slay them in symbolic battles of good over evil. But a few cultures, notably those of China and Japan, view dragons in a positive light and use them as symbols of good fortune. This may reflect the slightly different origins of dragons in different cultures, as well as cultural views on existing animals. In Europe, for example, dragons are the mythical equivalent of serpents, which have long been viewed by Europeans with fear and associated with evil. In Asia, dragons are associated with both serpents and fish, with dragons often depicted as having fish scales as skin. In addition, the Asian attitude toward snakes is generally more favorable than that of Europeans, perhaps due to more common exposure to the animals.

Dragons in Art, Literature, and Everyday Life

Dragons have been found in ancient art and literature from many cultures. They play an especially important role in Chinese and Japanese art. In modern times, dragons are one of the most readily recognized mythical creatures regardless of culture. The fantasy literature and art genres in particular use dragons frequently, and have developed many modern variations on dragon myth and legend. Notable literary works focusing on dragons include the *Dragonriders of Pern* series by Anne McCaffrey (begun in 1968) and *The Hobbit* by J. R. R. Tolkien (1937). Many films have also focused on dragons, including *Dragonslayer* (1981), *Dragonheart* (1996), and *Reign of Fire* (2002).

Read, Write, Think, Discuss

The *Inheritance Trilogy* is a best-selling series of fantasy books written by Christopher Paolini and first published in 2002. The books focus on Eragon, a poor boy who finds a dragon's egg and trains to become a Dragon Rider in the land of Alagesia, where all existing Dragon Riders have been destroyed by a vengeful king named Galbatorix. The first two volumes of the series, *Eragon* and *Eldest*, had sold over eight million copies as of 2007.

SEE ALSO *Beowulf*; George, St.; *Nibelungenlied, The*; Tiamat

Dreamtime

Myth Overview

Nationality/Culture
Australian Aboriginal

Pronunciation
DREEM-time

Alternate Names
The Dreaming, Alcheringa

Appears In
Australian Aboriginal oral mythology

In the mythology of the Australian Aborigines, Dreamtime, or the Dreaming, is the period of creation when the world took shape and all life began. During Dreamtime, ancestral beings created the landscape, made the first people, and taught the people how to live.

The Aborigines believe that the spirits of ancestral beings that sleep beneath the ground emerged from the earth during Dreamtime. As they wandered across the land, the ancestral beings took on the forms of humans, animals, plants, stars, wind, or rain. During their epic journey, they created hills, plains, and other natural formations. Some of the beings brought forth rain. Some created the first people, and some established the laws by which people would live.

When the ancestral beings lay down upon the wet and still soft rocks, they often left impressions of themselves. The Aborigines believe that the ancestral beings continue to live in the places that bear their mark. There, deep down in the earth, they left various forces, including "child-spirits," which take on human form through a father and a mother on earth. One of the ways in which humans trace their origin to the ancestral beings of Dreamtime is through the child-spirits.

Dreamtime did not end at the time of creation, because the ancestral beings and the child-spirits are eternal. When a life ends, the child-spirit returns to the earth and remains there until it comes back again in

Petroglyph believed to have been made by Aboriginal ancestors during the formation of the landscape during Dreamtime, New South Wales, Australia. WERNER FORMAN/ART RESOURCE, NY.

another human form. Moreover, by participating in certain rituals, individuals can reenact the journeys of their ancestors. Ancestral beings and human beings are thus closely and forever linked.

Different Aboriginal groups tell various Dreamtime stories about their ancestral beings. One group from northern Australia describes how an ancestral being in the form of a snake sent bats for humans to eat during the Dreamtime. However, the bats flew so high that the people could not capture them. The snake gave up one of his ribs to create the boomerang. Using this weapon, the people could hunt and eat the bats.

The Arrernte people of central Australia speak of a great lizard ancestor. They describe how the lizard created the first people in Dreamtime and gave them tools for survival, such as stone knives and spears. The Arrernte, who consider the lizard sacred, believe that certain waterholes and rock formations mark the places where the great lizard did his work.

Dreamtime in Context

The term "Dreamtime" was coined by anthropologist Francis James Gillen in about 1896. It reflects the fact that the Northern Arrernte, one of the first Aboriginal groups studied, use the same word to mean both "dream" and "the period of the creation of the world." In other tribes with similar beliefs, the two words are not related. Dreamtime is not meant to refer to sleep, although dreams are considered by some tribes to be a way to access the parallel world of the Dreamtime, which is not just an event that happened long ago, but is always occurring.

Key Themes and Symbols

The myth of Dreamtime is complex and symbolizes a way of life completely different from other cultures. Some elements that can be easily distinguished include the theme of creation, the idea of the snake as a sacred ancestor, and the theme of **reincarnation** or rebirth as illustrated by the child-spirits. The Dreamtime also represents a parallel world that is eternal and exists outside of time.

Dreamtime in Art, Literature, and Everyday Life

The myth of Dreamtime is most often seen in the work of artists who have been raised in the Australian culture. The 1977 film *The Last Wave* by Australian director Peter Weir focuses mainly on the clash between Aboriginal and white cultures, and includes elements of the Dreamtime as an important part of the plot. Some artists outside Australia have also been inspired by the myth: the English band The Stranglers released a successful album titled *Dreamtime* in 1986, which also contained a song by the same name.

Read, Write, Think, Discuss

The importance of dreams has long been debated by philosophers, psychologists, doctors, and others. What function, if any, do you think dreams serve? Is their purpose medical, cultural, personal, spiritual, or some combination of these? Do you think it is possible that a parallel world, such as the Dreamtime, could exist and be accessed while sleeping? Why or why not?

SEE ALSO Australian Mythology

Durga

See **Devi.**

Dwarfs and Elves

Character Overview

In myths and tales, dwarfs and elves are small humanlike creatures, often endowed with magical powers. Dwarfs generally look like old men with long beards and are sometimes ugly or misshapen. Elves, known for their mischievous pranks, tend to be smaller in stature than dwarves. Though usually associated with Scandinavian mythology, dwarfs and elves appear in the myths of many cultures, along with similar creatures such as fairies, gnomes, pixies, and **leprechauns**.

In **Norse mythology**, dwarfs and elves are usually male and often live in forests, in mountains, or in out-of-the-way places. There are two kinds of elves: the Dökkalfar (pronounced DOH-kahl-fahr), or dark elves, and the Ljosalfar (pronounced YOHL-sah-fahr), or light elves. The Dökkalfar dwell in caves or dark woods. The Ljosalfar live in bright places or in the sky.

Dwarfs and elves of the mountains are highly skilled metalworkers and artisans who have supernatural powers and make special gifts for the gods, such as a magic spear for **Odin**, the king of the gods; a ship for **Freyja** (pronounced FRAY-uh), the goddess of love and beauty; and a hammer for **Thor**, the god of thunder. But dwarfs and elves of the mines, who keep guard over underground stores of gold and precious stones, are unpredictable and spiteful. This association of dwarfs and elves with mining and precious metals exists in many legends and fairy tales.

In Germanic mythology, elves are tiny creatures who can bring disease to people and to cattle or can cause nightmares by sitting on a sleeper's chest. They also steal newborn babies and replace them with deformed elf children, called "changelings." In Central American myths, dwarfs are associated with caves, forests, and fertility. In one story, a Red Dwarf uses his ax to cause sparks that a fortune-teller interprets. The Bushpeople of South Africa tell of the Cagn-Cagn, dwarfs who killed the god Cagn with the help of ants and later restored him to life.

In North America, dwarf people appear in various Native American myths. For instance, the Awakkule are strong mountain dwarfs who act as helpful spirits in Crow mythology. The Wanagemeswak are thin,

Nationality/Culture
Various

Alternate Names
Ljosalfar, Dökkalfar (Norse), Cagn-Cagn (South African), Awakkule, Wanagemeswak, Djogeon (American Indian)

Appears In
Various myths around the world

Dwarfs, such as the ones from the story of "Snow White and the Seven Dwarfs" are portrayed as both helpful and suspicious. THE ART ARCHIVE/JOHN MEEK/THE PICTURE DESK, INC.

river-dwelling dwarfs in the mythology of the Penobscot Indians. The Senecas have legends about the Djogeon, little people who live in caves, in deep ditches, or along streams. The Djogeon warn humans about dangers and sometimes bring good fortune.

Dwarfs and Elves in Context

Dwarfs are sometimes represented as helpful creatures or wise advisors. More commonly, though, they are unpleasant, stubborn, and distrustful with an air of mystery about them. They may act in deceitful ways, or they may be openly hostile. In some stories, dwarfs steal food or carry off children and beautiful maidens.

Elves take on a variety of forms. Different cultures have identified elves as nature spirits, minor gods, imaginary beings, dream creatures, and souls of the dead. Like dwarfs, elves have both positive and negative images. In the legend of Santa Claus, they work hard in Santa's toy shop. In other stories, they are mischievous beings who play pranks on humans and animals, such as leading travelers astray.

The mythology surrounding elves and dwarfs likely has multiple roots. The earliest cultures tended to be pantheistic, believing in many gods, and people often believed that individual spirits inhabited specific ponds, trees, hills, and other natural features. These nature spirits probably evolved into the elves of later folklore. The pounding, rumbling, and shaking exhibited by volcanic mountains have often been associated with "miner" gods living beneath the ground, and this likely gave rise to legends of the dwarfs.

Key Themes and Symbols

Regardless of the culture in which they are found, dwarfs and elves are almost always linked to nature in some way. Dwarfs are often associated with the earth, as in Norse mythology, where they are believed to live deep in the ground. Likewise, elves are often associated with trees, forests, and rivers. This connection with nature is often magical, as with the dwarfs who create many of the powerful enchanted weapons and gadgets used by Norse gods. One theme common to all myths about elves and dwarfs is the idea of a parallel, mostly hidden race of creatures that exists alongside humans, sometimes providing benefits and sometimes causing great harm. They are often organized in groups similar to humans; in Norse mythology, for example, dwarfs are craftsmen that toil away in mines and at blacksmith fires. They may even represent exaggerated versions of human artisans common in Norse society.

Dwarfs and Elves in Art, Literature, and Everyday Life

Dwarfs and elves have become common fixtures in modern fantasy art, literature, and film. Although both were common in European folktales prior to the mid–twentieth century, it was the publication of J. R. R. Tolkien's *The Lord of the Rings* trilogy that earned these mythical races a permanent place in popular culture. Tolkien included several elf and dwarf characters in his books, most notably the elf Legolas and the dwarf Gimli. In the decades after Tolkien's trilogy was published, elves and dwarfs became standard in many works of fantasy. In addition to books, dwarfs and elves are also common in role-playing games and fantasy films—again, most influentially, in games and movies based on Tolkien's books. The 1937 Walt Disney movie *Snow White and the Seven Dwarfs* is also a popular story featuring dwarfs.

Elves have also remained a common part of the mythology of Santa Claus and Christmas. These elves, much different from those found in Tolkien and most works of fantasy, are found in most modern versions of the Santa Claus myth. They commonly appear in holiday films, such as the 2003 film *Elf* starring Will Ferrell and the *Santa Clause* series starring Tim Allen.

Read, Write, Think, Discuss

Dwarfism is a genetic disorder that results in a full-grown adult size of less than about 4 feet 10 inches in height. Dwarfism can lead to numerous health problems as well as negative treatment by others, some of whom might view those with dwarfism as "freaks." Do you think modern mainstream depictions of mythical dwarfs—such as Gimli in the *Lord of the Rings* books and films—help or hurt the public image of those with dwarfism? Explain your answer and include reasons to support your position.

SEE ALSO Leprechauns; Norse Mythology

Dybbuks

Character Overview

In Jewish folklore, a dybbuk is the spirit or soul of a dead person that enters a living body and takes possession of it. *Dybbuk* is a Hebrew word meaning "attachment."

Nationality/Culture
Jewish

Pronunciation
DIB-uhk

Alternate Names
Dibbuk

Appears In
Jewish folktales

Lineage
Varies

According to tradition, a dybbuk is a restless spirit that must wander about—because of its sinful behavior in its previous life—until it can "attach" itself to another person. The dybbuk remains within this person until driven away by a religious ceremony.

Dybbuks in Context

Belief in possessing spirits such as dybbuks was common in eastern Europe during the 1500s and 1600s. Sometimes people who had nervous or mental disorders were assumed to be possessed by a dybbuk. Often a special rabbi was called to exorcise, or drive out, the evil spirit. Exorcisms of dybbuks still take place in modern times, though they are rare and not considered a typical part of Jewish culture.

Key Themes and Symbols

Like ghosts in many cultures, dybbuks usually symbolize restlessness, unresolved conflict, or pain. Dybbuks are seldom identified with people who led happy, fulfilling lives. Dybbuks also serve as a reminder of the soul's continued existence after a person dies, which reinforces a belief in the **afterlife**.

Dybbuks in Art, Literature, and Everyday Life

Shloime Ansky wrote a play in Yiddish called *The Dybbuk* in 1916. It concerns a rabbinical student named Khonnon who calls upon **Satan** to help him win Leye, the woman he loves. When Khonnon dies, he becomes a dybbuk and takes possession of Leye. After she is freed of the spirit, Leye dies, and her spirit joins that of Khonnon. In 1974, composer Leonard Bernstein and choreographer Jerome Robbins created a ballet titled *Dybbuk* that was based on Ansky's play.

Read, Write, Think, Discuss

Some churches still practice exorcism as a way to remove a demonic spirit from the body of someone who has been declared possessed, usually a child. Many cases of exorcism around the world have resulted in death or injury to the supposed victim of the possession. Do you think the practice of exorcism should be protected under the banner of religious freedom? Why or why not?

E

Character

Deity

Myth

Theme

Culture

Nationality/Culture
Greek

Pronunciation
EK-oh

Alternate Names
None

Appears In
Ovid's *Metamorphoses*

Lineage
Unknown

Echo

Character Overview

In **Greek mythology**, Echo was a mountain nymph who annoyed **Hera** (pronounced HAIR-uh), queen of the gods, by talking to her constantly. Echo's chatter distracted Hera and prevented her from discovering the love affairs of her husband, **Zeus** (pronounced ZOOS). As punishment, Hera took away Echo's power of speech so that she could say nothing except the last words spoken by someone else.

Other myths tell of Echo's falling in love with **Narcissus** (pronounced nar-SIS-us), the handsome son of a river god. However, Narcissus rejected Echo because she could only repeat his words. She was so upset that she faded away until only her voice was heard as an echo. Another myth states that **Pan**, god of the woods, pursued Echo but that she escaped him by running away. The angry Pan caused some shepherds to go mad and tear Echo apart, leaving nothing but her voice to echo through the mountains.

Echo in Context

In many cultures, myths arise as a way to explain why something exists the way it does in nature. For example, a myth might explain why the giraffe has such a long neck. It is likely that the myth of Echo originated as a way to explain the reflected sounds heard by ancient Greeks;

329

One myth involving the nymph Echo tells of her love for Narcissus, who did not return her love because she could only repeat what he said. RÉUNION DES MUSÉES NATIONAUX/ART RESOURCE, NY.

this is supported by the fact that Echo was a mountain nymph, and mountainous areas are more likely to result in the reflected sounds we know today as echoes.

Key Themes and Symbols

One of the main themes of the myth of Echo is unrequited love, or love that is not felt and returned by the other person. In the myth, Echo loves Narcissus, even though she cannot tell him. Narcissus rejects Echo, and she simply fades away. The myth can also be seen as a warning of the dangers of talking too much; Echo is cursed by Hera after the goddess is distracted by Echo's constant chatter.

Echo in Art, Literature, and Everyday Life

Although Echo's story was widely known among the ancient Greeks, it was the subject of relatively few existing works of art and literature. Ovid's *Metamorphoses* is the most notable telling. The myth remained well-known through the Renaissance; William Shakespeare's classic play *Romeo and Juliet* includes a passage about Echo.

In modern times, the myth of Echo lives on in the term "echo," which refers to the reflection of a sound back to a listener, usually in enclosed areas or open places with hard vertical surfaces such as cliff faces.

Read, Write, Think, Discuss

Echo wastes away after Narcissus refuses to love her as she loves him. This theme of unrequited love is popular in modern books and movies. Find an example of unrequited love in a book you have read or a movie you have seen, and describe how the theme is handled in the story you have selected.

SEE ALSO Hera; Narcissus; Pan

Eden, Garden of

Myth Overview

According to the book of Genesis in the Bible, the Garden of Eden was an earthly paradise that was home to **Adam and Eve**, the first man and woman. The Bible says that God created the garden, planting in it "every tree that is pleasant to the sight, and good for food." Eden was a well-watered, fertile place from which four rivers flowed out into the world.

After creating Adam, God placed him in the garden so that he could take care of it. God told Adam that he could eat the fruit from any tree except one: the tree of knowledge of good and evil. God then created animals and birds and gave Adam the task of naming them. Realizing that Adam needed a companion, God caused him to fall asleep, then took one of his ribs and created Eve from it.

Nationality/Culture
Judeo-Christian

Pronunciation
GARD-n uhv EED-n

Alternate Names
None

Appears In
The Old Testament, the Talmud

Shortly afterward, the serpent—the most cunning of all the animals—approached Eve and asked if God had forbidden her to eat from any of the trees. Eve replied that she and Adam were not allowed to eat from the tree of knowledge of good and evil. The serpent told her that God knew that if they ate from the tree of knowledge they would become like gods. He persuaded Eve to eat the fruit of that tree, and Eve convinced Adam to take a bite as well. After they ate, their eyes were opened to the knowledge of good and evil. They realized they were naked and sewed together fig leaves to cover themselves.

Soon they heard God walking through the garden and, ashamed of their nakedness, they hid themselves. God called out to them, and when Adam replied that he was hiding because he was naked, God knew that he had eaten the forbidden fruit. Adam admitted that Eve had given him the fruit to eat. When God asked Eve why she had done this, she told him that the serpent had tempted her. God then expelled them from the garden and punished them by causing women to bear children in pain and forcing men to work and sweat for the food they need to live.

The Garden of Eden in Context

The peoples of ancient Mesopotamia also believed in an earthly paradise named Eden, located somewhere in the east. According to some ancient sources, the four main rivers of the ancient Near East—the Tigris, Euphrates, Halys, and Araxes—flowed out of the garden. Scholars today debate the origin of the word *Eden*. Some believe it comes from a Sumerian word meaning "plain." Others say it is from the Persian word *heden*, meaning "garden."

Key Themes and Symbols

The story of the Garden of Eden is an allegory, which means the characters and events are symbolic and represent other things, usually to drive home a message or moral. The serpent in the garden symbolizes temptation, while the fruit symbolizes sin. The main theme of the myth is mankind's fall from grace or perfection. The myth also serves as a warning to resist temptation.

The Garden of Eden in Art, Literature, and Everyday Life

The myth of the Garden of Eden has been a popular subject for artists, especially during the Middle Ages and Renaissance. Depictions of the

Garden of Eden have been painted by artists such as Michelangelo, Peter Paul Rubens, Masaccio, Albrecht Dürer, and Lucas Cranach. One of the most famous depictions of the Garden of Eden is found in the *Garden of Earthly Delights* altarpiece by Hieronymus Bosch, painted around 1504.

In modern usage, the term "Garden of Eden" is often used to describe any place that appears to be a natural paradise untouched by the progress of humans—specifically, a place with lush vegetation, wildlife, and a plentiful water supply.

Read, Write, Think, Discuss

The Garden of Eden is described as a place of unspoiled natural beauty. In our modern world, places of unspoiled natural beauty are being destroyed at an alarming rate in the name of progress. Do you think humankind would be better served by returning to a more natural environment instead of developing new industries and technologies, or by moving forward with the hope that technological progress will result in more efficient and less harmful uses for our natural resources? What sacrifices might be required to accomplish each of these goals?

SEE ALSO Adam and Eve; First Man and First Woman; Serpents and Snakes

Egyptian Mythology

Egyptian Mythology in Context

Bordered by deserts, Egypt's Nile River valley was relatively isolated from other centers of civilization in the ancient Near East for thousands of years. As a result, Egyptian religion remained almost untouched by the beliefs of foreign cultures. The religion included a large and diverse pantheon, or collection of recognized gods and goddesses, and around these deities arose a rich mythology that helped explain the world.

Conquest by the Macedonian ruler Alexander the Great in 332 BCE and by the Romans about three hundred years later weakened the

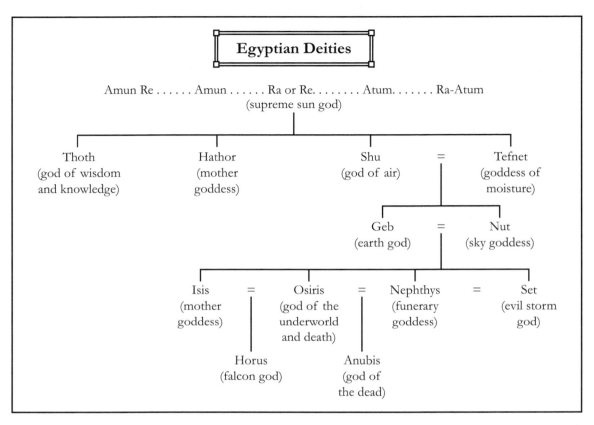

Egyptian Deities

Amun Re . . . . . . Amun . . . . . . Ra or Re. . . . . . . Atum. . . . . . . Ra-Atum
(supreme sun god)

Thoth
(god of wisdom
and knowledge)

Hathor
(mother
goddess)

Shu
(god of air)

=

Tefnet
(goddess of
moisture)

Geb
(earth god)

=

Nut
(sky goddess)

Isis
(mother
goddess)

=

Osiris
(god of the
underworld
and death)

=

Nephthys
(funerary
goddess)

=

Set
(evil storm
god)

Horus
(falcon god)

Anubis
(god of
the dead)

ILLUSTRATION BY ANAXOS, INC./CENGAGE LEARNING, GALE.

Egyptian religion. By about 400 CE, Christianity had become the dominant faith of the land.

Core Deities and Characters

Religion and religious cults (groups who worship specific gods) played a central role in all aspects of ancient Egyptian society. The king, or pharaoh, was the most important figure in religion as well as in the state. His responsibilities included ensuring the prosperity and security of the state through his relationship with the gods.

The ancient Egyptians believed that the king was a divine link between humans and the gods. As a living god, he was responsible for supporting religious cults and for building and maintaining temples to the gods. Through such activities, he helped maintain order and harmony.

Because of his critical role in promoting the welfare of Egyptian society, the pharaoh was in some ways more important than any individual god. His official names and titles reflected his special relationship to the gods, particularly to the **sun** god **Ra** and the sky god **Horus** (HOHR-uhs). Some kings sought to gain full status as gods during their lifetimes. Others achieved that position after their deaths.

Ancient Egypt had a remarkably large and diverse pantheon, with many national, regional, and local gods and goddesses. Unlike the gods of some cultures, who lived in a special place in the heavens, Egyptian deities were thought to inhabit the temples of their cults. Daily temple rituals involved caring for the gods and providing them with food, clothing, and other necessities.

Most Egyptian religious cults centered on a temple and the daily rituals performed there. Each temple contained images of the cult's god, generally kept in the innermost part of the building. Daily ceremonies involved clothing, feeding, and praising the god's image. The pharaoh had overall responsibility for all cults, but the temple priests supervised the daily rituals. Although temple rituals affected the welfare of all the people, common Egyptians rarely took part in them. They attended only special festivals, which often included processions of the god's images and reenactments of popular myths.

Egyptian gods tended to have shifting identities. Many did not have clearly defined characters, and their personalities might vary from one myth to another. Although most deities were known by certain basic associations—such as the connection of the god Ra (pronounced RAH) with the sun—these associations often overlapped with those of other gods. Some deities possessed a collection of names to go with the different sides of their personality. For example, the goddess **Hathor** (pronounced HATH-or), who helped the sun god, was also called the Eye of Ra. Sometimes the names and characters of two or more gods were combined to form one deity, such as the combination of the sky god **Amun** (pronounced AH-muhn) and Ra (sometimes Re) into Amun-Ra. The creator god Atum (pronounced AH-tuhm) merged with Ra to become Ra-Atum. Nevertheless, such deities might continue to exist separately as well as in their combined forms.

Egyptian gods also could assume different forms, often combining both human and animal features. If a deity was closely associated with a particular animal or bird, he or she might be shown in art with a human body and the head of that animal or entirely in animal form. Thus,

Horus appears with the head of a falcon, Sekhmet (pronounced SEK-met) with the head of a cat, and **Set** (pronounced SET) is portrayed as a donkey or huge dog. Sometimes a god was linked to several animals, each reflecting a different side of his character.

The gods were powerful and for the most part immortal (able to live forever), but their influence and knowledge had limits. Still, they had the ability to be in several places at the same time and could affect humans in many ways. Although generally benevolent, or helpful to humans, gods could bring misfortune and harm if humans failed to please them or care for them properly.

Egyptian deities were often grouped together in various ways. The earliest grouping was the *ennead* (pronounced EN-ee-ad), which consisted of nine gods and goddesses. The most important of these, the Great Ennead of the city of Heliopolis (pronounced hee-lee-OP-uh-luhs) in northern Egypt, contained the deities associated with creation, death, and rebirth. Another major grouping was the *ogdoad* (pronounced OG-doh-ad)—four pairs of male and female deities. Triads, found mainly in local centers, generally consisted of a god, a goddess, and a young deity (often male).

Although Egypt had thousands of gods and goddesses, only a few were regarded as major deities. The sun god Ra (sometimes Re) was a deity of immense power, considered to be one of the creators of the universe. The combined god Amun-Ra, a mysterious creator spirit, was the source of all life. Ra-Atum represented the evening sun that disappeared each night below the horizon and rose again at dawn. Another sun god, **Aten** (pronounced AHT-n), became the focus of religious reform in the 1300s BCE, when the pharaoh Akhenaten (pronounced ahk-NAHT-n) tried to make him the principal god of Egypt.

Osiris (pronounced oh-SYE-ris), **Isis** (pronounced EYE-sis), and Horus, who made up the best-known Egyptian triad of deities, played leading roles in some of the major Egyptian myths. Osiris, the lord of the **underworld** and god of death and resurrection (rebirth), was the brother and husband of Isis, a mother goddess of Egypt. Horus was their son. Osiris and Isis were the children of the earth god Geb (pronounced GEB) and the sky goddess **Nut** (pronounced NOOT). Set, another child of Geb and Nut, changed from a benevolent god to an evil one and murdered his brother Osiris.

One of the oldest goddesses of Egypt was the sky goddess Hathor, a mother goddess sometimes known as a deity of fertility, love, and beauty.

Egyptians believed that the first god appeared as a Benu bird, a long-legged, wading heron. WERNER FORMAN/ ART RESOURCE, NY.

Ptah (pronounced PTAH), another ancient deity, was credited in some myths with creating the world and other gods. **Thoth** (pronounced TOHT), a god of wisdom and arts, was said to have invented hieroglyphics, astronomy, mathematics, and medicine, as well as to have written the Egyptian Book of the Dead. **Anubis** (uh-NOO-bis), a god of the dead, presided over funerals and guided dead souls through the underworld or land of the dead.

In Egyptian mythology, goddesses were sometimes much more powerful than gods. When angered, they could cause warfare and destroy those who crossed them. Among the most powerful and terrifying goddesses were Neith (pronounced NEYT) and Sekhmet. Neith, associated with hunting and warfare, gave birth to the giant snake Apophis (pronounced uh-POH-fis) when she spat into the primeval waters. During

Major Egyptian Deities

Amun: supreme god, combined with the sun god Ra to form a new deity called Amun-Ra, who was king of the gods and creator of the universe.

Anubis: god of the dead.

Aten: personification of the sun and later an all-powerful and creator god under the pharaoh Akhenaten.

Atum: god of the sun and creation.

Geb: god of the earth.

Hathor: mother goddess associated with fertility and love, goddess of the sky.

Horus: sun god and sky god, ruler of Egypt, identified with the pharaoh.

Isis: mother goddess.

Nut: goddess of the sky and mother goddess.

Osiris: god of the underworld and judge of the dead.

Ptah: creator god, patron of sculpting and metalworking.

Ra (Re): sun god, combined with the supreme god Amun to form a new deity called Amun-Ra, who was king of the gods and creator of the universe.

Set: god of violent and chaotic forces.

Thoth: god of wisdom and knowledge, patron of scribes.

the struggle between Horus and Set, she threatened to make the sky fall if the other gods did not take her advice for resolving the dispute. Sekhmet, portrayed as a terrifying lioness, was killed by rebellious humans during the early years after creation. The Egyptians sometimes sacrificed criminals to her, and it was thought that she used contagious diseases as her messengers.

Magic played an important role in Egyptian religion, often providing a way to avoid or control misfortune. Magical spells might include versions of myths. All gods had secret, divine names that carried magical powers. One spell told the story of how Isis discovered the secret name of Ra, which she then used to increase her own magical skills. Many spells were used to treat the bites of snakes and scorpions, generally regarded as symbols of the forces of chaos. The god Thoth, a patron of wisdom, was closely connected with magic.

Major Myths

Very few actual Egyptian myths have been preserved from ancient times. Modern scholars have reconstructed stories from such sources as hymns, ritual texts, images on temple walls, and decorations on tombs and coffins. Some myths about major deities were known and valued throughout Egypt. But many gods and the legends about them had only regional significance. Even the widespread myths often changed or adapted to new situations over the centuries, resulting in numerous variations of a particular story.

Creation Myths The Egyptian creation myth has many versions. According to one account, the world was originally a dark, endless chaos of primitive waters. The forces of chaos were represented by an ogdoad consisting of four pairs of deities: Nun (pronounced NOON) and Naunet, the god and goddess of the waters; Kek and Ketet, the forces of darkness; Her and Hehet, the spirits of boundlessness; and Amun and Amaunet, the invisible powers. In some versions of the myth, the god Ptah is associated with Nun and plays a central role in creation.

Within the waters of chaos, the spirit of creation waited to take form. When a mound rose above the waters, Amun (or Ra) emerged and used divine powers to establish order (*ma'at*) out of the chaos. The spirit of creation (Amun or Ra—or sometimes Ptah) then made other gods and humans to inhabit the world. Some accounts say that the gods were formed from the sweat of the creator spirit and that humans came from his tears.

Another part of the Egyptian creation myth concerned the formation of the Great Ennead of Heliopolis. The first of these nine gods was Ra-Atum, who emerged from the primeval waters and created Shu (pronounced SHOO), the god of air, and Tefnut, the goddess of moisture. Shu and Tefnut united to produce the earth god Geb and sky goddess Nut. Geb and Nut stayed very close together, leaving no room for anything to exist between them. Finally Shu separated the two, providing space for other creatures. Geb and Nut eventually had two pairs of male-female **twins**: Osiris and Isis, and Set and Nephthys (pronounced NEF-this). The birth of these gods and goddesses completed the ennead.

Solar Myths Another group of Egyptian myths involved the sun gods and the daily cycle of their movement. According to one story, the sun god was born each day at dawn and crossed the sky in a boat filled with other gods and spirits. At nightfall, he descended to the underworld, where he traveled throughout the night, only to be born again the next day. During his passage through the sky and the underworld, the sun god faced dangers from a giant snake named Apophis and other enemies who tried to interrupt his journey.

The Egyptians celebrated the sun's cycle daily in temples and sang hymns and incantations to help ensure that the sun god would escape danger and continue his journey. They believed that the movements of the sun god made it possible for the world to be created anew each day.

Myths of Osiris According to Egyptian mythology, Osiris was one of the most important pharaohs. In time, his cult rivaled those of Ra and Amun, and myths about Osiris were widespread. Most of the stories involve three basic themes: the struggle between good and evil, the cycle of birth and rebirth, and the judgment of the dead.

As pharaoh, Osiris civilized the Egyptian people by introducing agriculture, establishing laws, and teaching them to worship the gods. Osiris decided to travel around in the world to bring civilization to other peoples. During his absence, he left his sister-wife, Isis, in charge.

By the time Osiris returned to Egypt, his evil brother Set had concocted a plot to kill him. Set had craft workers build a beautifully decorated box to the measurements of Osiris's body. At a lavish banquet, Set displayed the box and announced that he would give it to the person whose body fit in it exactly. When Osiris lay in the box, Set and his supporters closed the top and nailed it shut. Then they carried the box to the Nile River and threw it in the water.

When Isis heard of Set's treachery, she was overcome with grief and set out to find her husband's body. During the course of her travels, she learned that the box had floated to the shores of the land of Byblos (pronounced BIB-luhs) and had become trapped in the branches of a tree. The tree had grown to a great size, and the king of Byblos had cut it down to make a pillar for one of the rooms in his palace.

Isis went to Byblos and recovered the box. Then she brought it back to Egypt and hid it. However, Set discovered the box and cut Osiris's body into many pieces, scattering them all over Egypt. Accompanied by her son Horus and sister Nephthys, Isis gathered the pieces and used her magical powers to bring the dead Osiris back to life. Osiris then became the king of the gods and the underworld.

To avenge his father and to punish Set for his evil deeds against Osiris, Horus fought his uncle three times. Their battles represented a struggle between good and evil. Horus won each battle, and in the end,

The pyramids built in Giza, Egypt, honored the powerful kings of Egypt and provided them with a home in the afterlife. IMAGE COPYRIGHT FATIH KOCYILDIR, 2008. USED UNDER LICENSE FROM SHUTTER-STOCK.COM.

the gods decided that he was the rightful heir to the thrones of both Upper and Lower Egypt. Set was forced to accept this judgment. With Horus as pharaoh, Isis went to live with Osiris in the underworld, where he ruled as lord of the dead.

When the dead person's soul reached Osiris's throne room, it was placed on a scale balanced by a white feather symbolizing truth. Osiris, assisted by Horus, Anubis, and Thoth, sat in judgment. Individuals found innocent of various sins could live among the gods until their bodies were one day resurrected and reunited with the soul. Those found guilty were condemned to eternal torment.

Key Themes and Symbols

The idea of order, or *ma'at*, was a basic concept in Egyptian belief, reflecting such notions as truth, cooperation, and justice. Egyptians imagined their world as being surrounded by chaos or disorder that constantly threatened to overwhelm *ma'at*.

Another important theme in Egyptian mythology is the **afterlife**. When humans died, their souls began a difficult journey through the underworld. Spells and incantations helped them on their way, and these eventually were collected in a group of texts known as the Book of the Dead. The importance of the afterlife can be seen in the myths of Osiris.

Egyptian Mythology in Art, Literature, and Everyday Life

The influence of Egyptian mythology and religion extended beyond the kingdom's borders. The ancient Greeks and Romans adopted some of Egypt's gods and myths, suitably modified to fit their cultures. Egyptian cults, particularly that of Isis, also spread to Greece and Rome. In his book *The Golden Ass*, Roman philosopher Lucius Apuleius (pronounced ap-yuh-LEE-uhs) mentions festivals of Isis, and the Roman historian Plutarch (pronounced PLOO-tahrk) wrote down one of the most complete versions of the myth of Osiris and Isis.

Egyptian mythology has inspired modern writers, artists, and composers as well. The novel *The Egyptian* (1949) by Finnish author Mika Waltari refers to the supremacy of Aten over other gods. The opera *Aida* (1869) by Italian composer Giuseppe Verdi is set in ancient Egypt and mentions the god Ptah. Loosely interpreted Egyptian mythology has played a part in numerous films, including the 1994 science fiction film *Stargate*, the classic Universal horror film *The Mummy*, and its more action-oriented 1999 remake of the same name starring Brendan Fraser and Rachel Weisz.

Read, Write, Think, Discuss

Using your library, the Internet, or other available resources, research the topic of Egyptian mummification. How did the Egyptians preserve the bodies of the dead? What was the purpose in preserving these bodies? What other items were placed in Egyptian burial chambers, and why? Did the Egyptians practice mummification on animals as well?

SEE ALSO Afterlife; Amun; Animals in Mythology; Anubis; Aten; Creation Stories; Hathor; Horus; Isis; Nut; Osiris; Ra; Set; Thoth; Underworld

El

Character Overview

In the mythology of the ancient Near East, El was the supreme god of the Canaanites. He was the creator deity, the father of gods and men,

Nationality/Culture
Canaanite

Pronunciation
ELL

Alternate Names
Il

Appears In
Ugaritic texts and inscriptions

Lineage
Father of humankind

and the highest judge and authority in all divine matters and human affairs. In the Bible, the creator deity is referred to as El, Elohim (pronounced ay-LOH-heem, a form of El), or Yahweh (pronounced YAH-way).

Major Myths

One story from Ugarit concerned Aqhat, son of King Danel. In return for the king's hospitality, the craftsman god Kothar gave Aqhat his bow and arrows. The goddess Anat wanted the bow and tried to buy it with gold and silver. When Aqhat refused, the goddess offered to give him immortality (eternal life) in exchange for the bow. Aqhat rudely rejected her offer, telling the goddess that she could not make immortal a man destined to die.

The god El. THE ART AR-CHIVE/NATIONAL MUSEUM DAMASCUS SYRIA/GIANNI DAGLI ORTI/THE PICTURE DESK, INC.

Angry about having her offer rejected, Anat asked for and received El's permission to have Aqhat killed. The young man's death brought drought and crop failure. Anat cried over his death and said she would bring him back to life so that the earth might be fertile again. Unfortunately, the tablets containing this myth are in such bad condition that the ending of the story is difficult to interpret.

El in Context

Despite his religious significance, El did not play an active role in Canaanite mythology. Most myths were about the actions of others and involved El indirectly. The true nature of El is further confused by the fact that "El" could be used to refer to any god, and not just the supreme deity of the Canaanites. This is similar to how the word "god" can refer to any deity of any religion, but is commonly used—with a capital "G"—to refer to the supreme being in Judeo-Christian beliefs.

Key Themes and Symbols

In Canaanite mythology, El was usually represented as an elderly man with a long beard. He was believed to live on Mount Saphon, near the ancient Syrian city of Ugarit. A highly respected deity, El was all-knowing and all-powerful, wise and compassionate. He was sometimes referred to as "the Bull" and was generally shown as a seated figure wearing a crown with bull's horns. The bull suggested El's strength and creative force.

El in Art, Literature, and Everyday Life

El appears throughout ancient Middle Eastern religious texts and inscriptions. Over time, however, other names began to appear more frequently in references to the supreme being. These include Elohim and Yahweh. Although early Christian leaders recognized El as the first Hebrew name of God, the term is usually associated with beliefs and practices that existed in times before the Bible.

Read, Write, Think, Discuss

It is widely recognized that Judaism, Christianity, and Islam all arose in the same region of the world and from the same core belief in a single supreme being, with El being one of the names of this deity. However, modern followers of these three religions each typically view members of the other two religions as completely different in their beliefs. Using your library, the Internet, or other available resources, research the basic beliefs of these three religions and write down at least three common elements found in all of them.

SEE ALSO Semitic Mythology

El Dorado

Myth Overview

The legend of El Dorado (pronounced el doh-RAH-doh) was about a fabulously wealthy city of gold and the king who ruled over it. The story

Nationality/Culture
Spanish/Muisca

Pronunciation
el doh-RAH-doh

Alternate Names
None

Appears In
Juan Rodriguez Freyle's *El Carnero*

This model raft made of gold symbolizes the El Dorado legend in which a wealthy South American king supposedly threw gold into a lake from a raft as an offering to the gods. The legend sparked a search for El Dorado by gold-hungry Spanish explorers to South America. THE PICTURE DESK, INC. REPRODUCED BY PERMISSION.

sprang up shortly after the first Spanish explorers landed in Central and South America.

Local people told tales of a rich king who plastered his body with gold dust and then dived into a sacred lake to wash it off. Afterward, he would toss gold into the lake as an offering to the gods. The Spanish called the king El Dorado—The Gilded One—because his body was gilded, or covered in gold. As the tale spread, the city he ruled came to be called El Dorado. Eventually, the meaning of the name changed to include any mythical region that contained great riches.

An early version of the El Dorado legend placed the city near Lake Guatavita, a circular lake formed in a volcanic crater not too far from modern Bogotá, Colombia. The story was based on the Muisca people who performed a ceremony similar to that in the legend. The Muisca king, covered with gold dust, boarded a raft in the lake and made offerings to the gods. Both Spaniards and Germans searched the region in 1538 but failed to find El Dorado. They even attempted to drain the lake in an effort to locate gold; today, Lake Guatavita still bears a deep groove along its crater rim that was cut by Spanish explorers.

El Dorado in Context

One of the reasons Spanish explorers aimed to conquer the Americas was to find new sources of wealth—specifically, gold. The myth of El Dorado appealed strongly to these Spanish explorers because it played into their desire to locate untold riches and claim it for their country (and themselves).

Local inhabitants usually claimed that El Dorado was somewhere far away in the hope that the Europeans would search elsewhere and leave them in peace. Men as famous as English explorer Sir Walter Raleigh (1552–1618) spent years in South America looking for legendary golden cities such as Manoa and Omagua. Other places mentioned in stories were Paititi, a land of gold located in Paraguay, and the City of the Caesars, an invisible golden city in Chile. Several bloody expeditions were launched to find these imaginary kingdoms. One of the most tragic was led by a rebel soldier named Lope de Aguirre, a brutal madman who proclaimed himself king and was murdered by one of his followers.

Key Themes and Symbols

The myth of El Dorado symbolized riches beyond imagining to Spanish explorers. The idea of a place where gold was so common that it could be tossed into a lake also represents the way different cultures viewed wealth, and what is considered precious. Also contained within the myth is the underlying notion that Native Americans were too uncivilized to understand or appreciate the value of their resources; this was often used as a justification for conquering native tribes throughout the Americas.

El Dorado in Art, Literature, and Everyday Life

El Dorado was such an appealing myth to Europeans that it made its way into literature. In *Candide*, a 1759 novel by the French writer Voltaire, the main character accidentally discovers the rich city. Edgar Allan Poe's poem "Eldorado" refers to the legend, as does *Paradise Lost* by English poet John Milton. More recently, the myth of El Dorado was the basis of the 2000 Dreamworks animated film *The Road to El Dorado*, featuring voice work by Kevin Kline and Kenneth Branagh.

Today, the term "El Dorado" is often used to refer to a mythical place of untold riches. Several cities and towns in the United States have used the name, and Cadillac has even named one of its cars the Eldorado.

Read, Write, Think, Discuss

Mythical places such as El Dorado usually offer something that cannot be found in the real world. For El Dorado, it is untold wealth; for the mythical Buddhist city of Shambhala (renamed Shangri-La in a 1933 British novel called *Lost Horizons*), it is perfect peace and harmony. To the Arawak Indians, the mythical land of Beemeenee offered eternal youth. If you could journey to a mythical land that offered something not available in the real world, what one thing would you like to find there? Why?

Electra

Character Overview

In **Greek mythology**, there are two figures called Electra. The earlier Electra was one of seven daughters of the Titan **Atlas** (pronounced AT-luhs) and Pleione (pronounced PLEE-oh-nee). The seven sisters together were known as the Pleiades (pronounced PLEE-uh-deez) and eventually became a constellation, or group of stars, by the same name. According to the story, Electra was the mother of Dardanus (pronounced DAR-dun-us), the founder of the city of Troy. When the Greeks destroyed Troy during the Trojan War, she left her place in the constellation to avoid seeing the city's destruction.

The second and more well-known Electra appears in plays by the Greek writers Aeschylus (pronounced ES-kuh-luhs), Sophocles (pronounced SOF-uh-kleez), and Euripides (pronounced yoo-RIP-i-deez). In this legend, Electra was the daughter of **Agamemnon** (pronounced ag-uh-MEM-non), the leader of the Greeks in the Trojan War, and his wife, Clytemnestra (pronounced klye-tem-NES-truh). While Agamemnon was

Nationality/Culture
Greek

Pronunciation
ee-LEK-truh

Alternate Names
None

Appears In
Hyginus's *Fabulae*

Lineage
Varies

away at war, Clytemnestra took a lover named Aegisthus (pronounced ee-JIS-thuhs), and they plotted to murder Agamemnon when he returned. Clytemnestra wanted revenge on Agamemnon because he had sacrificed their daughter to the gods in return for success in the war. They also wanted to kill Orestes (pronounced aw-RES-teez), Agamemnon's young son, but his sister Electra rescued him and sent him away to live in safety.

As an adult, Orestes returned home with his cousin Pylades (pronounced PIL-uh-deez) to avenge his father's murder. Although Orestes disguised himself to enter the palace, Electra recognized him. She helped her brother and Pylades murder Clytemnestra and Aegisthus. It was said that Electra later married Pylades.

Electra in Context

Matricide is the term used to refer to a person murdering his or her mother. The killing of a parent is a common theme in ancient mythology, particularly with the Greeks, even though it was considered an unthinkable act in ancient Greek society. The Greek gods themselves came to power through a chain of patricide (father-killing): the Titan **Cronus** (pronounced KROH-nuhs) killed his father **Uranus** (pronounced YOOR-uh-nuhs), and **Zeus** (pronounced ZOOS) later killed his father Cronus and became king of the gods. There is a similar pattern of family killings in the case of Electra and her family, starting with Agamemnon's **sacrifice** of his daughter, which led to his murder by Clytemnestra, which in turn led to her murder by Electra and Orestes. Electra is motivated by a desire to avenge the death of her father rather than a quest for power, which makes an unthinkable crime justified in the eyes of the ancient Greeks. As is the case with many ancient societies, the ancient Greeks believed in an "eye for an eye" system of justice, meaning that the murder of a murderer is the right thing to do. The ancient Greeks did not view the murder Clytemnestra commits as "eye for an eye" justice because, as a woman, she should not have attacked her husband and king; her role as an avenger is further damaged because she betrayed Agamemnon by taking a lover while he was away at war.

Key Themes and Symbols

One of the main themes of the myth of Electra is vengeance, or the seeking of justice for an unpunished crime. Electra and Orestes both seek vengeance for the murder of their father Agamemnon. Another

Electra recognized her brother Orestes and his friend Pylades when they returned home in disguise to avenge the murder of their father Agamemnon. Electra helped them carry out their revenge. © MARY EVANS PICTURE LIBRARY/THE IMAGE WORKS.

important theme is the idea that violence inevitably results in more violence. Both of these themes are emphasized even more when looking at the larger myth: Clytemnestra murdered Agamemnon as an act of vengeance, because he sacrificed their daughter in order to gain favorable passage for his army during the Trojan War.

Electra in Art, Literature, and Everyday Life

Electra appears in Greek playwright Aeschylus's play the *Oresteia*, first performed in 458 BCE. Modern versions of Electra appear in the play *Mourning Becomes Electra*, written by Eugene O'Neill in 1931, and the 1909 opera *Elektra* by Richard Strauss. The Marvel comics character

Electra Complex

In psychology, the term "Electra complex" refers to the emotional problems suffered by a woman whose unresolved love for her father harms her relationships with other men. It is based on the psychoanalytical theories of Sigmund Freud (1856–1939), considered the "father" of modern psychiatry. It is an offshoot of Freud's concept of the "Oedipus complex," which theorizes that a son's complicated feelings of attraction toward his mother lead him for a time to feel hostility toward his father. Likewise, Freud theorized, a daughter's complicated feelings of love and attraction toward her father might cause her to feel hostility toward her mother.

Elektra, portrayed in a 2005 film of the same name by Jennifer Garner, was also loosely inspired by the mythological character.

Read, Write, Think, Discuss

Though few people experience a family life as violent and dysfunctional as Electra's, many believe that children who are raised in a "broken" home—where one parent is not present or involved in the upbringing—are much more likely to have a wide range of problems later in life. Others counter that the great majority of people raised in single-parent households are as well-adjusted as those raised in homes with both parents. What do you think? Craft a persuasive argument to support your opinion; you can do research to find statistics that support your point.

SEE ALSO Agamemnon

Nationality/Culture
Judeo-Christian

Pronunciation
ee-LYE-juh

Alternate Names
Eliyahu, Elias, Ilyas (Arabic)

Appears In
Hebrew and Christian Bibles, the Qur'an

Lineage
Unknown

Elijah

Character Overview

In **Semitic mythology**, Elijah was one of the most important figures in the tales of early Christianity and Judaism. According to legend, he was a priest and a prophet, or a person who could communicate the word of

Yahweh (God) to humankind. He is mentioned in the Bible as one of two figures—along with Moses—who appeared and spoke to Jesus during an event called the Transfiguration, where God is said to have confirmed that Jesus was his son.

Nothing is known of Elijah's early life, but he is referred to as "the Tishbite," suggesting he came from the city of Tishbe in Gilead. According to some sources, he lived sometime during the ninth century BCE. Elijah appeared at the court of King Ahab of Israel and warned the king that his worship of the god **Baal** (pronounced BAY-uhl) would lead to a disastrous drought in his land. Elijah was then directed by Yahweh to leave Israel for two years; during that time, a drought devastated the region. Elijah then returned to Ahab and challenged him and his people to a test of the gods. An altar was built upon a mountaintop in honor of Baal, with wood and animal sacrifices placed upon it, and the followers of Baal prayed for their god to light a **fire** there. After several hours, no fire had been lit. Elijah then built a similar altar for Yahweh and doused it with water. When he offered the **sacrifice** to Yahweh, a bolt of lightning shot down from the heavens and lit the sacrifice on fire. The audience was convinced of Yahweh's power, and the drought ended.

After uniting much of Israel in its worship of Yahweh and fiercely punishing those who worshipped other gods, Elijah left the world in a most unique way. He approached the Jordan River and struck it with his cloak, which caused the waters to separate, allowing him and his companion to cross. Then a fiery chariot appeared in the sky and lifted Elijah in a whirlwind, leaving behind no trace of the man except his cloak.

Elijah in Context

Although Elijah was a key figure in early tales of Judaism, he enjoys less popularity among Christian followers, which reflects some of the differences in belief between the two groups. One reason for this may be due to the controversy surrounding his ascension into **heaven** aboard a fiery chariot. According to some versions of the New Testament, Jesus states that no one else has ascended to heaven before him. If this statement is accepted as true, then the story of Elijah's departure from earth must be false—unless he was simply transported to a location other than heaven. It is also believed that Elijah is supposed to return to earth before the coming of the Messiah (pronounced muh-SYE-uh), or the

The prophet Elijah's condemnation of Ahab's sins meant that his life was often in danger. HIP/ART RESOURCE, NY.

savior of humankind usually believed to be the son of God. According to Jewish tradition, this has not yet happened. According to Christian tradition, which contends that Jesus was the Messiah, John the Baptist was Elijah in his returned form.

Key Themes and Symbols

One of the main themes of the stories of Elijah is the wrath of God—the punishment that is administered by God to those who disobey esta-

Ascension Myths Around the World

Ascension myths are popular around the world. Many ancient cultures described death as climbing a mountain or a tree; the act of going upward, or ascending, has always been associated with death and spiritual renewal. Ancient Egyptians believed their kings would ascend into heaven after death and become reunited with the supreme deity. Korean legends and epics tell of the hero's ascension into heaven, after which he becomes divine. Christian and Jewish ascension myths adopted this worldwide motif.

Probably the earliest ascension myths revolved around the shaman's journey to other worlds through the Axis Mundi, or World Axis. This was a mythological pole running through the centers of the earth, sky, and underworld. In trance, the shaman would ascend the pole and enter the spirit world. Symbolically, ascension signifies going beyond the human condition and acquiring spiritual power.

blished religious practices and teachings. Elijah warns Ahab of God's wrath over the continued worship of Baal. This leads to a devastating drought throughout his kingdom. The power of God's wrath is also seen in the punishment of King Ahab, his wife, and their son, and in the death of soldiers that attempt to arrest Elijah after he predicts awful ends for Ahab and his family.

Elijah in Art, Literature, and Everyday Life

Although he is featured in the major religious books for Judaism, Christianity, and Islam, Elijah has been the subject of relatively little attention from later artists and writers. Elijah was depicted in a well-known sculpture by the Italian artist Lorenzetto, and his life was the basis for a grand musical work by composer Felix Mendelssohn. In some Jewish sects, Elijah is still an important presence in traditional activities. During the feast of Passover, for example, a table setting is left empty for Elijah, just in case the prophet should decide to appear. Similarly, an empty chair is provided at Jewish circumcision ceremonies so that Elijah can serve as a witness to the proceedings.

Read, Write, Think, Discuss

As stated above, Elijah is also mentioned in the most important Islamic religious text, the Qur'an. Using your library, the Internet, or other available resources, research Elijah's appearance in the Qur'an. What role does he play? How is it different from his role in the Hebrew and Christian bibles?

SEE ALSO Baal; Semitic Mythology

Enkidu

See **Gilgamesh.**

Enuma Elish

Nationality/Culture
Babylonian

Pronunciation
ee-NOO-muh eh-LISH

Alternate Names
None

Appears In
Ancient Babylonian creation mythology

Myth Overview

Enuma Elish was the creation myth of the people of Babylonia (pronounced bab-uh-LOH-nee-uh), a civilization of the ancient Near East. Written in the form of an epic poem, *Enuma Elish* gives the Babylonian account of the origin of the world. The myth is similar to the biblical story of creation in the book of Genesis.

The poem, inscribed on seven tablets, probably dates from around 1100 BCE, although earlier, unrecorded versions of it may have existed long before that time. Its title, meaning "when on high," comes from the first line of the epic, which begins: "When on high the **heaven** had not been named/Firm ground below had not been called by name."

Enuma Elish tells how the Babylonian deities were born from a goddess named **Tiamat** (pronounced TYAH-maht), a vast ocean of formless chaos or disorder, sometimes described as a dragon. **Marduk** (pronounced MAHR-dook), the protector god of the city of Babylon, defeated Tiamat and her army of monsters. He then divided her corpse into two parts, one of which became heaven and one earth. He also killed Tiamat's ally, Kingu (pronounced KIN-goo), and created human beings from Kingu's blood to serve the gods. Marduk's victory brought order to the universe.

Enuma Elish in Context

Enuma Elish had political as well as religious meaning for the Babylonians. By identifying the heroic creator god as Marduk of Babylon, the myth justified the city's dominance over the region. For hundreds of years, celebrations to mark the beginning of the new year in Babylon included a recital of *Enuma Elish* in many of the city's main temples.

Key Themes and Symbols

One of the main themes of *Enuma Elish* is creation. More specifically, though, the myth describes creation of the world from the body and blood of the gods. In this myth, the heavens, earth, and humans are not only created by the gods—they are created out of the material of the gods Tiamat and Kingu. This represents the presence of the divine influence in the world and its people.

Another main theme of *Enuma Elish* is conflict between two opposing forces. The creation of the world comes about due to a battle between Marduk and his supporters on one side, and Tiamat and her minions on the other side. This theme of struggle between light and darkness, good and evil, or order and disorder is common in creation myths around the world.

Enuma Elish in Art, Literature, and Everyday Life

Although it was first written down over three thousand years ago, *Enuma Elish* was unknown to modern scholars until the mid-nineteenth century, when it was discovered on a set of tablets in the ruins of an ancient library in Iraq. Because of this, *Enuma Elish* has appeared in very few other pieces of art or literature. However, it likely inspired other similar creation myths centuries after its development.

Read, Write, Think, Discuss

The *Enuma Elish* was discovered in Iraq, a region known for both its rich human history and its tragic conflicts. In the chaos that followed the U.S. invasion of Iraq in 2003, countless priceless, ancient artifacts have been looted from Iraqi museums and archaeological sites. Use library resources and the Internet to find out more about at least four major Iraqi archeological sites. Then write a paper explaining the historical significance of the sites, their current status, and what steps, if any, should be taken to protect them.

SEE ALSO Creation Stories; Marduk; Tiamat

Eos
See **Aurora.**

Eros

Nationality/Culture
Greek

Pronunciation
AIR-ohs

Alternate Names
Amor, Cupid (Roman)

Appears In
Hesiod's *Theogony*, Ovid's *Metamorphoses*, Virgil's *Aeneid*

Lineage
Son of Aphrodite and Ares

Character Overview

In **Greek mythology**, Eros was the god of passionate or physical love. The Romans called him Amor (pronounced AY-mor) or Cupid (pronounced KYOO-pid), from the words *amor* meaning "love" and *cupido* meaning "desire." His role in mythology changed over time, as did images of him in sculpture and other works of art. Eros became specifically identified with passionate love and fertility. The Greeks portrayed him as a handsome young man with a bow and arrow. The people he struck with his arrows were bound to fall in love. The Romans, however, had a different image of Eros, naming him "Cupid" and portraying him as a mischievous chubby winged boy or infant.

Major Myths

Many different accounts of Eros's birth exist. One of the oldest is found in the *Theogony* (History of the Gods), written by the Greek Hesiod around 700 BCE. Hesiod claimed that Eros, like **Gaia** (pronounced GAY-uh) the earth goddess, was one of the offspring of the primitive emptiness called Chaos (pronounced KAY-oss). He believed Eros to be one of the first powers in the universe, representing the force of attraction and harmony that filled all of creation. The Greeks spoke of Eros as the son of **Aphrodite** (pronounced af-ro-DYE-tee), the goddess of love, and **Ares** (pronounced AIR-eez), the god of war. In this way, the Greeks demonstrated their view of romantic love as a force that would produce violent emotions.

In some myths, Eros makes mischief with his ability to make gods and mortals alike fall in love. His arrow forced the god **Apollo** to fall in love with Daphne, a river nymph who did not love Apollo in return. His mother Aphrodite ordered him to make a beautiful mortal woman named **Psyche** (pronounced SYE-kee) fall in love with the ugliest creature he could find because men were paying more attention to Psyche than to her. Instead, Eros himself fell in love with Psyche. The two married, but Eros kept his identity a secret from Psyche, and only visited her at night when she could not see him. Psyche's jealous sisters convinced her that her husband was actually a monster, telling her to take a lamp and a knife to bed. Psyche did so, only to learn that her husband was a beautiful god. Her mistrust caused Eros to leave her, but she eventually won him back by completing a series of difficult tasks put to her by Aphrodite.

Eros in Context

In ancient Greece, a distinction was generally made between the types of love represented by Eros and Aphrodite. While Aphrodite was the goddess who oversaw love between men and women, Eros reigned over love between a man and a boy. To the wealthy and noble classes of the ancient Greeks, the idea of such a relationship was considered normal, healthy, and masculine. Men and boys often exercised and performed athletics in the nude together, and soldiers fighting together often formed bonds as couples. Only rarely is sexual intercourse specifically mentioned as part of the relationship, though it is sometimes suggested. The lower classes of ancient Greek society were not as involved in this practice.

Key Themes and Symbols

Eros is an enduring symbol of romantic love. His bow and arrow symbolize how love can strike the heart of any person without warning. The blindfold he is sometimes shown to be wearing symbolizes the seeming randomness of love, sometimes resulting in the most unlikely or unexpected pairings. Eros also represents adolescence, a time when many first experience feelings of romantic love.

A popular image of the god Eros was as Cupid, a mischievous young boy with wings. RÉUNION DES MUSÉES NATIONAUX/ART RESOURCE, NY.

Eros in Art, Literature, and Everyday Life

Eros appears throughout literature in works such as the *Aeneid* by Virgil and the *Metamorphoses* by Ovid as well as in the poems *Endymion* and *Ode to Psyche* by the English poet John Keats (1795–1821).

In later art, the Roman conception of Cupid became the most popular depiction of Eros. He was often seen holding his bow and arrow and wearing a blindfold. Artists sometimes multiplied him into many small winged figures. After the rise of Christianity, these little cupids became identified with baby **angels**.

In modern times, Eros—under his Roman name Cupid—has become synonymous with the Valentine's Day holiday. The character of Cupid has appeared in many films, television shows, and commercials, including the 1998 series *Cupid* starring Jeremy Piven as a man who may or may not be the god sent to Earth in human form as punishment by **Zeus**.

Read, Write, Think, Discuss

Since ancient times, the onset of love has been described as something that can happen suddenly, even violently—like an arrow to the heart. Even the phrase "falling in love" carries the implication of a sudden, painful accident. Recently, scientists have begun to piece together what actually happens inside the mind and body of someone "shot by Eros." Using the library and the Internet, find out more about the physiology of love, and write a paper summarizing what you find out.

SEE ALSO Aphrodite; Apollo; Greek Mythology; Psyche

Eurydice

Character Overview

In **Greek mythology**, Eurydice was a dryad, a nymph (female nature spirit) associated with trees, who became the bride of **Orpheus** (pronounced OR-fee-uhs), a hero legendary for his musical skills. While walking in the countryside one day not long after their wedding, Eurydice met Aristaeus (pronounced a-ris-TEE-uhs), the son of the god **Apollo** (pronounced uh-POL-oh). Aristaeus tried to seize her. Eurydice fled but was bitten by a poisonous snake and died. Overcome with grief at his wife's death, Orpheus decided to go to the **underworld** and bring her back.

Orpheus gained entrance to the underworld by charming its guardians with his singing and playing of the lyre (a stringed instrument). The beauty of his music persuaded **Hades** (pronounced HAY-deez), the ruler of the underworld, to allow Eurydice to follow

Nationality/Culture
Greek

Pronunciation
yoo-RID-uh-see

Alternate Names
None

Appears In
Ovid's *Metamorphoses*, Pausanias's *Description of Greece*

Lineage
Unknown

Orpheus back up to the world of the living, but Hades made one condition: Orpheus must not look back at Eurydice as they left his realm. The couple set out on the long, difficult journey back to earth. Toward the end of their trip, just as the darkness of the underworld gave way to the light of earth, Orpheus turned back to Eurydice to share his joy with her. But as he looked at her, Eurydice disappeared, returning to the underworld forever.

Eurydice in Context

The myth of Eurydice and Orpheus reflects the ancient Greek emphasis on the power of music to stir the soul. Greeks used music as an integral part of their most important ceremonies, including marriages and funerals. This may explain why music is so closely associated with both love and death in Greek culture. Several musical instruments, such as the lyre and the double-reed flute known as an *aulos*, were either invented or popularized in ancient Greece. Music was practiced by many members of the upper classes, and it accompanied events not normally associated with music, such as sports. Some groups used music as a way to worship, drawing themselves into altered states of behavior that they interpreted as closeness with the god they worshipped.

Orpheus attempted to lead his dead wife Eurydice out of the underworld, but failed when he disobeyed an order not to look back at her until they were back among the living. PHOTO BY HULTON ARCHIVE/GETTY IMAGES.

Key Themes and Symbols

One of the main themes of the myth of Eurydice is the power of true love. Although Eurydice has died and passed on to the underworld, Orpheus refuses to let her go. He displays determination and cunning, but above all, he never falters in his unending love for his wife. Another important theme in this myth is the power of music. The lyre of Orpheus symbolizes this power. Orpheus uses it to gain entrance to the underworld, and his skill at playing music convinces Hades to let him take Eurydice back to the land of the living.

Another important theme in this myth is obedience to the gods. Eurydice dies when she flees from Aristaeus; though the gods do not directly cause her death, it is clear that her submission to the will of Apollo's son would have resulted in her remaining alive. Later, when Orpheus disobeys Hades by looking back at Eurydice before they reach the surface, he breaks his agreement with Hades, and Eurydice must return to the underworld.

Eurydice in Art, Literature, and Everyday Life

Even though the myth of Eurydice is similar to other ancient Greek tales in which someone dies at a young age and an attempt is made to bring him or her back from the underworld, it has retained a great deal of popularity through the centuries. Renaissance painters such as Peter Paul Rubens and Titian created depictions of Eurydice and Orpheus, and several operas were written about the pair during the seventeenth, eighteenth, and nineteenth centuries. The most famous of these is Jacques Offenbach's 1858 burlesque operetta *Orpheus in the Underworld*, which includes one piece known popularly as the music played during the French dance called the "Can Can."

More recently, the story of Eurydice and Orpheus was adapted for the 1959 film *Black Orpheus* by Marcel Camus. The 1997 Disney animated film *Hercules* also used elements of the myth of Eurydice and Orpheus, instead having Hercules travel to the underworld in an attempt to save his love, Megara. Both Eurydice and Orpheus also appear in *The Sandman*, a comic series written by Neil Gaiman.

Read, Write, Think, Discuss

In the myth, Eurydice dies and travels to the underworld. Orpheus later rescues her and almost succeeds in bringing her back to the land of the living. Some people who have experienced severe medical trauma claim to have visited or seen the realm of the dead before being brought back to life by doctors. These are typically known as "near-death experiences." Research the topic of near-death experiences and express your opinion on the subject. Do you think some people have actually journeyed to the **afterlife**? What evidence exists that supports this? Is there any evidence that something else might be behind these experiences?

SEE ALSO Greek Mythology; Hades; Orpheus; Underworld

F

Character

Deity

Myth

Theme

Culture

Fates, The

Character Overview

The Fates were three female goddesses who shaped people's lives. In particular, they determined how long a man or woman would live. Although a number of cultures held the notion of three goddesses who influenced human destiny, the Fates were most closely identified with **Greek mythology**. The parentage of the Fates is something of a mystery. Hesiod described them as daughters of Nyx (pronounced NIKS), the goddess of night, but he also said that they were the children of **Zeus** (pronounced ZOOS), the chief of the gods, and Themis (pronounced THEEM-is), the goddess of justice.

The Greek image of the Fates developed over time. The poet Homer, credited with composing the *Iliad* and the *Odyssey*, spoke of Fate as a single force, perhaps simply the will of the gods. Another poet, Hesiod, portrayed the Fates as three old women. They were called the Keres (pronounced KARE-ays), which means "those who cut off" or the Moirai (pronounced MOY-rye), "those who allot." They may have originated as goddesses who were present at the birth of each child to determine the course of the child's future life.

Hesiod called the Fates Clotho (pronounced KLO-thoh, "the spinner"), Lachesis (pronounced LAK-uh-sis; "the allotter"), and Atropos (pronounced AY-truh-pos; "the unavoidable"). In time, the name Clotho,

Nationality/Culture
Greek

Pronunciation
FAYTS

Alternate Names
Moirae, Parcae (Roman)

Appears In
Hesiod's *Theogony*, Ovid's *Metamorphoses*, Homer's *Iliad*

Lineage
Daughters of Zeus and Themis

The three Fates. ALINARI/ART RESOURCE, NY.

with its reference to spinning thread, became the basis for images of the three Fates as controlling the thread of each person's life. Clotho spun the thread, Lachesis measured it out, and Atropos cut it with a pair of shears to end the life span. Literary and artistic works often portray the Fates performing these tasks.

The Romans called the Fates Parcae (pronounced PAR-see), "those who bring forth the child." Their names were Nona (pronounced NOH-nuh), Decuma (pronounced DEK-yoo-muh), and Morta (pronounced MOR-tuh). Nona and Decuma were originally goddesses of childbirth, but the Romans adopted the Greek concept of the three weavers of Fate and added a third goddess to complete the triad. In addition, they sometimes referred to fate or destiny as a single goddess known as Fortuna (for-TOO-nuh).

Goddesses Three

A triad of goddesses linked with human destiny appears in various forms in mythology. In addition to the Moirai, the Greeks recognized a triad of goddesses called the Horae (pronounced HOR-ee), who were associated with the goddess Aphrodite. Their names were Eunomia (pronounced yoo-NOH-mee-uh; "order"), Dike (pronounced DYE-kee; "destiny"), and Eirene (pronounced eye-REEN-ee; "peace"). The Norse called their three Fates the Norns: Urth, "the past"; Verthandi (pronounced WURT-hand-ee), "the present"; and Skuld (pronounced SKOOLD), "the future." Sometimes the Norns were referred to as the Weird Sisters, from the Norse word *wyrd*, meaning "fate." The Celts had a triad of war goddesses, collectively known as the Morrigan (mor-REE-gan), who determined the fate of soldiers in battle. The image of a triple goddess may be linked to very ancient worship of a moon goddess in three forms: a maiden (the new moon), a mature woman (the full moon), and a crone (the old moon).

Major Myths

The Fates had power over Zeus and the gods, and many ancient authors, including the Roman poet Virgil, stressed that even the king of the gods had to accept the decisions of the Fates. Occasionally, however, fate could be changed through clever action. According to one myth, **Apollo** (uh-POL-oh) tricked the Fates into letting his friend Admetus (ad-MEE-tuhs) live beyond his assigned lifetime. Apollo got the Fates drunk, and they agreed to accept the death of a substitute in place of Admetus.

The Fates in Context

The ancient Greeks believed that human lives were ruled by destiny—the idea that a person's path in life has already been decided by the gods, and regardless of whatever action the person might take, the path will not change. Destiny can be seen as a way of explaining why things happen the way they do, despite a person's best efforts to bring about a different outcome. The counterpoint to the concept of destiny is the idea of free will, which holds that people have the power to choose their own paths in life. Whether a person's life is predetermined or under his own control has been the subject of debate for thousands of years.

Key Themes and Symbols

The threads of the loom controlled by the Fates represent the lives of all mortals, and suggest the fragile nature of a person's life. The threads also symbolize how the lives of humans are interwoven.

The Fates in Art, Literature, and Everyday Life

In the realm of art and literature, the Fates are somewhat overshadowed by the similar Norse goddesses known as the Weird Sisters. These Norse goddesses appear most notably in William Shakespeare's play *Macbeth* and Richard Wagner's opera *Twilight of the Gods*. In recent years, the Fates have appeared in numerous video games and Japanese comics. A modernized version of the Fates appeared in the 1994 Stephen King novel *Insomnia*, and the Fates also appeared in the 1997 Disney animated film *Hercules*. More recently, the Fates appeared in Rick Riordan's 2005 novel *The Lightning Thief.*

Read, Write, Think, Discuss

The ancient Greeks believed in the power of the Fates to control human destiny. Many people still believe that things happen because of "fate." Others argue that if every person left their futures up to fate, no one would ever strive to accomplish anything unless they were assured to be successful. Do you think the path of humans is largely beyond their individual control, based instead on the environment and conditions in which they live? Or do you think any person is capable of achieving any goal, regardless of their circumstances? Is it possible to subscribe to both these beliefs, to a certain degree?

Nationality/Culture
Norse

Pronunciation
FEN-reer

Alternate Names
Fenris, Vanargand

Appears In
The Eddas

Lineage
Son of Loki and Angrboda

Fenrir

Character Overview

Fenrir, a monstrous wolf, was one of three terrible children of the Norse trickster god **Loki** (pronounced LOH-kee) and the giantess Angrboda (pronounced AHNG-gur-boh-duh). Their other children—Jormungand

Wolves of Legend

Wolves feature prominently in legends from around the world. Sometimes they are seen as monsters, sometimes as nobility. Since, until recently, wolves were a very real threat to humans in Europe, there are many folktales and children's stories involving wolves, including "Little Red Riding Hood" and "The Boy Who Cried Wolf." The fear of wolves also sparked a belief in werewolves—creatures that are human at times, but under certain conditions become ferocious wolves—throughout much of Europe, especially during the Middle Ages.

In Roman mythology, however, it is a wolf who makes Roman civilization possible. The twin orphan babies Romulus and Remus were, according to legend, nursed by a she-wolf. Romulus went on to found Rome.

(pronounced YAWR-moon-gahnd), a giant serpent, and **Hel**, the goddess of the dead—were thrown out of Asgard (pronounced AHS-gahrd), the home of the gods, by **Odin** (pronounced OH-din). But Odin felt that the gods should look after Fenrir.

In time, Fenrir grew incredibly large, and only Odin's son **Tyr** (pronounced TEER) was brave enough to approach and feed him. The gods finally decided to chain the beast, but Fenrir broke the two huge chains they made to restrain him. Asked by the gods to create something that would hold Fenrir, the dwarves produced a silky ribbon called Gleipnir (pronounced GLAYP-nir). To make it, they used the sound of a cat moving, the beard of a woman, the roots of a mountain, the sinews of a bear, the breath of a fish, and the spit of a bird.

The gods took Fenrir to an isolated island and challenged him to prove that he was stronger than Gleipnir. Because the ribbon seemed so weak, Fenrir suspected it was magical. He allowed himself to be bound with it only after Tyr agreed to put his hand in Fenrir's mouth. When Fenrir found that he could not break Gleipnir, he bit off Tyr's hand. The gods put a sword in Fenrir's open mouth, with the tip of the blade against the roof, to quiet him. Saliva ran from his howling open mouth, and formed a river called Van Hope.

According to legend, Fenrir will be released just before **Ragnarok** (pronounced RAHG-nuh-rok), the final battle in which the gods of

Asgard will be killed. It is written that Fenrir will swallow Odin during the battle and then be killed by Odin's son.

Fenrir in Context

The Eurasian wolf is the most commonly found wolf in Scandinavia, though it is much rarer in western Europe. They are known for hunting strategically in packs and swallowing large amounts of prey, which they then regurgitate for others after returning to the den. This is similar to Fenrir swallowing the god Odin during Ragnarok. To the Norse, who relied on hunting for much of their food, wolves were respected hunters, feared predators, and fierce competitors for available resources. It makes sense that a giant wolf would be seen as one of the greatest enemies of the gods.

Wolves have long been viewed as a threat throughout Europe and Asia, and have been documented as the cause of many human deaths over the centuries. In areas such as England and Scotland wolves were completely eliminated through bounties and other programs initiated by royal leaders. Some Scandinavian governments still view wolves as a threat to human and livestock safety, even though wolf populations have dwindled and the animals are protected under the laws of the European Union.

Key Themes and Symbols

In **Norse mythology**, Fenrir represents savagery that ultimately cannot be controlled, even by the gods. Although they subdue Fenrir with Gleipnir, the wolf will eventually grow large enough to break his bonds and kill Odin. The wolf is widely recognized as a symbol of wild ferocity. Fenrir also represents fate, or the unfolding of events that have already been foretold. The gods attempt to prevent Fenrir's devastation by binding him, but the creature is destined to continue growing and eventually break free despite all efforts to keep him bound. Specifically, Fenrir symbolizes the fate of the Norse gods, who are destined to fall during Ragnarok.

Fenrir in Art, Literature, and Everyday Life

The image of Fenrir as a giant wolf has inspired northern European artists and writers for centuries. Fenrir has served as inspiration for many similar characters, including Fenris Ulf (also known as Maugrim) from

The monstrous wolf Fenrir bit off the hand of Tyr when the gods tricked him into being bound with magic rope.
© ROYAL LIBRARY, COPEN-HAGEN, DENMARK/THE BRIDGEMAN ART LIBRARY.

the 1950 C. S. Lewis novel *The Lion, the Witch, and the Wardrobe.* The legend of Fenrir inspired the character of Fenrir Greyback in the *Harry Potter* series by novelist J. K. Rowling.

Read, Write, Think, Discuss

K. A. Applegate's *Everworld* series, first published in 1999, tells of four high school students who follow a mysterious girl into a realm inhabited by mythological characters and creatures from all the legends of the world. In the first book in the series, *The Search for Senna*, the mythical giant wolf Fenrir breaks through to our world and kidnaps Senna for his father, Loki. This sends the rest of the group on a quest through strange and dangerous lands to find and rescue her. The *Everworld* series consists of twelve volumes, and was written by the same author as the popular *Animorphs* series.

SEE ALSO Animals in Mythology; Norse Mythology; Ragnarok; Tyr

Finn

Nationality/Culture
Irish/Celtic

Pronunciation
FIN

Alternate Names
Finn MacCumhail, Finn MacCool

Appears In
The Fenian Cycle

Lineage
Son of Cumhail

Character Overview

Finn, also known as Finn MacCumhail or Finn MacCool, is the hero of a series of Irish legends known as the Fionn (or Fenian) Cycle. Finn was the son of Cumhail, who led a band of warriors called the Fianna (pronounced FEE-uh-nuh). Members of this group were chosen for their bravery and strength and took an oath to fight for the king and defend Ireland from attack. In time, Finn became the leader of the Fianna and was the greatest warrior of all.

Finn was born with the name Deimne, but earned the nickname Finn (meaning "fair") when his hair turned white at a young age. As a boy, Finn became the pupil of a druid, a Celtic priest. The druid had been told that he would gain all the world's knowledge if he caught and ate a certain salmon. He caught the fish and instructed Finn to cook but not to eat it. While preparing the fish, Finn touched it and burned his thumb. He sucked the thumb to ease the pain and received the knowledge that was meant for the druid. Later, he found he could suck on his thumb to gain additional insight or knowledge whenever he needed it.

Finn later traveled to Tara, the court of the Irish king, Cormac MacArt. Every year a fire-breathing demon came and destroyed Tara. Finn managed to kill the demon and save the hall. As a reward, the king named Finn the leader of the Fianna. Under his leadership, the Fianna performed many amazing deeds, such as traveling to the **underworld** (land of the dead) and defeating supernatural enemies.

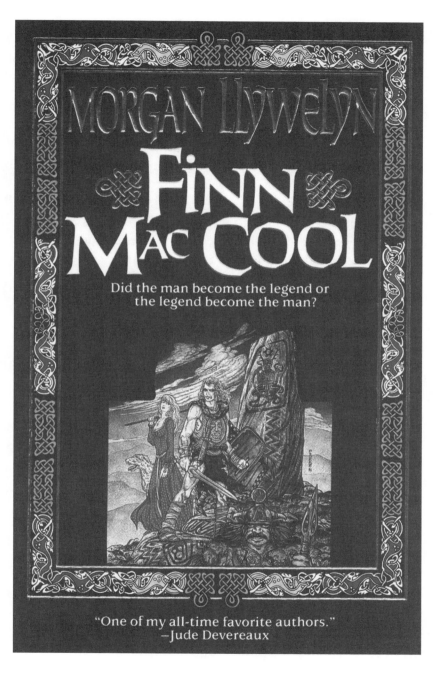

The 1994 novel **Finn Mac-Cool** *is a modern retelling of the legend of the Irish hero Finn.* FITZPATRICK, JIM, ILLUSTRATOR. FROM A COVER OF *FINN MACCOOL* BY MORGAN LLYWELYN. TOR BOOKS, 1995. REPRODUCED BY PERMISSION.

Always a select group, the Fianna became even more exclusive when Finn invented tests of strength and courage for all those who wanted to join.

Several legends concern Finn's death. However, some stories say he is not dead at all, but sleeping in a cave or a hollow tree, and that he will awaken when Ireland once again needs his help.

Finn in Context

For the Irish people, an important element of the myth of Finn was the idea of the dormant or sleeping leader. This idea suggested that Finn was immortal, or able to live forever, which only increased his status as a hero. It also provided comfort that the Irish would have a defender to lead them in a future time of need.

Although Ireland is now a prosperous country, it was marked by grinding poverty for centuries. The Irish were also repressed, often brutally, by the British government, which controlled all of Ireland starting in the 1200s. The Irish rose up against the British many times, and at last began to achieve some success in the late nineteenth and early twentieth centuries. In the nineteenth century, an organization named the Fenian Brotherhood was created in the United States. Named after the Fianna, the organization aimed to support Irish citizens in their efforts to re-establish Ireland as an independent republic free of England's control. Legendary characters like Finn served as a unifying force for the Irish culture. The Irish were able to achieve independence for most of Ireland by 1937.

Key Themes and Symbols

In **Celtic mythology**, Finn represents the courage and cleverness of the Irish people. His white hair symbolizes wisdom, which he achieved at a very young age. This knowledge is also symbolized by the salmon he cooks, of which he accidentally consumes a small portion. In Celtic mythology, fish, and salmon in particular, are associated with knowledge. Finn may also represent eternal vigilance or guardianship, always ready when needed to protect Ireland.

Finn in Art, Literature, and Everyday Life

Finn appears in several literary works, especially those of Irish and Scottish writers. He appears throughout James Joyce's 1939 novel *Finnegan's Wake*, and is the subject of James MacPherson's 1761 epic poem *Fingal,* which the author claimed was based on an existing Scottish work (though many scholars doubt this). In 1994, historical fantasy author Morgan Llewellyn (also spelled Llywelyn) created a retelling of the stories of the Fenian Cycle in her novel *Finn MacCool.*

Read, Write, Think, Discuss

Finn is viewed by many Irish citizens as a mythical protector of Ireland. Modern comic book superheroes are often viewed the same way by the fictional cities they inhabit. Superman, for example, is viewed by the residents of Metropolis as their guardian against crime. Can you think of other examples? What are the qualities that these protectors have in common?

SEE ALSO Celtic Mythology

Finnish Mythology

Finnish Mythology in Context

Finnish mythology, like that of many other cultures, tells the stories of gods and legendary **heroes**. Most of the myths date from pre-Christian times and were passed from generation to generation by storytellers. A work called the *Kalevala* (pronounced kah-luh-VAH-luh), which the Finnish people consider their national epic, contains many of the legends. Compiled by Finnish scholar Elias Lönnrot in the early 1800s, the *Kalevala* is based on traditional poems and songs that Lönnrot collected over a long period of time.

The myths of the *Kalevala* reflect several unique aspects of Finnish culture. First, they suggest a long-standing conflict with a neighboring cultural group, referred to in the epic as Pohjola. Second, the tales of the *Kalevala* focus on characters who exhibit many human characteristics, as opposed to just the heroic ideals of so many other mythologies. The stories also emphasize violence and the search for love. This seems to suggest a lack of cultural unity among early groups, with the stories of the *Kalevala* perhaps documenting real conflicts between groups and even building on actual events of the ancient past. The doomed search for love may reflect the uneasy relationship between cultural groups, with individuals attempting to marry outside their group but finding themselves blocked by conflicts between groups.

Core Deities and Characters

The word *Kalevala*, which means "land of the descendants of Kaleva," is an imaginary region associated with Finland. The epic's fifty poems or songs—also known as cantos or runes—recount the stories of various legendary heroes and of gods and goddesses and describe mythical events such as the creation of the world.

Vainamoinen (pronounced vye-nuh-MOY-nen), one of the heroes in the *Kalevala*, is a wise old seer who can see the future and work magic through the songs that he sings. His mother is Ilmatar (pronounced EEL-mah-tar), the virgin spirit of air, who brought about creation. Another great hero of the epic, Lemminkainen (pronounced LEM-in-kye-nen), appears as a handsome, carefree, and romantic adventurer.

Vainamoinen and Lemminkainen have certain experiences and goals in common. In their adventures, both men meet Louhi (pronounced LOH-hee), the evil mistress of Pohjola (the Northland), and both of them seek to wed Louhi's daughter, the beautiful Maiden of Pohjola. A third suitor for the maiden's hand, Ilmarinen (EEL-mah-ree-nen), is a blacksmith who constructs a *sampo*, a mysterious object like a mill that can produce prosperity for its owner.

A number of other figures become involved with these leading characters. Kuura, another hero, joins Lemminkainen on his journey to Pohjola. Joukahainen (pronounced YOH-kuh-hye-nen), an evil youth, challenges Vainamoinen to a singing contest. His sister Aino (pronounced EYE-noh), who is offered in marriage to Vainamoinen, drowns herself rather than wed the aged hero. Another character, Kullervo (pronounced KOO-ler-vaw), commits suicide after unknowingly raping his own sister. Marjatta (pronounced MAR-yah-tah), the last major character introduced in the *Kalevala*, is a virgin who gives birth to a king.

Major Myths

The *Kalevala* begins with the story of Ilmatar, who descends from the heavens to the sea, where she is tossed about for seven hundred years. During that time, a seabird lays eggs on her knee. When Ilmatar moves, the eggs break, and the pieces form the physical world and the **sun** and the moon. She then has a son, Vainamoinen, who begins life as a wise old man.

Soon after Vainamoinen's birth, the evil Joukahainen challenges him to a singing contest after hearing that the hero is noted for his magic songs. Vainamoinen accepts the challenge and wins the contest, causing Joukahainen to sink into a swamp. Fearing that he will drown, Joukahainen offers Vainamoinen his sister Aino in exchange for his rescue.

Vainamoinen plans to marry Aino, and her parents encourage the match. But she refuses to wed the old man. When her mother tries to persuade her to change her mind, Aino goes to the sea and drowns herself. Vainamoinen follows the girl and finds her in the form of a fish. He catches the fish, but she slips back into the water and escapes.

Unhappy that he has lost Aino, Vainamoinen sets off for Pohjola, the Northland, in search of another wife. Along the way Joukahainen, still bitter over losing the singing contest, shoots at the hero but only hits his horse. Vainamoinen falls into the sea and escapes. He finally arrives at Pohjola, where the evil Louhi promises him her daughter, the Maiden of Pohjola, if he will build a magic *sampo* for her. Unable to do this by himself, Vainamoinen seeks help from Ilmarinen, the blacksmith. However, after Ilmarinen completes the *sampo*, Louhi gives her daughter to him instead of to Vainamoinen.

The Adventures of Lemminkainen The next section of the *Kalevala* recounts the adventures of the hero Lemminkainen, who marries Kyllikki (pronounced KYOO-luh-kee), a woman from the island of Saari. But she is unfaithful to him, and he leaves her and goes to Pohjola to find a new wife. When he reaches his destination, Louhi promises him her daughter if he can complete several tasks. While Lemminkainen is working on the last task, he is killed by a blind cattle herder whom he has insulted. The herder

This painting, **The Curse of Kullervo***, by Akseli Gallén-Kallela, shows the Finnish character Kullervo reacting in anger to the discovery that the Maiden of Pohjola put a stone in his bread.* © BIBLIOTHEQUE DES ARTS DECORATIFS, PARIS, FRANCE/ARCHIVES CHARMET/THE BRIDGEMAN ART LIBRARY.

Gods and Spirits

Finnish mythology includes many gods and spirits not mentioned in the *Kalevala*. One of the most important gods was Ukko, the god of thunder, whose rainfall helped nourish crops. The god of the forest was Tapio (pronounced TAH-pee-oh), sometimes depicted as a fierce creature, part human and part tree. Many spirits with very changeable natures also lived in the forest. Hunters used to make offerings to these spirits and avoided making loud noises so as not to anger them.

cuts the hero's body into many pieces, but Lemminkainen's mother manages to collect the pieces and restore him to life with magic spells.

Meanwhile, Louhi gives her daughter to Ilmarinen as a bride. Angry at not being invited to the wedding, Lemminkainen storms Louhi's castle, kills her husband, and then returns home. Discovering that his house has been burned by raiders from Pohjola, Lemminkainen returns there with his companion Kuura. They try to destroy the land but are defeated.

The Tragedy of Kullervo The *Kalevala* next tells the tragic tale of Kullervo, who is sent by his family to the home of Ilmarinen and the Maiden of Pohjola. The Maiden takes a strong dislike to the youth, and one day she puts a stone in his bread. In revenge, Kullervo kills the Maiden and flees. After wandering for some time, he finds his family and works for them. On his way home one day, he meets a woman and rapes her. Later he finds out that the woman is his sister. When the sister discovers that she has been raped by her own brother, she throws herself into a river and drowns. Kullervo also kills himself because of what he has done.

Battle for the *Sampo* In the next section of the epic, the three heroes—Vainamoinen, Ilmarinen, and Lemminkainen—travel together to Pohjola to steal the magic *sampo*, which has brought great riches to the evil Louhi. They succeed in stealing the mysterious object, but Louhi and her forces pursue them. A great battle takes place, during which the *sampo* is lost in the sea. Furious at the loss, Louhi tries to destroy Vainamoinen and his land. In the end, however, Vainamoinen emerges victorious.

Major Characters of the *Kalevala*

Aino: Joukahainen's sister, drowns herself after being offered in marriage to Vainamoinen.

Ilmarinen: blacksmith, makes a magical object called a *sampo* that brings prosperity to its owner.

Ilmatar: virgin spirit of the air and creator goddess.

Joukahainen: evil youth, challenges Vainamoinen to a singing contest.

Kuura: hero, joins Lemminkainen on his journey to Pohjola.

Lemminkainen: hero, handsome adventurer.

Louhi: evil woman and mother of the Maiden of Pohjola.

Maiden of Pohjola: beautiful young woman sought in marriage by Ilmarinen, Lemminkainen, and Vainamoinen.

Vainamoinen: hero, wise old seer who sings magical songs.

A Virgin Birth The last story of the *Kalevala* deals with the virgin Marjatta and the birth of her son. As the time approaches for the boy to be baptized, Vainamoinen arrives to investigate. He decides that the boy must be put to death, but the boy scolds him severely. Later the boy is baptized and becomes king. An angry Vainamoinen leaves the land. Most of the characters and tales in the *Kalevala* reflect pre-Christian ideas, but the story of Marjatta and of Vainamoinen's flight suggests a transition from non-Christian to Christian beliefs since it is similar to the virgin birth of Jesus.

Key Themes and Symbols

One recurring theme in the *Kalevala* is revenge. Joukahainen tries to kill Vainamoinen after losing a singing contest against him. Kullervo kills the Maiden of Pohjola after she puts a stone in his bread. Lemminkainen is killed as an act of revenge by a man he insulted, though he is later brought back to life. Later, Lemminkainen kills Louhi's husband after she fails to invite him to her daughter's wedding. Lemminkainen also seeks revenge against raiders from Pohjola after they burn down his house.

Another recurring theme in the *Kalevala* is unfortunate romantic entanglement. Vainamoinen wishes to marry Aino, but she refuses because he appears to be an old man; she decides to drown herself rather than marry him. Lemminkainen's first wife, Kyllikki, is unfaithful to him so he leaves her. Three men—Vainamoinen, Ilmarinen, and Lemminkainen—all seek the hand of Louhi's daughter, and Louhi promises her to all of them. In the end, Ilmarinen claims her. And in perhaps the darkest tale, Kullervo rapes a woman who he later discovers is his own sister. Both end up committing suicide.

Finnish Mythology in Art, Literature, and Everyday Life

The *Kalevala* helped create a national identity for the Finnish people by presenting a common mythology filled with familiar heroes and gods. The work also inspired many literary and artistic works by Finns and others.

Among the most famous individuals to make use of the *Kalevala* was Finnish composer Jean Sibelius, who wrote a number of symphonies and other musical works based on its characters and tales. Another Finnish composer, Robert Kajanus, also created several pieces of music inspired by the *Kalevala*, and Finnish artist Akseli Gallén-Kallela painted many works based on its stories. The American poet Henry Wadsworth Longfellow used the rhythmic patterns of the *Kalevala* as the basis for his poem *The Song of Hiawatha*. Some of the scenes and events in the poem are modeled after the Finnish work as well.

Read, Write, Think, Discuss

The Songs of Power: A Finnish Tale of Magic, Retold from the Kalevala by Aaron Shepard (2007) offers a retelling of the *Kalevala* aimed at young readers. Shepard is the author of several books based on mythological tales from around the world.

Fire

Theme Overview

In ancient times, people considered fire one of the basic elements of the universe, along with water, air, and earth. Fire can be a friendly, comforting thing, a source of heat and light, as anyone who has ever sat by a campfire in the dark of night knows. Yet fire can also be dangerous and deadly, racing and leaping like a living thing to consume all in its path. In mythology, fire appears both as a creative, cleansing force and as a destructive, punishing one, although positive aspects of fire generally outweigh negative ones.

Major Myths

Agni (pronounced AG-nee), the god of fire in Hindu mythology, represents the essential energy of life in the universe. He consumes things, but only so that other things can live. Fiery horses pull Agni's chariot, and he carries a flaming spear. Agni created the **sun** and the stars, and his powers are great. He can make worshippers immortal, or able to live forever, and can purify the souls of the dead from sin. One ancient myth about Agni says that he consumed so many offerings from his worshippers that he was tired. To regain his strength, he had to burn an entire forest with all its inhabitants.

Chinese mythology includes stories of Hui Lu (pronounced hwee-LOO), a magician and fire god who kept one hundred firebirds in a gourd. By setting them loose, he could start a fire across the whole country. There was also a hierarchy—or an ordered ranking—of gods in charge of fire. At its head was Lo Hsüan (pronounced loh-SWAHN), whose cloak, hair, and beard were red. Flames spurted from his horse's nostrils. He was not unconquerable, however. Once when he attacked a city with swords of fire, a princess appeared in the sky and quenched his flames with her cloak of mist and dew.

The bringers of fire are legendary **heroes** in many traditions. **Prometheus** (pronounced pruh-MEE-thee-uhs) of **Greek mythology**, one of the most famous fire-bringers, stole fire from the gods and gave it to humans. The gods punished him severely for his crime. Similar figures appear in the tales of other cultures.

Some American Indian tribes believed that long ago some evil being hid fire so that people could not benefit from it. A hero had to recover it and make it available to human beings. In many versions of the story, Coyote steals fire for people, but sometimes a wolf, woodpecker, or other animal does so. According to the Navajo, Coyote tricked two monsters that guarded the flames on Fire Mountain. Then he lit a bundle of sticks tied to his tail and ran down the mountain to deliver the fire to his people.

African traditions also say that animals gave fire to humans. According to the myths of the San of South Africa, Ostrich guarded fire under his wing until a praying mantis stole it. Mantis tricked Ostrich into spreading his wings and made off with the fire. The fire destroyed Mantis, but from the ashes came two new Mantises.

Indians of the Amazon River basin in Brazil say that a jaguar rescued a boy and took him to its cave. There the boy watched the jaguar cooking food over a fire. The boy stole a hot coal from the fire and took it to his people, who then learned to cook.

Legends in the Caroline Islands of the Pacific link fire to Olofat, a mythical trickster hero who was the son of the sky god and a mortal woman. As a youth, Olofat forced his way into **heaven** to see his father. Later Olofat gave fire to human beings by allowing a bird to fly down to earth with fire in its beak. The Admiralty Islanders of the Pacific Ocean have a myth in which a snake asks his human children to cook some fish. The children simply heat the fish in the sun and eat it raw, so the snake gives them fire and teaches them to use it to cook their food.

A myth from Assam, in northern India, says that after losing a battle with Water, Fire hid in a bamboo stalk. Grasshopper saw it and told Monkey, who figured out how to use Fire. But a man saw Monkey and decided that he should have Fire, so he stole it from Monkey. Like many stories, this myth portrays ownership of fire as a human right. Even partial control over such a powerful force of nature is one of the things that gives human society its identity.

Fire in Context

People in all parts of the world tell myths and legends about fire. Numerous stories explain how people first acquired fire, either through their own daring or as a gift from an animal, god, or hero. The ability to make and control fire—which is necessary for cooking, making pottery and glass, and metalworking—sets people apart from other living things.

Because fire warms and gives off light like the sun, it often represents the sun or a sun god in mythology. In some tales, it is linked with the idea of the hearth, the center of a household. Fire can also be a symbol of new life, as in the case of the **phoenix** (pronounced FEE-niks), the mythical bird that is periodically destroyed by flames to rise reborn from its own ashes.

Fire's energy is not always a good thing. Flames can bring punishment and suffering as in the Christian image of **hell** as a place

Women known as "Vestal Virgins" attended to the sacred fire of Vesta, the Roman goddess of the hearth.
© MUSEE DES BEAUX-ARTS, LILLE, FRANCE/LAUROS/ GIRAUDON/THE BRIDGEMAN ART LIBRARY.

of fiery torment. Some myths about the end of the world predict that the world will end in fire—but it may be a purifying, cleansing fire that will allow the birth of a fresh new world.

Because fire can be treacherous and destructive, mythical figures associated with it may be **tricksters**, not always to be trusted. The Norse god **Loki**'s (pronounced LOH-kee) shifty and malicious character may have been based on the characteristics of a forest fire. Another deity, or god, associated with fire is the Greek **Hephaestus** (pronounced hi-FES-tuhs), god of metalworking, who is usually portrayed as deformed and sullen.

Fighting Sorcery with Fire

In Europe and America, individuals accused of being witches were once burned at the stake. Many cultures have held the belief that fire destroys sorcery, or black magic. The Assyrians of ancient Mesopotamia called upon fire to undo the effects of evil witchcraft aimed at them. They used these words:

> *Boil, boil, burn, burn! . . . As this goat's skin is torn asunder and cast into the fire, and as the blaze devours it . . . may the curse, the spell, the pain, the torment, the sickness, the sin, the misdeed, the crime, the suffering, that oppress my body, be torn asunder like this goat's skin! May the blaze consume them today.*

In many cultures, people practice rituals or ceremonies related to fire. These rituals are often based on myths and legends about fire or fire gods. In ancient Rome, a sacred flame associated with the goddess Vesta (pronounced VESS-tuh) represented national well-being. Women called the Vestal Virgins had the holy duty of keeping that flame alive. The Aztecs of ancient Mexico believed that the fire god Huehueteotl (pronounced hway-hway-tay-OH-tul) kept earth and heaven in place. At the end of each cycle of 52 years, they extinguished all fires, and Huehueteotl's priests lit a new flame for the people to use. In northern Europe, which has long, dark, cold winters, fire was especially honored. Pre-Christian fire festivals such as lighting bonfires on May 1 have continued into modern times in European communities.

Many cultures have practiced cremation, the burning of the dead. In cremation, fire represents purification, a clean and wholesome end to earthly life. The Pima people of the southwestern United States say that fire appeared in the world to solve the problem of how people should dispose of the dead.

Fire in Art, Literature, and Everyday Life

Fire is a common element in ancient mythical art and literature. It is frequently associated with **dragons** and the **underworld**. Although fire in modern times may not be viewed with as much supernatural wonder as it once was, there are some contemporary examples of fire as a mythological force. In the 1967 animated Disney adaptation of *The Jungle Book*, King Louie the orangutan abducts the human boy Mowgli and tries to get the boy to teach him the secret of how to make fire.

Russian composer Igor Stravinsky composed the score for a 1910 ballet called *Firebird*, which was based on a Russian legend about a magical bird of flame. Another "firebird"—a phoenix—appears as the wizard Albus Dumbledore's companion in the Harry Potter novels written by J. K. Rowling. Prometheus, the fire-stealer, has fascinated artists and writers for centuries. Romantic poets Johann von Goethe, Lord Byron, and Percy Shelley all wrote poems about him in which Prometheus is unrepentant for his action. Prometheus appears as the subject of numerous paintings and recently became the inspiration for a groundbreaking Web-based artwork called *Prometheus Bound* by Tim Rollins and the Kids of Survival (http://www.diacenter.org/kos/home.html). The Web site contains readings, modern translations, and meditations on the myth of Prometheus.

Read, Write, Think, Discuss

Some ancient cultures believed that cremating the dead would purify their souls so they could pass on to the next world. Other cultures such as the ancient Egyptians believed that a dead person needed his or her body preserved so that it could transport the soul to the **afterlife**. In many modern cultures, burial is the most common way to handle the dead. What do you think this says about modern beliefs about the afterlife? Do modern cultures show a preference for preserving or purifying the dead? How?

SEE ALSO Floods; Hell; Hephaestus; Loki; Phoenix; Prometheus

Firebird

Myth Overview

The firebird is a magical bird with golden feathers and crystal eyes that appears in many Russian folk stories. Several of the tales involve young Prince Ivan, son of the tsar, or leader of Russia.

Nationality/Culture
Russian

Alternate Names
Zhar-ptitsa (Russian)

Appears In
Russian folktales

In one story, the firebird stole magical golden apples from the tsar's garden. The tsar promised his kingdom to the son who could catch the firebird. The youngest son, Ivan, found a magic gray wolf, which helped him capture the bird. While Ivan and the wolf were on their journey, they met a beautiful princess and a horse with a golden mane. When Ivan's two jealous brothers saw them, they killed Ivan and took the horse and princess for themselves. The wolf found Ivan and brought him back to life just in time to stop Ivan's older brother from marrying the princess. When their father heard the full story, he imprisoned his two evil sons and allowed Ivan to marry the princess.

In another tale, Ivan captured the firebird in a castle garden but set it free in exchange for a magic feather from the firebird. Thirteen princesses came out of the castle and told Ivan that the owner was an evil magician who turned people into stone. But Ivan, who fell in love with one of the princesses, ignored the warning and decided to face the magician and his demons. The magic feather protected Ivan, and the firebird cast a spell on the demons. When the bird showed the prince an egg that contained the magician's soul, Ivan broke the egg, killing the magician and freeing the princesses.

The Firebird in Context

Although the main character of many tales about the firebird is a young prince, the tales themselves also offer an appealing message to more common people. In some tales, the firebird steals from the rich—as with the golden apples from the tsar's garden—and gives those riches to the peasants. The firebird is also believed to drop pearls from its beak when passing over peasant villages, to give the poor something to trade for food and other necessities. In this way, the firebird is a folk hero for the Russian people.

Key Themes and Symbols

In Russian folklore, the firebird represents a treasure that is rare and difficult to possess. This is emphasized by descriptions of the bird, which often refer to its golden or glowing feathers and eyes that resemble jewels. The fact that just one of its feathers contains magic suggests the great power of the bird. The color gold is used repeatedly in the tales of the firebird to indicate not only material riches, but also magical power.

The Firebird in Art, Literature, and Everyday Life

Folktales about the firebird inspired Russian composer Igor Stravinsky to write a ballet called *The Firebird* in 1910. The animated Disney film *Fantasia 2000* used a suite of Stravinsky's music from *The Firebird* as the inspiration and score for its final segment. "Firebird" has also been used as the name of a car created by Pontiac, a Marvel Comics superheroine, and a line of electric guitars made by Gibson.

Read, Write, Think, Discuss

In Russian mythology, the firebird is a one-of-a-kind creature that is rarely seen. In recent times, some birds have been discovered to be nearly extinct, often because humans have destroyed their natural habitats. Do you think humans should be required to protect animal species that exist only in small numbers, or do you think extinction should be allowed to happen as a natural part of the animal world? Does your opinion depend upon whether or not humans helped contribute to the disappearance of the species?

SEE ALSO Animals in Mythology

First Man and First Woman

Character Overview

In the mythology of the Navajo of North America, First Man and First Woman—known as Altsé hastiin and Altsé asdzáá, respectively—were beings who prepared the world for the creation of people. Created when the winds blew life into two special ears of **corn**, the couple led the creatures that would become the Navajo on a journey from a series of lower worlds up to the surface of the earth. In some stories, First Man and First Woman are joined by two other original leaders: First Boy and First Girl.

In each of the lower worlds, the followers of First Man and First Woman discovered different resources. The couple taught their followers how to survive in the unfamiliar surroundings and urged them to learn new skills, such as planting beans and corn for food. The two helped

Nationality/Culture
American Indian/Navajo

Alternate Names
Altsé hastiin and Altsé asdzáá

Appears In
Navajo creation myths

Lineage
Created by the Holy People

their people overcome various crises, including a great flood that surged over the land in powerful waves. They also had to deal with the troublesome Coyote, who quarreled and played many tricks on the people.

In one of the lower worlds, First Man and First Woman had a bitter dispute about whether men and women need each other to live. As a result of their dispute, First Man led all of the men away from the women for four years. Following this period of separation, some of the young women gave birth to terrible monsters that preyed on the people. Eventually, the men and women realized that they needed each other, and they agreed to live together again.

First Man and First Woman also raised the Navajo deity, or god, known as **Changing Woman** (Asdzáá nádleehé), whom they found as a child. They gave Changing Woman the medicine bundle of creation, a bag or collection of sacred objects that became the source of her power. Changing Woman and her sister, White Shell Woman (Yolgai asdzáá), gave birth to **twins** who became warriors and killed the monsters that threatened their people.

First Man and First Woman in Context

Corn was one of the most important sources of food for the Navajo people. The fact that First Man and First Woman are created from ears of corn illustrates the importance of corn in the Navajo diet. Similarly, the fact that the first Navajo people were brought forth from lower worlds reflects the importance of the earth and nature in Navajo life. In the myth, First Man leads the men away to live on their own for four years. This reflects traditional Navajo beliefs about the duties of men as being separate from the duties of women.

Key Themes and Symbols

First Man and First Woman represent fatherhood and motherhood, raising the Navajo people into their current human form. The two figures also represent both creation and destruction in Navajo myth, since the Navajo believed that both must exist together to maintain a balance in the world. The journey of the Navajo people from deep within the earth can be seen as a progression from the non-living world to the living world, or as a parallel to development from a seed, like a plant that eventually sprouts above the ground.

First Man and First Woman in Art, Literature, and Everyday Life

First Man and First Woman are depicted in traditional Navajo art forms, including rugs and sand painting. Spider Rock, a unique formation within the Canyon de Chelly National Monument, is said to be the location where First Man and First Woman learned the art of weaving from **Spider Woman**.

Read, Write, Think, Discuss

First Man and First Woman reflect the Navajo belief that people should live in balance with the natural world. This contrasts with the traditional Western view that nature is a resource meant to be controlled and adapted to human needs. What do you think are the consequences of each of these views? What are the benefits of each? What are the shortcomings?

SEE ALSO Changing Woman; Corn; Creation Stories; Floods; Native American Mythology

Floods

Theme Overview

Floods are among the most powerful and devastating of natural events. Long after the water has gone, people remember and talk about the loss and destruction. Sometimes, the scale of devastation is great enough to convince people that the flooding is the work of supernatural beings.

It is no surprise that flood myths occur in cultures around the world. One of the most common tells of a great flood that occurred in the distant past. The biblical story of **Noah** (pronounced NOH-uh) and the ark (a boat) he built to save certain people and animals from the flood is just one version of a much older myth from Mesopotamia. Similar stories appear wherever people have experienced floods.

Major Myths

Although the details of the stories differ, flood myths from around the world have many similarities. The themes of punishment, survival, and rebirth or renewal occur frequently.

Ancient Near East The basic flood myth of the ancient Near East, in which the flood was sent as a divine punishment, originated among the Sumerian cities in southern Mesopotamia. Over a period of several thousand years, the Babylonians, the Hebrews, and other civilizations developed their own versions.

The Sumerian myth tells how the human race, which the gods had created to do their work, became so numerous and noisy that the god Enlil (pronounced EN-lil) sent a flood to destroy it. However, another god, Enki (pronounced EN-kee), wanted to save King Ziusudra (pronounced zee-oo-SOO-druh). Forbidden by Enlil to warn the king, Enki spoke to the king's reed house. The king overheard the warning, built a boat, and saved his family and a collection of animals.

The Babylonian version of the flood myth appears in the *Epic of Gilgamesh*. In this account, the survivor is a man called Utnapishtim (pronounced oot-nuh-PISH-tim). Warned of the flood by a dream in which he heard a god whispering to his reed house, Utnapishtim built a boat, took aboard his family and a selection of craftspeople and animals, and rode out a terrible storm that raged for six days and six nights. Finally the boat landed on a mountaintop, the only land above the flood. Utnapishtim and his wife became immortal, or able to live forever, as a reward for following the advice of the god in the dream.

The Hebrew version of the story, told in the book of Genesis in the Bible, places greater emphasis on the sinfulness of humankind. The flood was not a cruel whim or mistake of the gods but a deliberate punishment. Like Utnapishtim, Noah was a good man who received a warning and instructions to build a boat. He and his family, and two of every sort of living thing, survived the flood and landed upon the peak of Mount Ararat.

Egypt The Egyptian flood myth begins with the **sun** god **Ra** (pronounced RAH), who feared that people were going to overthrow him. He sent the goddess **Hathor** (pronounced HATH-or), who was his eye, to punish the people. But she killed so many that their blood, flowing into the Nile River and the ocean, caused a flood. Hathor greedily drank the bloody water. Feeling that things had gone too far, Ra ordered slaves to make a lake of beer, dyed red to look like blood. Hathor drank the beer, became very drunk, and failed to finish the task of wiping out humanity. The survivors of her bloodbath started the human race anew.

Ancient Greece The Greek flood myth says that **Zeus** (pronounced ZOOS), father of the gods, sent a mighty inundation to destroy the human race. Some versions say that Zeus was angry at the Titan **Prometheus** (pronounced pruh-MEE-thee-uhs) for stealing **fire** from the gods and giving it to people. Others say that the flood was punishment for human sinfulness. Prometheus warned his son Deucalion (pronounced doo-KAY-lee-uhn) to escape the flood by building a boat. Deucalion and his wife survived, and when the flood waters retreated, they were the only humans left on earth. The couple began the race of people who inhabit the world today. The story of the flood, along with many other Greek myths, appears in the *Metamorphoses* by the Roman poet Ovid.

China For thousands of years, the Chinese people have suffered from the flooding of the two great rivers that flow through their land, the Chang Jiang (Yangtze) and the Huang He (Yellow) Rivers. Taming the rivers was one of the chief goals of early Chinese civilization. The story of Yu, one of several Chinese flood myths, celebrates a victory in the long struggle against floods.

In the myth, a man named Gun tried for nine years to dam the destructive waters that covered the land. Because he failed, the supreme god executed him. Gun's son, Yu, took up the task of taming the waters. Instead of building a dam, he decided to drain away the floodwaters through channels. A winged dragon flew in front of him, marking with his tail where Yu should dig the channels. Yu worked for many years, too busy even to see his family. In the end, however, he tamed the rivers, making the land along them suitable for farming. As his reward, Yu became emperor of China.

The Yao people of southern China have a myth that tells how the thunder god caused a great flood. A man captured the god to stop the rains, but the god convinced the man's son and daughter to set him free, and the flooding resumed. The man built a boat and floated to

heaven to ask the other gods to help. They were too helpful. The water god drained the flood away so rapidly that the boat crashed to earth, killing the man. His children, meanwhile, were the only survivors of the flood. They floated on the water in a large gourd that grew from a tooth the thunder god had given them. They became the parents of a new human race.

India The flood legend of India begins with a creator god named **Manu** (pronounced MAN-oo) washing himself with water from a jar. A fish in the jar asked for Manu's protection and promised to save him from a great flood that would occur in the future. Manu raised the fish until it was one of the largest fish in the world, and then he released it into the sea. The fish told Manu what year the flood would come and advised him to build a ship. Manu built the ship, and when the flood came, the fish towed it to a mountaintop. Manu alone survived the flood. The fish is generally identified as one form of the god **Vishnu** (VISH-noo).

North and Central America In many American Indian myths, floods occur as punishment for human misdeeds. The Chiricahua Apache maintain that the Great Spirit sent a flood to drown the whole earth because people did not worship him. According to the Navajo, a series of floods forced the people to emerge from deep in the earth through several higher worlds. The final flood was caused by Water Monster, who became angry when Coyote stole his child. This flood, which drove the people to the surface of the present world, ended when Coyote returned the Water Monster's baby. The Cheyenne say that the gods use floodwaters to control people's movements.

Floods also have positive powers. In myths of the Arikara and Caddo people, floods wipe out evil **giants** and make the world safe for humans. Several Indian mythologies in Mexico and the American West tell of cycles of destruction in which one whole world creation was destroyed by flood, while others ended in fire, ice, wind, or other disasters. The Aztecs believed that the first age of creation ended in a flood. In the Mayan creation story, a flood washed away the wooden people made by the gods in an early attempt to create human beings.

Australia Several groups among the Aborigines, the native people of Australia, believe that a vast flood swept away a previous society. Perhaps

The Lost Continent of Atlantis

The ancient Greek philosopher Plato mentioned in his writings a highly advanced civilization that existed around 9000 BCE that was swallowed by the sea in one disastrous day of earthquakes and flooding: it was called Atlantis. Whether or not Atlantis ever actually existed has been the subject of debate ever since, as geographers, adventurers, and historians through the centuries have proposed different possible locations of the lost civilization and different theories about how it met its end. Many cultures have similar "lost civilization" legends that describe privileged, wise people who are suddenly destroyed—often by a flood.

these myths grew out of conditions at the end of the last Ice Age, when sea levels rose, and coastal regions flooded.

One group of Aborigines says that their ancestral **heroes**, the Wandjina (pronounced wand-JIN-uh), caused the flood and then re-created society in its present form. Another version of the myth tells that a huge half-human snake called Yurlunggur (pronounced YUR-lun-gur) brought on the flood to punish two sisters for sexual misbehavior, that is, for breaking tribal rules concerning proper partners. Yurlunggur swallowed the sisters, but after the floodwaters withdrew, he spat them out and allowed them to start a new society.

Floods in Context

Some scholars believe that memories of real disasters, such as the violent and unpredictable floods that occurred along Mesopotamia's Tigris and Euphrates Rivers, underlie mythological accounts of catastrophic rains and floods. These stories give meaning and purpose to events in the natural world. In myths, floods become part of a cycle of destruction and rebirth.

Mythological floods are not local. They take place on a grand scale, generally covering the whole world. Though the direct cause of the rising waters may be heavy rainfall, gods or other supernatural beings are responsible. Often the flood is sent as punishment for the wrongdoings of humankind.

In some traditions, a flood reproduces the original mythological conditions of creation—the formless, empty expanse out of which the world was created. The flood not only destroys the old world but also sets the stage for a brand new one. In myths in which the flood was sent to punish people for their sins, the new world that follows the flood is purified. The religious ritual of baptism reenacts the flood myth on an individual level. The baptismal water is believed to wash away sins, allowing people to be reborn in a purified state. In India, Hindus bathe in the sacred Ganges River to purify themselves.

According to many myths about great floods, a few virtuous individuals survive the deluge, perhaps with the help or advice of a friendly deity (god). Those survivors repopulate the world, becoming the parents of the present human race. In this way, flood myths are often myths of human origins as well.

Floods in Art, Literature, and Everyday Life

Of all the floods in mythology, the flood described in the Bible has inspired more artists than any other. Images of Noah and the biblical deluge can be found throughout European and American art, with famous examples by Michelangelo, Gustave Doré, Jacopo Bassano, and Edward Hicks. Mythological floods have even appeared on film; the Disney animated film *Fantasia 2000* contains a sequence re-telling the myth of Noah with Donald Duck filling the role, while the 2007 comedy *Evan Almighty* casts Steve Carell as a modern-day version of Noah.

Read, Write, Think, Discuss

When Hurricane Katrina struck the United States Gulf Coast on August 29, 2005, it caused massive flooding. Hundreds were killed as the world watched in helpless horror. Soon after, dozens of religious and political leaders claimed the disaster was proof that God was punishing the United States. Some pointed the finger at the "wickedness" of the city of New Orleans, which was particularly hard-hit. Others said American policy in the Middle East had caused the divine punishment. What do you think of these ideas? Why do some people see natural disasters as a sort of divine punishment?

SEE ALSO Creation Stories; Gilgamesh; Manu; Noah

Flowers in Mythology

Theme Overview

From new life to death, from purity to passion, flowers have had many meanings in myths and legends. Swelling from tender bud to full bloom, flowers are associated with youth, beauty, and pleasure. But as they wilt and die, flowers represent fragility and the swift passage from life into death. Specific flowers such as roses and lilies have assumed symbolic significance in mythology.

Major Myths

Many flowers from around the world appear in mythology. The anemone, carnation, hyacinth, lily, lotus, narcissus, poppy, rose, sunflower, and violet are among those that are associated with stories or customs from various cultures.

Anemone Greek mythology linked the red anemone, sometimes called the windflower, to the death of **Adonis** (pronounced uh-DON-is). This handsome young man was loved by both **Persephone** (pronounced per-SEF-uh-nee), queen of the **underworld** (land of the dead), and **Aphrodite** (pronounced af-ro-DYE-tee), goddess of love. Adonis enjoyed hunting, and one day when he was out hunting alone, he wounded a fierce boar, which stabbed him with its tusks. Aphrodite heard the cries of her lover and arrived to see Adonis bleeding to death. Red anemones sprang from the earth where the drops of Adonis's blood fell. In another version of the story, the anemones were white before the death of Adonis, whose blood turned them red.

Christians later adopted the symbolism of the anemone. For them its red represented the blood shed by Jesus Christ on the cross. Anemones sometimes appear in paintings of the crucifixion.

Carnation Composed of tightly packed, fringed petals of white, yellow, pink, or red, carnations have many different meanings. To the Indians of Mexico, they are the "flowers of the dead," and their fragrant blooms are piled around corpses being prepared for burial. For the Koreans, three carnations placed on top of the head are a form of divination, or predicting the future. The flower that withers first indicates which phase of the person's life will contain suffering and hardship. To the Flemish people of Europe, red carnations symbolize love, and a kind of carnation called a pink was traditionally associated with weddings.

Hyacinth The Greek myth of Hyacinthus (pronounced high-uh-SIN-thuhs) and **Apollo** (pronounced uh-POL-oh) tells of the origin of the hyacinth, a member of the lily family. Hyacinthus, a beautiful young man of Sparta, was loved by the **sun** god Apollo. One day the two were amusing themselves throwing a discus, a heavy disc used in Greek athletic games, when the discus struck Hyacinthus and killed him. Some accounts say that Zephyrus, the god of the west wind, directed the discus out of jealousy because he also loved Hyacinthus.

While Apollo was deep in grief, mourning the loss of his companion, a splendid new flower rose out of the bloodstained earth where the young man had died. Apollo named it the hyacinth and ordered that a three-day festival, the Hyacinthia, be held in Sparta every year to honor his friend.

Lily To the ancient Egyptians, the trumpet-shaped lily was a symbol of Upper Egypt, the southern part of the country. In the ancient Near East, the lily was associated with **Ishtar** (pronounced ISH-tahr), also known as Astarte (pronounced a-STAR-tee), who was a goddess of creation and fertility. The Greeks and Romans linked the lily with the queen of the gods, called **Hera** (pronounced HAIR-uh) by the Greeks and Juno (pronounced JOO-noh) by the Romans. The lily was also one of the symbols of the Roman goddess Venus.

In later times, Christians adopted the lily as the symbol of Mary, who became the mother of Jesus while still a virgin. Painters often portrayed the angel Gabriel handing Mary a lily, which became a Christian symbol of purity. Besides being linked to Mary, the lily was also associated with virgin saints and other figures of exceptional purity of body.

Lotus The lotus shares some associations with the lily. Lotus flowers, which bloom in water, can represent female sexual power and fertility as well as birth or rebirth. The ancient Egyptians portrayed the goddess **Isis** (pronounced EYE-sis) being born from a lotus flower, and they placed lotuses in the hands of their mummified dead—dried and preserved before burial—to represent the new life into which the dead souls had entered.

The Language of Flowers

In Europe during the late 1800s, the idea that flowers represented feelings grew into a system of communicating through flower arrangements. Code books guided those who wanted to compose or read floral messages. According to one book, the apple blossom meant "Will the glow of love finally redden your delicate cheeks?" Field clover signified "Let me know when I can see you again." A red rose petal meant "Yes!", a white one "No!" Spurge, a green flower, carried the message: "Your nature is so cold that one might think your heart made of stone." Users of this elaborate language needed not only a code book but also the ability to recognize blooms.

In Asian mythology the lotus often symbolizes the female sexual organs, from which new life is born. Lotuses appear in both Hindu and Buddhist mythology. Hindus refer to the god **Brahma** (pronounced BRAH-muh) as "lotus-born," for he is said to have emerged from a lotus that was the navel, or center, of the universe. The lotus is also the symbol of the goddess Padma (pronounced PAD-muh), who appears on both Hindu and Buddhist monuments as a creative force.

The holiness of the flower is illustrated by the legend that when the Buddha walked on the earth he left lotuses in his trail instead of footprints. One myth about the origin of Buddha relates that he first appeared floating on a lotus. According to a Japanese legend, the mother of Nichiren (pronounced NITCH-er-en) became pregnant by dreaming of sunshine on a lotus. Nichiren founded a branch of Buddhism in the 1200s. The phrase "Om mani padme hum," which both Hindus and Buddhists use in meditation, means "the jewel in the lotus" and can refer to the Buddha or to the mystical union of male and female energies.

Narcissus The Greek myth about the narcissus flower involves the gods' punishment of human shortcomings. Like the stories of Adonis and Hyacinth, it involves the transfer of life or identity from a dying young man to a flower.

Narcissus (pronounced nar-SIS-us) was an exceptionally attractive young man who scorned the advances of those who fell in love with him, including **Echo** (pronounced EK-oh), a nymph (female nature deity). His lack of sympathy for the pangs of those he rejected angered the gods, who caused him to fall in love with his own reflection as he bent over a pool of water. Caught up in self-adoration, Narcissus died—either by drowning as he tried to embrace his own image or by pining away at the edge of the pool. In the place where he had sat gazing yearningly into the water, there appeared a flower that the **nymphs** named the narcissus. It became a symbol of selfishness and coldheartedness. Today psychologists use the term "narcissist" to describe someone who directs his or her affections inward rather than toward other people.

Poppy A type of poppy native to the Mediterranean region yields a substance that can be turned into opium, a drug that was used in the ancient world to ease pain and bring on sleep. The Greeks associated poppies with both **Hypnos** (pronounced HIP-nohs), god of sleep, and Morpheus (pronounced MOR-fee-uhs), god of dreams. Morphine, a drug made from opium, gets its name from Morpheus.

Rose The rose, a sweet-smelling flower that blooms on a thorny shrub, has had many meanings in mythology. It was associated with the worship of certain goddesses and was, for the ancient Romans, a symbol of beauty and the flower of Venus, the Roman goddess of love. The Romans also saw roses as a symbol of death and rebirth, and they often planted them on graves.

When Christians adopted the rose as a symbol, it still carried connections with ancient mother goddesses. The flower became associated with Mary, the mother of Christ, who was sometimes addressed as the Mystic or Holy Rose. In time, the rose took on additional meanings in Christian symbolism. Red roses came to represent the blood shed by the martyrs who died for their faith; white ones stood for innocence and purity. One Christian legend says that roses originally had no thorns. But after the sin of **Adam and Eve**—for which they were driven out of the Garden of **Eden**—the rose grew thorns to remind people that they no longer lived in a state of perfection.

Sunflower Sunflowers turn their heads during the day, revolving slowly on their stalks to face the sun as it travels across the sky. The Greek myth of Clytie (pronounced KLY-tee) and Apollo, which

The lotus flower's association with rebirth made it a prominent flower in ancient Egyptian tombs, as a way of promoting the rebirth of the dead into the afterlife. Here the wife of the Egyptian nobleman Nebamun is shown holding lotus flowers on a wallpainting in his tomb. WERNER FORMAN/ART RESOURCE, NY.

exists in several versions, explains this movement as the legacy of a lovesick girl.

Clytie, who was either a water nymph or a princess of the ancient city of Babylon, fell in love with Apollo, god of the sun. For a time the god returned her love, but then he tired of her. The forlorn Clytie sat, day after day, slowly turning her head to watch Apollo move across the sky in his sun chariot. Eventually, the gods took pity on her and turned her into a flower. In some versions of the myth, she became a heliotrope or a marigold, but most accounts say that Clytie became a sunflower.

Violet The violet, which grows low to the ground and has small purple or white flowers, appeared in an ancient Near Eastern myth that probably inspired the Greek and Roman myth of Aphrodite (pronounced af-ro-DYE-tee) and Adonis. According to this story, the great mother goddess **Cybele** (pronounced SIB-uh-lee) loved Attis, who was killed while hunting a wild boar. Where his blood fell on the ground, violets grew.

The Greeks believed that violets were sacred to the god **Ares** (pronounced AIR-eez) and to Io (pronounced EE-oh), one of the many human loves of **Zeus** (pronounced ZOOS). Later, in Christian symbolism, the violet stood for the virtue of humility, or humble modesty, and several legends tell of violets springing up on the graves of virgins and saints. European folktales associate violets with death and mourning.

Flowers in Context

Many plants bloom for only a few weeks, often in the spring or early summer, and the individual flowers tend to be short-lived. At their peak, flowers are delicate, colorful, and frequently sweet-scented. From these qualities emerge the symbolic meanings of flowers and, in some cultures, floral goddesses.

Many cultures connect flowers with birth, with the return of spring after winter, with life after death, and with joyful youth, beauty, and merriment. Yet because they fade quickly, flowers are also linked with death, especially the death of the young. Together the two sets of associations suggest death followed by heavenly rebirth, which may be one reason for the tradition of placing or planting flowers on graves. People also offer flowers to their gods at shrines and decorate churches with them.

In many societies, certain colors of flowers have acquired symbolic meanings. White blossoms, for example, represent both purity and death, while red ones often symbolize passion, energy, and blood. Yellow flowers may suggest gold or the sun. In the Chinese Taoist tradition, the highest stage of enlightenment—or supreme understanding and perception of the world—was pictured as a golden flower growing from the top of the head.

The shapes of flowers also have significance. Blossoms with petals projecting outward like rays of light from the sun have been associated with the sun and with the idea of the center—of the world, the universe, or consciousness.

The Aztecs, who dominated central Mexico before the early 1500s CE, had a goddess of sexuality and fertility named Xochiquetzal (pronounced soh-chee-KATE-sahl), which means "flower standing upright." She carried a bouquet of flowers and wore a floral wreath in her hair. Fragments of surviving poetry show that the Aztecs recognized the double symbolism of flowers as emblems of both life and death:

> The flowers sprout, and bud, and grow, and glow. . . . Like a flower in the summertime, so does our heart take refreshment and bloom. Our body is like a flower that blossoms and quickly withers. . . . Perish relentlessly and bloom once more, ye flowers who tremble and fall and turn to dust.

The Greeks also had a floral goddess, Chloris (pronounced KLOR-iss), who was married to Zephyrus (pronounced ZEF-er-uhs), the god of the west wind. The Romans called her Flora (pronounced FLOR-uh) and honored her each year with a celebration known as the Floralia. She was often portrayed holding flowers or scattering them; her blossom-crowned image appeared on coins of the Roman republic.

Flowers in Art, Literature, and Everyday Life

As mentioned above, ancient art and literature often associate certain gods with specific flowers.

This Roman fresco of 79 CE shows the Roman goddess Flora gathering flowers. ALINARI/ ART RESOURCE, NY.

Additionally, gods associated with fertility and the seasons are often pictured surrounded by flowers. In more recent times, flowers were used as symbols of the impermanence of beauty, as in sixteenth-century French poet Pierre Ronsard's "Ode to Cassandra." The poet likens Cassandra to a rose that is beautiful now, but will soon wither. In the past century, flowers have mostly been depicted in realistic and natural ways, without much emphasis on myth. John McCrae's 1915 poem "In Flanders Fields," which focuses on an image of poppies growing over the graves of those killed during battle in World War I, is a rare modern example of flowers achieving a mythical significance. In the 2003 Tim Burton fantasy film *Big Fish*, adapted from a novel by Daniel Wallace, the main character somehow gathers all the daffodils (also known as narcissus) within five states and plants them in a field to impress his love.

Even in everyday life, flowers connected to certain myths often retain a special meaning. In Korea, carnations are presented as symbols of gratitude and love to one's parents on May 8, also known as Parents Day. In the United States, pink carnations have become the flower most associated with Mother's Day. In predominantly Christian regions, lilies are closely associated with the Easter holiday, and are often used as decoration during this time. The red rose is still one of the most recognized symbols of love in the world.

Read, Write, Think, Discuss

As shown by the myths mentioned here, certain flowers tend to be given mythical significance in many different cultures, while some other flowers are rarely associated with gods, goddesses, or myths. What characteristics do you think help the flowers discussed above to achieve mythic status over other flowers?

SEE ALSO Adonis; Fruit in Mythology; Hypnos; Ishtar; Isis; Narcissus

Frey

See **Freyr.**

Freya

See **Freyja.**

Freyja

Nationality/Culture
Norse

Pronunciation
FRAY-uh

Alternate Names
Freya, Vanadis

Appears In
The Eddas

Lineage
Daughter of Njord

Character Overview

In **Norse mythology**, Freyja was the goddess of love and fertility, associated with affairs of the heart. Her identification with love and passion led other gods to condemn her behavior. The trickster god **Loki** (pronounced LOH-kee) claimed that Freyja was the lover of all of the gods and accused her of sleeping with her twin brother, **Freyr** (pronounced FRAY), the god of fertility and prosperity. Freyja, Freyr, and their father Njord (pronounced NYORD) were originally part of the group of gods known as the Vanir (pronounced VAH-nir), who battled the other gods of Norse mythology before forming an alliance with them.

In addition to being concerned with matters of love, Freyja had links with death and the world of the dead. Half of all the warriors who died in battle were given to her; the other half went to **Odin** (pronounced OH-din), ruler of the gods. According to oral tradition, Odin receives warriors who fight in lands away from their homes, while Freyja receives those who die defending their own homes or families.

Major Myths

One story about Freyja explained how she acquired her favorite possession, the Necklace of the Brisings, made by four dwarfs. She agreed to spend a night with each of the dwarfs in exchange for the necklace. However, Loki later crept into Sessrumnir, Freyja's heavenly home, while Freyja was sleeping and stole the precious necklace. When she discovered the theft, she knew that only Loki could have stolen it, and she demanded its return. Odin agreed that the necklace should be returned to her, but only on condition that she start a war between two kings and give the slain new life so they could fight again. Freyja agreed, and got back her necklace. This myth combines two of Freyja's primary roles: her role as a goddess of love, and her association with war and the death of warriors. Another version of the myth leaves out the theft of the necklace, and has Odin condemning Freyja for paying such a price for the necklace. As her penance, he orders her to start the war between the kings.

Freyja in Context

Freyja was associated with **Frigg** (pronounced FRIG), goddess of marriage. Some scholars have suggested that the two goddesses represent different aspects of the same deity, who oversaw both love and motherhood. The group of gods known as the Vanir, which included Freyja, were viewed as primitive when compared to the other Norse gods. Freyja's father is said to have married his sister, an act forbidden among the other gods (and the Scandinavian people) but allowed among the Vanir. This may have reflected Scandinavian views about previous generations or nearby cultures that were eventually overtaken by the Norse culture. The condemnation of Freyja by the other gods may also reflect societal views toward women who have relationships with more than one man.

Key Themes and Symbols

In Norse mythology, Freyja represents many things. As a symbol of fertility, she represents both the growth of crops and the creation of children. Freyja also symbolizes romantic and physical love. At the same time, Freyja is an agent of the land of the dead to some warriors.

One of the animals commonly associated with Freyja is the falcon, which symbolizes magic and the ability to travel between worlds. The boar is also sometimes associated with Freyja and can symbolize both fertility and protection for warriors. She is also associated with cats, which were said to pull her chariot.

Freyja in Art, Literature, and Everyday Life

Freyja is often depicted in Scandinavian art riding in a chariot drawn by cats, or with a falcon perched on her hand. She is often shown wearing the Necklace of the Brisings. Her most famous appearance is in the Richard Wagner opera cycle known as *The Ring of the Nibelung*, first performed in its entirety in 1876. More recently, Freyja has served as the inspiration for numerous characters in Japanese comics, animation, and video games, most notably in games created by the Japanese developer Square-Enix.

Freyja continues to play a part in modern Scandinavian life. The element vanadium was named after the goddess (who is sometimes known as Vanadis), and the name Freja (a variant of Freyja) is one of the most popular female names in Denmark.

Read, Write, Think, Discuss

Using your library, the Internet, or other available resources, research the geographic extent of the Norse culture. Which modern-day countries were part of the Norse culture? Do those areas still retain elements of their Norse heritage today?

SEE ALSO Freyr; Frigg; Loki; Norse Mythology

Freyr

Character Overview

In **Norse mythology**, Freyr was the god of fertility and prosperity and the twin of **Freyja** (pronounced FRAY-uh), the goddess of love and fertility. He and his sister were the children of the sea god Njord (pronounced NYORD) and the female giant Skadi (pronounced SKAY-dee). Freyr belonged to the race of gods known as the Vanir (pronounced VAH-nir). When these gods went to war with another group of gods called the Aesir (pronounced AY-sur), Freyr was taken hostage. The Aesir eventually released Freyr, and the Norse came to consider him a member of both groups of gods.

Freyr used many magical items during his adventures. These included a horse named Blodughofi and a magnificent boar with a glowing mane, Gullinbursti, which pulled his chariot. Thus, both boars and horses were associated with Freyr. From the dwarfs, Freyr received a ship that could travel in any direction regardless of which way the wind was blowing. When Freyr was not using the ship, he could fold it up and put it in his pocket. Another magnificent treasure was a sword that could fight by itself.

Major Myths

One of the best-known legends about Freyr explains how he fell in love with a female giant named Gerda (pronounced GAIR-duh). The moment he saw her, Freyr decided to make her his bride. He sent his servant Skirnir (pronounced SKEER-nir) to try to convince Gerda to

Nationality/Culture
Norse

Pronunciation
FRAY

Alternate Names
Frey

Appears In
The Eddas

Lineage
Son of Njord

The Norse god Freyr was associated with boars. A magnificent boar named Gullinbursti pulled his chariot. © CHARLES WALKER/TOPFOTO/ THE IMAGE WORKS.

marry him. She refused at first but later agreed. Freyr gave his magic sword to Skirnir in return for winning Gerda for him. Unfortunately, without his sword to fight with during **Ragnarok** (pronounced RAHG-nuh-rok)—the final battle of the gods—Freyr is destined to die while fighting a giant named Surtr (pronounced SURT).

Freyr in Context

Freyr gives up his magic sword in order to get Gerda as his wife. In other words, the warrior gives up his ability to fight and instead chooses love. The warrior's sword is often seen as a symbol of manhood. The ancient Scandinavians placed great importance on the ability to fight, and while they also recognized the vital role of women, sacrificing the ability to defend oneself and one's family would not have been favored. Indeed, during Ragnarok, when Freyr is once again called to fight, legend has it that he will die because he has given up his sword.

Key Themes and Symbols

Freyr served as a symbol of fertility and growth of crops. Boars, such as Freyr's Gullinbursti, were also associated with fertility. His magical ship, which always enjoys a favorable wind, is a symbol of Freyr's ability to control nature. Freyr is also seen as a symbol of peace and happiness to humans. Freyr is linked to Sweden and the Swedish people, especially the region of Bohuslan, which was thought to have once been ruled by elves.

Freyr in Art, Literature, and Everyday Life

Like his twin sister Freyja, Freyr is an important figure in Norse art and literature. He is usually depicted with his magical sword and boar. His most famous appearance is in the Richard Wagner opera cycle known as *The Ring of the Nibelung*, first performed in its entirety in 1876. More recently, he has appeared as a character in the Marvel Comic series *Thor*. He has also appeared in the *Stargate SG-1* series (1997–2007) in a most unusual form: as an alien, a member of the advanced Asgard race based on the Norse gods.

Read, Write, Think, Discuss

In many modern cultures, just as in ancient Scandinavia, weapons are often seen as symbols of manhood. Guns are the most prominent weapons of the modern world. Do you think the symbolic connection between guns and manhood plays a part in people's views on issues like gun control and wildlife hunting? Why or why not?

SEE ALSO Dwarfs and Elves; Freyja; Norse Mythology

Frigg

Character Overview

In **Norse mythology**, Frigg was the wife of **Odin** (pronounced OH-din), father of the gods. She was associated with marriage and the birth of children. In earlier Germanic mythology, Frigg was called Frija, from which the word "Friday" is derived. For many years, Germans considered Friday a lucky day to be married. Even though her main role was guardian of marriage, Frigg did not live with Odin. Instead, she made her home in a place called Fensalir and was attended by several maids.

Nationality/Culture
Norse

Pronunciation
FRIG

Alternate Names
Frija, Fricka

Appears In
The Eddas

Lineage
Daughter of Fjorgyn

Major Myths

One of the best-known stories about Frigg concerns her attempt to make her son **Balder** (pronounced BAWL-der) immortal, or able to live forever. She obtained promises from every thing under the sky, except one, not to harm him. The one thing she neglected to ask was the mistletoe plant, which she considered too small and weak to be of any danger. However, the trickster god **Loki** found this out and tricked Balder's blind brother into throwing mistletoe at Balder, which killed him. Frigg mourned her son, and attempted to get him released from the land of the dead, but without success.

Frigg in Context

Frigg was a dutiful and supportive wife to Odin. This reflects the importance of a dutiful and loyal wife to the ancient Scandinavian people. It is important to note that Frigg was not viewed as a servant of Odin, but as an equal in many ways. In Norse myths, Frigg is the only person other than Odin permitted to sit on his throne, which allows him to watch over all the worlds. This suggests that the importance of women's duties in Scandinavian culture was recognized, even if those duties were not emphasized as much as the duties of men.

Key Themes and Symbols

Frigg is a symbol of marriage, motherhood, and childbirth, and is often closely linked to **Freyja**, the goddess of romantic love and fertility. In some areas it was believed that the two were actually the same goddess. One of Frigg's most important functions in Norse mythology is as a strong and supportive wife to Odin, a symbol of the benefits of marriage. Frigg is also associated with fate and destiny—the idea that human actions have already been foretold—though she does not reveal her knowledge or make predictions. Objects associated with Frigg include a spinning wheel—which symbolizes domestic life and which she uses to spin the clouds—and keys, which symbolize her role as protector of the home.

Frigg in Art, Literature, and Everyday Life

Frigg was often depicted at a spinning wheel or beside her husband Odin. As with many Norse gods, her most famous appearance is in the Richard Wagner opera cycle known as *The Ring of the Nibelung*, where she is referred to as Fricka. The plant known as lady's bedstraw, which has sedative properties and was often used to calm women during childbirth, is also known as "Frigg's grass."

Read, Write, Think, Discuss

Frigg attempts to protect her son Balder by making him immortal, though she fails to protect him against mistletoe. In recent years, parents—and lawmakers—have gone out of their way to keep their children from being exposed to anything that might be physically harmful: hands are sanitized to kill germs; helmets are worn while skateboarding and riding bicycles; special toddler seats are required when young children are riding in a car. Do you think these measures actually result in a safer environment for children? Or do you think "kid-proofing" an environment can keep a child from developing a sense of caution and natural defenses to threats?

SEE ALSO Balder; Loki; Odin

Frija

See **Frigg.**

Fruit in Mythology

Theme Overview

Fruit appears in myths from around the world. Often it is a symbol of abundance, associated with goddesses of fertility, plenty, and the harvest. Sometimes, however, fruit represents earthly pleasures, overindulgence, and temptation. Specific kinds of fruit have acquired their own symbolic meanings in the myths and legends of different cultures.

Major Myths

Many of the most significant fruits in world mythology, such as the apple, have different meanings to different cultures. Sometimes the same fruit can represent different things in different myths within the same culture. This section examines each of the major fruits found in mythology and provides examples from the myths of various cultures.

Apple Apples are brimming with symbolic meanings and mythic associations. In China they represent peace, and apple blossoms are a symbol of women's beauty. In other traditions, they can signify wisdom, joy, fertility, and youthfulness.

Apples play an important part in several Greek myths. **Hera** (pronounced HAIR-uh), queen of the gods, owned some precious apple trees that she had received as a wedding present from **Gaia** (pronounced GAY-uh), the earth mother. Tended by the Hesperides (pronounced hee-SPER-uh-deez), the Daughters of Evening, and guarded by a fierce dragon, these trees grew in a garden somewhere far in the west. Their apples were golden, tasted like honey, and had magical powers. They could heal the sick or injured, they renewed themselves as they were eaten, and if thrown, they always hit their target and then returned to the thrower's hand.

For the eleventh of his twelve great labors, the hero **Heracles** (pronounced HAIR-uh-kleez), also known as Hercules, had to obtain some of these apples. After a long, difficult journey across North Africa, he enlisted the help of the giant **Atlas** (pronounced AT-luhs), who entered the garden, strangled the dragon, and obtained the fruit. Heracles took the apples to Greece, but **Athena** (pronounced uh-THEE-nuh) returned them to the Hesperides.

A golden apple stolen from Hera's garden caused the Trojan War, one of the key events in **Greek mythology**. Eris (pronounced EER-iss), the goddess of discord or conflict, was angry not to be included among the gods asked to attend a wedding feast. Arriving uninvited, she threw one of the apples, labeled "For the Fairest" onto a table at the feast. Hera, Athena, and **Aphrodite** (pronounced af-ro-DYE-tee) each assumed that the apple was meant for her. They asked Paris (pronounced PAIR-iss), a prince of Troy, to settle the matter, and he awarded the apple to Aphrodite. In revenge, Hera and Athena supported the Greeks in the war that led to the fall of Troy. People still use the phrase "apple of discord" to refer to something that provokes an argument.

In **Norse mythology**, apples are a symbol of eternal youth. Legend says that the goddess **Idun** (pronounced EE-thoon) guarded the magical golden apples that kept the gods young. But after the trickster god **Loki**

The Horn of Plenty

The cornucopia (pronounced korn-uh-KOH-pee-uh), a curved horn with fruits and flowers spilling from its open mouth, is a common symbol of abundance and the earth's bounty. The symbol's origin lies in Greek mythology. Legend says that Zeus (pronounced ZOOS), the king of the gods, was raised by a foster mother named Amalthaea (pronounced am-uhl-THEE-uh), who was either a goat or a goddess who tended a goat. Either way, she fed the infant god goat's milk. One day one of the goat's horns broke off. Amalthaea filled the horn with fruits and flowers and gave it to Zeus, who graciously placed it in the sky, where it became a constellation.

(pronounced LOH-kee) allowed Idun to be carried off to the realm of the **giants**, the gods began to grow old and gray. They forced Loki to recapture Idun from the giants. **Celtic mythology** also mentions apples as the fruit of the gods and of immortality, or the ability to live forever.

Today the apple is often associated with an episode of temptation described in Genesis, the first book of the Bible. **Adam and Eve**, the first man and woman, lived in a garden paradise called **Eden** (pronounced EED-n). God forbade them to eat the fruit of one tree that grew in the garden—the tree of the knowledge of good and evil. When they gave in to temptation and tasted the fruit, God drove them out of the Garden of Eden for breaking his commandment. Many people picture the forbidden fruit as an apple because it has been portrayed that way for centuries in European artworks. However, the apple was unknown in the Near East when the Bible was written there. The biblical description of the tree in the Garden of Eden does not name a specific fruit, and in some traditions, the forbidden fruit has been imagined as a fig, a pear, or a pomegranate.

Breadfruit The breadfruit—a round fruit that can be baked and eaten like bread—is an important staple food in Polynesia. Myths about the origin of the breadfruit are found on several Polynesian islands. One story told in Hawaii takes place during a famine. A man named Ulu (pronounced OO-loo), who died in the famine, was buried beside a spring. During the night, his family heard the rustle of flowers and leaves drifting to the ground. Next came a thumping sound of falling fruit. In the morning, the people found a breadfruit tree growing near the spring, and the fruit from the tree saved them from the famine.

Peach Peaches can symbolize immortality or fertility. One hero of Japanese folklore, Momotaro, is said to have been sent from **heaven** to Earth inside a giant peach found floating down a river by an old woman. In some versions of the myth, the old woman and her husband eat pieces of the peach and become younger. One Chinese legend tells of the goddess Xi Wang Mu (pronounced shee wang MOO), in whose garden the peaches of immortality were gathered by the gods every six thousand years. Peaches were commonly believed to extend life to those who ate them.

Coconut People in tropical regions consume the milk and meat of the coconut and use the oil and empty shells for various purposes. According to a legend from Tahiti, the first coconut came from the head of an eel named Tuna (pronounced TOO-nuh). When the moon goddess Hina (pronounced HEE-nuh) fell in love with the eel, her brother, **Maui** (pronounced MAH-wee), killed it and told her to plant the head in the ground. However, Hina left the head beside a stream and forgot about it. When she remembered Maui's instructions and returned to search for the head, she found that it had grown into a coconut tree.

Fig Native to the Mediterranean region, the fig tree appears in some images of the Garden of Eden. After eating the forbidden fruit, Adam and Eve covered their nakedness with leaves that are usually said to be from the fig tree, and Islamic tradition mentions two forbidden trees in Eden—a fig tree and an olive tree. In Greek and **Roman mythology**, figs are sometimes associated with **Dionysus** (pronounced dye-uh-NYE-suhs), god of wine and drunkenness, and with Priapus (pronounced pry-AY-puhs), a satyr (half-man, half-goat) who symbolized sexual desire.

The fig tree has a sacred meaning for Buddhists. According to Buddhist legend, the founder of the religion, Siddhartha Gautama (pronounced see-DAHR-tuh GAW-tuh-muh), or the Buddha, achieved enlightenment one day in 528 BCE while sitting under a bo tree, a kind of fig tree. The bo or bodhi tree remains a symbol of enlightenment.

Pear In Greek and Roman mythology, pears are sacred to three goddesses: Hera, Aphrodite, and Pomona (pronounced puh-MOH-nuh), an Italian goddess of gardens and harvests.

The golden apple given by Paris to the goddess Aphrodite as a prize in a beauty contest began a chain of events that eventually led to the Trojan War. © FOGG ART MUSEUM, HARVARD UNIVERSITY ART MUSEUMS, USA/GIFT OF META AND PAUL J. SACHS/THE BRIDGEMAN ART LIBRARY.

The ancient Chinese believed that the pear was a symbol of immortality. (Pear trees live for a long time.) In Chinese the word *li* means both "pear" and "separation," and for this reason, tradition says that to avoid a separation, friends and lovers should not divide pears between themselves.

Plum The blossom of the plum tree, even more than the fruit, has meaning in East Asia. Appearing early in the spring before the trees have leaves, the blossoms are a symbol of a young woman's early beauty. The cover on a bridal bed is sometimes called a plum blossom blanket. The blossom has another meaning as well. Its five petals represent the five traditional Chinese gods of happiness.

Pomegranate For thousands of years, the pomegranate, a juicy red fruit with many seeds, has been a source of food and herbal medicines in the Near East and the eastern Mediterranean. Its many seeds made it a symbol of fertility, for out of one fruit could come many more. To the Romans, the pomegranate signified marriage, and brides wore pomegranate-twig wreaths.

Pomegranate seeds appear in the Greek myth of the goddess **Demeter** (pronounced di-MEE-ter), protector of grain, crops, and the earth's bounty, and her daughter **Persephone** (pronounced per-SEF-uh-nee). One day Persephone was picking flowers when **Hades** (HAY-deez), the king of the **underworld**, or land of the dead, seized her and carried her to his dark realm to be his bride. Grief-stricken, Demeter refused to let crops grow. All of humankind would have starved if **Zeus** had not ordered Hades to release Persephone. Hades let her go, but first he convinced her to eat some pomegranate seeds. Having once eaten the food of the underworld, Persephone could never be free of the place. She was fated to spend part of each year there. For those months, the world becomes barren, but when Persephone returns to her mother, the earth again produces flowers, fruit, and grain.

Strawberry Strawberries have special meaning to the Seneca of the northeastern United States. Because strawberries are the first fruit of the year to ripen, they are associated with spring and rebirth. The Seneca also say that strawberries grow along the path to the heavens and that they can bring good health.

Mythological Fruit in Context

Although there are many different kinds of fruit found throughout the world, a large number of myths are centered on a handful of different fruits. This may be due to the fact that growing regions for these fruits overlapped the larger ancient societies that are known for documenting their beliefs, such as the Greeks. Fruits such as bananas and oranges may be just as significant to other, smaller groups whose myths have yet to receive the same level of study. This favoring of certain fruits may also represent the cultural and dietary significance of some fruits over other fruits.

Mythological Fruit in Art, Literature, and Everyday Life

Many fruits have retained their mythical significance and symbolism into modern times through art and tradition. The apple is probably the most significant fruit in mythological art and literature, but this can be at least partially explained by how the word "apple" was used in previous centuries. The word was applied as a general term for many kinds of fruit, and was often used to mean simply "fruit."

The apple plays a significant role in the fairy tale of Snow White, especially the 1937 Disney animated adaptation *Snow White and the Seven Dwarfs*, in which an evil queen disguised as an old woman tempts Snow White with a beautiful red apple that turns out to be poisoned. Apples still signify knowledge, and are a traditional gift for teachers on the first day of the school year. New York City is nicknamed "The Big Apple." How it got its nickname is a matter of debate, but the general idea is that the apple symbolizes opportunity and plenty.

Other fruits have also made their mark on modern culture. In Asia, the word "peach" is frequently used as slang for a young woman or a bride, reflecting the fruit's association with youth and life. Pomegranates are often broken on the ground at Greek weddings to bring good luck to the couple.

Read, Write, Think, Discuss

Select a fruit not already mentioned above. (Oranges, bananas, and cherries are some possible suggestions, but you can choose any fruit you want.) In what regions of the world does your chosen fruit grow? What cultures are located in those regions? Can you find any myths about your fruit in any of those cultures? Provide a brief summary of at least one myth for your fruit.

SEE ALSO Adam and Eve; Atalanta; Demeter; Flowers in Mythology; Persephone

Furies

Character Overview

In Greek and **Roman mythology**, the Furies were female spirits of justice and vengeance. They were also called the Erinyes (pronounced ee-RIN-ee-eez; angry ones). Known especially for pursuing people who had

Nationality/Culture
Greek/Roman

Pronunciation
FYOO-reez

Alternate Names
Erinyes

Appears In
Hesiod's *Theogony*, Ovid's *Metamorphoses*, Virgil's *Aeneid*

Lineage
Born from the blood of Uranus

murdered family members, the Furies punished their victims by driving them mad. When not punishing wrongdoers on earth, they lived in the **underworld**, or land of the dead, and tortured the damned.

According to some stories, the Furies were sisters born from the blood of **Uranus** (pronounced YOOR-uh-nuhs), the ancient god of the sky, when he was wounded by his son **Cronus** (pronounced KROH-nuhs). In other stories, they were the children of Nyx (pronounced NIKS), goddess of night. In either case, their ancient origin set them apart from the other deities or gods in Greek and Roman mythology.

Most tales mention three Furies: Alecto (pronounced uh-LEK-toh; endless), Tisiphone (pronounced ti-SIF-uh-nee; punishment), and Megaera (pronounced muh-JEER-uh; jealous rage). Usually imagined as monstrous, foul-smelling hags, the sisters had bats' wings, coal-black skin, and hair entwined with serpents. They carried torches, whips, and cups of venom with which to torment wrongdoers. The Furies could also appear as storm clouds or swarms of insects.

Major Myths

The Furies appear in many myths and ancient literary works. They have a prominent role in *Eumenides* (pronounced yoo-MEN-uh-deez), a play written by the Greek dramatist Aeschylus (pronounced ES-kuh-luhs). This play tells of the Furies' pursuit of Orestes (pronounced aw-RES-teez), who had killed his mother, Clytemnestra (pronounced klye-tem-NES-truh), in revenge for her part in murdering his father, King **Agamemnon** (pronounced ag-uh-MEM-non) of Mycenae (pronounced mye-SEE-nee).

In *Eumenides*, Orestes' act was depicted as just, and the god **Apollo** (pronounced uh-POL-oh) protected him in his sacred shrine at **Delphi** (pronounced DEL-fye). But the Furies still demanded justice. Finally, the gods persuaded the Furies to allow Orestes to be tried by the Areopagus (pronounced ar-ee-OP-uh-guhs), an ancient court in the city of Athens. The goddess **Athena** (pronounced uh-THEE-nuh), the protector goddess of Athens, cast the deciding ballot.

Athena then calmed the anger of the Furies, who became known afterward as the Eumenides (soothed ones) or Semnai Theai (pronounced SEM-nay THEE-eye; honorable goddesses). Now welcomed in Athens and given a home there, they helped protect the city and its citizens from harm. The Furies also had shrines dedicated to them

The ghost of Clytemnestra summoned the Furies to avenge her murder by her children. The Furies were ugly hags who relentlessly pursued criminals to bring them to justice. © YALE CENTER FOR BRITISH ART, PAUL MELLON COLLECTION, USA/THE BRIDGEMAN ART LIBRARY.

in other parts of Greece. In some places, the Furies were linked with the three **Graces**, goddess sisters who represented beauty, charm, and goodness—qualities quite different from those usually associated with the Furies.

The Furies in Context

The need for maintaining order among the public was important in ancient Greece and Rome. Before the rise of complex laws and codes, the Furies represented the power needed to maintain order. As these ancient societies developed their own methods of justice, the Furies became associated primarily with punishing those who broke "natural laws": laws considered to be outside the scope of the normal justice system, such as killing a family member. Such a crime was considered so awful that no human method of punishment could be sufficient for it.

Although the Furies seemed terrifying and sought vengeance, they were not considered deliberately evil. On the contrary, they represented justice and were seen as defenders of moral and legal order. They punished the wicked and guilty without pity, but the good and innocent had little to fear from them.

Key Themes and Symbols

The Furies are symbols of the power of a guilty conscience. It is significant that they do not physically punish wrongdoers: they hound them into madness. This suggests that the Furies' power is within the mind of the guilty party.

The Furies in Art, Literature, and Everyday Life

The Furies appeared in many Greek dramas, especially those concerning Orestes and **Electra**. Perhaps the most famous artistic depiction of the Furies is the 1862 painting *The Remorse of Orestes* by William-Adolphe Bouguereau. The characters were the subject of a poem by Charles Marie René Leconte de Lisle titled *Les Erinnyes*, written in 1872. The Furies also appeared as characters in Jean-Paul Sartre's 1943 play *The Flies*, a retelling of the myth of Electra. More recently, the trio appeared as recurring characters in the adventure television series *Xena: Warrior Princess*, and in a storyline of Neil Gaiman's comic series *The Sandman*.

Read, Write, Think, Discuss

Literature is filled with characters who are tormented by their conscience after committing a crime or wrong of some sort. Some notable examples include William Shakespeare's tragedy *Macbeth*, Fyodor Dostoevsky's 1866 novel *Crime and Punishment*, and Edgar Allan Poe's 1843 short story "The Tell-Tale Heart." Think of some more examples of characters in books or films whose punishment for past crimes comes mainly from their own conscience. Do you think such a punishment is sufficient? Is it more or less suitable than a traditional punishment, like a jail sentence? Can you think of fictional characters who commit crimes and feel no pangs of conscience at all?

SEE ALSO Graces; Uranus

Where to Learn More

African

Altman, Linda Jacobs. *African Mythology*. Berkeley Heights, NJ: Enslow Publishers, 2003.

Ardagh, Philip, and Georgia Peters. *African Myths & Legends*. Chicago: World Book, 2002.

Giles, Bridget. *Myths of West Africa*. Austin, TX: Raintree Steck-Vaughn, 2002.

Husain, Shahrukh, and Bee Willey. *African Myths*. 1st ed. North Mankato, MN: Cherrytree Books, 2007.

Lilly, Melinda. *Spider and His Son Find Wisdom: An Akan Tale*. Vero Beach, FL: Rourke Press, 1998.

Lilly, Melinda. *Warrior Son of a Warrior Son: A Masai Tale*. Vero Beach, FL: Rourke Press, 1998.

Lilly, Melinda. *Zimani's Drum: A Malawian Tale*. Vero Beach, FL: Rourke Press, 1998.

Schomp, Virginia. *The Ancient Africans*. New York: Marshall Cavendish Benchmark, 2008.

Seed, Jenny. *The Bushman's Dream: African Tales of the Creation*. 1st American ed. Scarsdale, NY: Bradbury Press, 1975.

Anglo-Saxon/Celtic

Ardagh, Philip, and G. Barton Chapple. *Celtic Myths & Legends*. Chicago: World Book, 2002.

Crossley-Holland, Kevin, and Peter Malone. *The World of King Arthur and His Court: People, Places, Legend, and Lore*. New York: Dutton Children's Books, 2004.

Hicks, Penelope, and James McLean. *Beowulf*. New York: Kingfisher, 2007.

Lister, Robin, Alan Baker, and Sir Thomas Malory. *The Story of King Arthur.* Boston: Kingfisher, 2005.

Martell, Hazel Mary. *The Celts.* 1st American ed. New York: Peter Bedrick, 2001.

Morris, Gerald. *The Lioness & Her Knight.* Boston: Houghton Mifflin, 2005.

Whittock, Martyn J. *Beliefs and Myths of Viking Britain.* Oxford: Heinemann, 1996.

Williams, Marcia, ed. *Chaucer's Canterbury Tales.* London: Walker, 2008.

Asian/Pacific

Behnke, Alison. *Angkor Wat.* Minneapolis: Twenty-First Century Books, 2008.

Carpenter, Frances. *Tales of a Korean Grandmother.* Boston: Tuttle Pub., 1973.

Coburn, Jewell Reinhart. *Encircled Kingdom: Legends and Folktales of Laos.* Rev. ed. Thousand Oaks, CA: Burn, Hart, 1994.

Coulson, Kathy Morrissey, Paula Cookson Melhorn, and Hmong Women's Project (Fitchburg, MA). *Living in Two Worlds: The Hmong Women's Project.* Ashburnham, MA: K. M. Coulson and P. C. Melhorn, 2000.

Dalal, Anita. *Myths of Oceania.* Austin, TX: Raintree Steck-Vaughn, 2002.

Green, Jen. *Myths of China and Japan.* Austin, TX: New York: Raintree Steck-Vaughn Publishers, 2002.

Htin Aung, U., G. Trager, and Pau Oo Thet. *A Kingdom Lost for a Drop of Honey, and Other Burmese Folktales.* New York: Parents' Magazine Press, 1968.

Kanawa, Kiri Te. *Land of the Long White Cloud: Maori Myths, Tales, and Legends.* 1st U.S. ed. New York: Arcade Pub., 1989.

Sakairi, Masao, Shooko Kojima, and Matthew Galgani. *Vietnamese Fables of Frogs and Toads.* Berkeley, CA: Heian International, 2006.

Sakairi, Masao, Shooko Kojima, and Matthew Galgani. *Vietnamese Tales of Rabbits and Watermelons.* Berkeley, CA: Heian International, 2006.

Egyptian

Ardagh, Philip, and Danuta Mayer. *Ancient Egyptian Myths & Legends.* Chicago: World Book, 2002.

Broyles, Janell. *Egyptian Mythology.* 1st ed. New York: Rosen Pub. Group, 2006.

Cline, Eric H., and Jill Rubalcaba. *The Ancient Egyptian World.* California ed. New York: Oxford University Press, 2005.

Gleason, Katherine. *Ancient Egyptian Culture.* New York: Newbridge Educational Pub., 2006.

Kramer, Ann. *Egyptian Myth: A Treasury of Legends, Art, and History.* Armonk, NY: Sharpe Focus, 2008.

Kudalis, Eric. *The Royal Mummies: Remains from Ancient Egypt.* Mankato, MN: Capstone High-Interest Books, 2003.

McCall, Henrietta. *Gods & Goddesses in the Daily Life of the Ancient Egyptians.* Columbus, OH: Peter Bedrick Books, 2002.

Mitchnik, Helen. *Egyptian and Sudanese Folk-Tales.* New York: Oxford University Press, 1978.

Schomp, Virginia. *The Ancient Egyptians.* New York: Marshall Cavendish Benchmark, 2008.

Wyly, Michael J. *Death and the Underworld.* San Diego, CA: Lucent Books, 2002.

Greek/Roman

Bingham, Jane. *Classical Myth: A Treasury of Greek and Roman Legends, Art, and History.* Armonk, NY: M. E. Sharpe, 2008.

Hepplewhite, Peter, and Mark Bergin. *The Adventures of Perseus.* Minneapolis, MN: Picture Window Books, 2005.

Lister, Robin, Alan Baker, and Homer. *The Odyssey.* Reformatted ed. Boston: Kingfisher, 2004.

McCarty, Nick, Victor G. Ambrus, and Homer. *The Iliad.* Reformatted ed. Boston: Kingfisher, 2004.

Mellor, Ronald, and Marni McGee. *The Ancient Roman World.* New York: Oxford University Press, 2005.

Roberts, Russell. *Athena.* Hockessin, DE: Mitchell Lane Publishers, 2008.

Roberts, Russell. *Dionysus.* Hockessin, DE: Mitchell Lane Publishers, 2008.

Roberts, Russell. *Zeus.* Hockessin, DE: Mitchell Lane Publishers, 2008.

Schomp, Virginia. *The Ancient Romans.* New York: Marshall Cavendish Benchmark, 2008.

Spires, Elizabeth, and Mordicai Gerstein. *I Am Arachne: Fifteen Greek and Roman Myths.* New York: Frances Foster Books, 2001.

Whiting, Jim. *The Life and Times of Hippocrates.* Hockessin, DE: Mitchell Lane Publishers, 2007.

Hindu

Choudhury, Bani Roy, and Valmiki. *The Story of Ramayan: The Epic Tale of India.* New Delhi: Hemkunt Press; Pomona, CA: Distributed in North America by Auromere, 1970.

Dalal-Clayton, Diksha, and Marilyn Heeger. *The Adventures of Young Krishna: The Blue God of India.* New York: Oxford University Press, 1992.

Ganeri, Anita. *The* Ramayana *and Hinduism*. Mankato, MN: Smart Apple Media, 2003.

Ganeri, Anita, and Carole Gray. *Hindu Stories.* Minneapolis: Picture Window Books, 2006.

Ganeri, Anita, and Tracy Fennell. *Buddhist Stories.* Minneapolis: Picture Window Books, 2006.

Husain, Shahrukh, and Bee Willey. *Indian Myths.* London: Evans, 2007.

Kipling, Rudyard. *The Jungle Book.* New York: Sterling Pub., 2008.

Parker, Vic, and Philip Ardagh. *Traditional Tales from India.* Thameside Press; North Mankato, MN: Distributed in the United States by Smart Apple Media, 2001.

Sharma, Bulbul. *The* Ramayana *for Children*. Penguin Global, 2004.

Staples, Suzanne Fisher. *Shiva's Fire.* 1st ed. New York: Farrar Straus Giroux, 2000.

Judeo-Christian

Geras, Adele. *My Grandmother's Stories: A Collection of Jewish Folk Tales.* New York: Alfred A. Knopf, 2003.

Kimmel, Eric A., and John Winch. *Brother Wolf, Sister Sparrow: Stories about Saints and Animals.* 1st ed. New York: Holiday House, 2003.

Schwartz, Howard, and Barbara Rush. *The Diamond Tree: Jewish Tales from Around the World.* 1st Harper Trophy ed. New York: HarperTrophy, 1998.

Schwartz, Howard, and Stephen Fieser. *Invisible Kingdoms: Jewish Tales of Angels, Spirits, and Demons.* 1st ed. New York: HarperCollins Publishers, 2002.

Self, David, and Nick Harris. *Stories from the Christian World.* Englewood Cliffs, NJ: Silver Burdett Press, 1988.

Senker, Cath. *Everyday Life in the Bible Lands.* North Mankato, MN: Smart Apple Media, 2006.

Taback, Simms. *Kibitzers and Fools: Tales My Zayda (Grandfather) Told Me.* New York: Puffin, 2008.

Native American

Ardagh, Philip, and Syrah Arnold. *South American Myths & Legends.* Chicago: World Book, 2002.

Berk, Ari, and Carolyn Dunn Anderson. *Coyote Speaks: Wonders of the Native American World.* New York: Abrams Books for Young Readers, 2008.

Brown, Virginia Pounds, Laurella Owens, and Nathan H. Glick. *Southern Indian Myths and Legends.* Birmingham, AL: Beechwood Books, 1985.

Curry, Jane Louise. *The Wonderful Sky Boat and Other Native American Tales from the Southeast.* New York: Margaret K. McElderry, 2001.

Monroe, Jean Guard, and Ray A. Williamson. *They Dance in the Sky: Native American Star Myths.* Award ed. Boston: Houghton Mifflin, 1993.

Parker, Victoria. *Traditional Tales from South America.* North Mankato, MN: Thameside Press. Distributed in the United States by Smart Apple Media, 2001.

Philip, Neil. *The Great Mystery: Myths of Native America.* New York: Clarion Books, 2001.

Pijoan, Teresa. *White Wolf Woman: Native American Transformation Myths.* 1st ed. Little Rock, AR: August House Publishers, 1992.

Ramen, Fred. *Native American Mythology.* 1st ed. New York: Rosen Central, 2008.

Schomp, Virginia. *The Native Americans.* New York: Marshall Cavendish Benchmark, 2008.

Vogel, Carole G. *Weather Legends: Native American Lore and the Science of Weather.* Brookfield, CT: Millbrook Press, 2001.

Near Eastern/Islamic

Ganeri, Anita. *Islamic Stories.* 1st American ed. Minneapolis, MN: Picture Window Books, 2006.

Grimal, Pierre. *Stories from Babylon and Persia.* Cleveland, OH: World Pub, 1964.

Ibrahim, Abdullahi A. *Enuma Elish.* Austin, TX: Steck-Vaughn Co., 1994.

Jabbari, Ahmad. *Amoo Norooz and Other Persian Folk Stories.* Costa Mesa, CA: Mazda Publishers, 2000.

León, Vicki. *Outrageous Women of Ancient Times.* New York: Wiley, 1998.

Marston, Elsa. *Figs and Fate: Stories about Growing Up in the Arab World Today.* 1st ed. New York: George Braziller, 2005.

Marston, Elsa. *Santa Claus in Baghdad and Other Stories about Teens in the Arab World.* Bloomington: Indiana University Press, 2008.

McCaughrean, Geraldine. *Gilgamesh the Hero.* Oxford: Oxford University Press, 2002.

Podany, Amanda H., and Marni McGee. *The Ancient Near Eastern World.* New York: Oxford University Press, 2005.

Schomp, Virginia. *The Ancient Mesopotamians.* New York: Marshall Cavendish Benchmark, 2008.

Walker, Barbara K. *Turkish Folk-Tales.* Oxford: Oxford University Press, 1993.

Norse/Northern European

Andersen, H. C., Diana Frank, Jeffrey Frank, Vilhelm Pedersen, and Lorenz Frolich. *The Stories of Hans Christian Andersen: A New Translation from the Danish.* Durham: Duke University Press, 2005.

Ardagh, Philip, and Stephen May. *Norse Myths & Legends.* Chicago: World Book, 2002.

Branford, Henrietta, and Dave Bowyer. *The Theft of Thor's Hammer.* Crystal Lake, IL: Rigby Interactive Library, 1996.

D'Aulaire, Ingri, and Edgar Parin. *D'Aulaires' Book of Norse Myths.* New York: New York Review of Books, 2005.

Evan, Cheryl, and Anne Millard. *Usborne Illustrated Guide to Norse Myths and Legends.* London: Usborne, 2003.

Jones, Gwyn, and Joan Kiddell-Monroe. *Scandinavian Legends and Folk-Tales.* New ed. Oxford: Oxford University Press, 1992.

Osborne, Mary Pope. *Favorite Norse Myths.* New York: Scholastic, 2001.

Porterfield, Jason. *Scandinavian Mythology.* New York: Rosen Central, 2008.

Web Sites

American Folklore. http://www.americanfolklore.net/ (accessed on June 11, 2008).

The British Museum: Mesopotamia. http://www.mesopotamia.co.uk/menu.html (accessed on June 11, 2008).

The Camelot Project at the University of Rochester. http://www.lib.rochester.edu/CAMELOT/cphome.stm (accessed on June 11, 2008).

Common Elements in Creation Myths. http://www.cs.williams.edu/~lindsey/myths (accessed on June 11, 2008).

Egyptian Museum Official Site. http://www.egyptianmuseum.gov.eg/ (accessed on June 11, 2008).

Internet History Sourcebooks Project. http://www.fordham.edu/halsall/ (accessed on June 11, 2008). Last updated on December 10, 2006.

Iron Age Celts. http://www.bbc.co.uk/wales/celts/ (accessed on June 11, 2008).

Kidipede: History for Kids. http://www.historyforkids.org/ (accessed on June 11, 2008).

Mythography. http://www.loggia.com/myth/myth.html (accessed on June 11, 2008). Last updated on April 17, 2008.

National Geographic. http://www.nationalgeographic.com/ (accessed on June 11, 2008).

NOVA Online: The Vikings. http://www.pbs.org/wgbh/nova/vikings/ (accessed on June 11, 2008).

Perseus Project. http://www.perseus.tufts.edu/ (accessed on June 11, 2008).

Sanskrit Documents. http://sanskritdocuments.org/ (accessed on June 11, 2008). Last updated on February 2, 2008.

United Nations Educational, Scientific and Cultural Organization. http://portal. unesco.org/ (accessed on June 11, 2008).

World Myths & Legends in Art. http://www.artsmia.org/world-myths/artbyculture/index.html (accessed on June 11, 2008).

Index

Italic type indicates volume number; **boldface** type indicates main entries and their page numbers; (ill.) indicates photos and illustrations.

B

D

F

G

M

Q

S

U

V

X

BOCA RATON PUBLIC LIBRARY, FLORIDA

3 3656 0483295 2

201.3 UXL

U*X*L encyclopedia of world
 mythology